Interpersonal Process in
COGNITIVE THERAPY

Interpersonal Process in

COGNITIVE
THERAPY

JEREMY D. SAFRAN
& ZINDEL V. SEGAL

BASIC BOOKS, INC., PUBLISHERS
New York

To my teachers
—J.D.S.

To my parents, Icek and Mania
—Z.V.S.

The quotations on pages 1 and 248 are from Martin Buber, *I and Thou*, translated by Ronald Gregor Smith. Copyright © 1958, renewed 1986, by Charles Scribner's Sons. Reprinted by permission of Charles Scribner's Sons, an imprint of Macmillan Publishing Company.

The poem on page 223 is from Soiku Shigematsu, *Zen Forest: Sayings of the Masters*, 1981, Tanko-Weatherhill, Inc. Reprinted by permission of Tanko-Weatherhill, Inc.

Library of Congress Cataloging-in-Publication Data
Safran, Jeremy D.
    Interpersonal process in cognitive therapy / Jeremy
D. Safran & Zindel V. Segal.
      p.   cm.
    Includes bibliographical references.
    ISBN 0-465-06387-X: $24.95
    1. Cognitive therapy. 2. Interpersonal relations. I.
Segal, Zindel V., 1956-   . II. Title.
    [DNLM: 1. Cognitive Therapy. WM 425 S128i]
RC489.C63S24   1990
616.89'142—dc20
DNLM/DLC   90-108

Contents

Contents

PART II. PRACTICE

Acknowledgments

The thinking in this book has been influenced by sources too numerous to mention. The more important ones, however, are as follows: In the interpersonal tradition, Don Kiesler's work has been seminal, and his support and encouragement over time have been greatly appreciated. In the experiential tradition, Les Greenberg's friendship and collaboration over the years have been important influences, and Harvey Freedman's clinical wisdom has been tremendously influential. In many ways, Harvey is the embodiment of the more important principles articulated in this book. In the cognitive tradition, we would like to acknowledge Brian Shaw, who provided an open and supportive environment for integrative thinking about psychotherapy when the Cognitive Therapy Unit at the Clarke Institute was under his directorship from 1983 to 1986. We would also like to acknowledge Barry Wolfe for his helpful comments on an earlier draft of the manuscript, and Jo Ann Miller, our editor at Basic Books, for her feedback and support. Finally, we would like to thank Ed Cook for his dedicated and conscientious assistance in typing the manuscript, and Bob Leiper, who helped sow the seeds for this book many years ago.

PART I

THEORY

Spirit is not in the I, but between I and Thou. It is not like the blood that circulates in you, but like the air in which you breathe. Man lives in the spirit, if he is able to respond to his Thou. He is able to, if he enters into relation with his whole being. Only in virtue of his power to enter into relation is he able to live in the spirit.

—MARTIN BUBER

CHAPTER 1

Introduction

Cognitive Therapy in Evolution

These seem like good times for cognitive therapists. The cognitive revolution in psychotherapy, which sprang from a crack in a behavioral hegemony in the late 1960s, has become a mainstream psychotherapy tradition.

The vigorous debates about cognitive constructs and the value of mediation-based accounts of learning are now historical footnotes (Rachlin 1977; Mahoney 1977), and cognitive therapists can bask in the acceptance that their orientation has received as one of the most popular intervention formats among practitioners (Smith 1982).

In this salutary climate, it is easy to believe that cognitive behavioral theory and therapy have put their house in order and that future challenges concern only the continuing demonstration of efficacy and the wider dissemination of these findings. Yet, as in most times of plenty, there are those who remain unfulfilled; it is clear that more change is to come.

Cognitive therapists are questioning long-cherished theoretical assumptions and experimenting with new ideas and techniques from other psychotherapy traditions. Tension continues as calls for the development of new theory and techniques (Guidano and Liotti 1983; Mahoney and Gabriel 1987) intermingle with critiques of the old theory as inadequate and weakly supported (Beidel and Turner 1986; Coyne and Gotlib 1983), and theorists begin to question the theoretical foundations upon which much of cognitive treatment is based. With the recent explosion of interest in emotion has come a challenge

3

to traditional cognitive assumptions about the role of emotion in human functioning and the relationship between emotion and cognition. Cognitive therapists have shown growing interest in the role of unconscious processes and are questioning, on philosophical grounds, the assumption that there is such a thing as objective reality that people either perceive accurately or distort. And the list goes on.

In this book, we aim both to broaden the purview of cognitive behavior therapy by incorporating elements from interpersonal psychotherapy and other theoretical traditions and to move toward a cognitive-interpersonal perspective on how change in therapy takes place. Our objective is consistent with the growing trend toward integration in the psychotherapy field—a trend arising, as John Norcross (1986) has discussed, from the failure to find differential effectiveness among therapies, from the search for common ingredients of effective therapy, and from the growing realization that the "nonspecific factors" of therapy may be the most powerful components of successful treatment. Findings like these have spurred a re-examination of the belief in the adequacy of any single approach to therapy.

We favor the increasing trend toward psychotherapy integration, but not the proliferation of multiple, new, integrative schools of psychotherapy (Goldfried and Safran 1986). One rationale often advanced for developing new integrative approaches is that existing schools of pure-form psychotherapy are not flexible or versatile enough to adapt to individual patient differences. All too often, however, the new approaches provide systems that are less comprehensive and sophisticated than the schools of psychotherapy they are designed to replace because they lose the accumulated wisdom of years of practice and theoretical development in a particular tradition. Our intention is, thus, not to develop a new school of psychotherapy, but to initiate a process of conceptual and technical expansion in cognitive therapy that is informed by other therapy traditions.

Psychotherapy as a Human Encounter

In this book we focus on the role of the therapeutic relationship in cognitive therapy and the nature of the relationship between cognitive and interpersonal processes. In choosing this focus, our intent is to redress what we view as a fundamental imbalance in cognitive approaches to therapy, an imbalance that has a seriously detrimental impact on practice. Because the therapeutic relationship or nonspecific

4

aspects of therapy are less tangible and more difficult to operational-
ize than specific cognitive and behavioral techniques, cognitive therapists tend to see them as less important. Although in recent years
they have begun to pay more attention to the therapeutic relationship, they still tend to see it as something separate from the active
ingredients of therapy, as a prerequisite for the change process rather
than as an intrinsic part of it.

In our view, this perpetuates a mechanistic approach to therapy that
fails to recognize the fundamentally human nature of the therapeutic
encounter and the change process. The assertion that psychotherapy
is fundamentally a human encounter does not mean that there is no
theory for therapists to learn and no skills for them to acquire. It does
mean, however, that the relevant theory must clarify the process
through which this human encounter brings about change, and that
the relevant skills must include the ability to use one's own humanity
as a therapeutic instrument.

A fundamental postulate of the current approach, derived from the
interpersonal tradition of psychotherapy, is that the individual must
always be understood as part of the interpersonal system in which he
or she is participating. Thus, one cannot understand the patient in
therapy independent of the therapist. To paraphrase Harry Stack Sullivan, the therapist plays an inextricable role in everything that tran-
spires in therapy, and only by systemically clarifying his or her own
contribution to the interaction can the therapist come fully to understand the patient. The notion of an objective or neutral therapist is an
illusion. The therapist is a human being with his or her own blind
spots and particular areas of sensitivity, and these will inevitably
interact with the patient's problems and sensitivities. Sullivan defined
the therapeutic relationship as follows: "Two people, both with problems in living, who agree to work together to study those problems,
with the hope that the therapist has fewer problems than the patient"
(Kasin 1986). Therapy must thus involve an ongoing process of self-
exploration on the therapist's part.

A Process Perspective

One reason cognitive therapy has been popular is its focus on clear-
cut, easily specifiable techniques. This has obvious advantages for both
training and research. From a training perspective, this kind of spec-
ificity helps allay the therapist's anxiety in the face of the inherent

ambiguity of the clinical situation. The clearly operationalized nature of cognitive techniques gives therapists the reassuring feeling that they have something concrete and tangible to offer their patients. The existence of a host of different cognitive techniques provides them with the sense of having a large therapeutic armamentarium at their disposal, thereby further enhancing their sense of potential efficacy.

From a research perspective, the clear-cut technical focus of cognitive therapy makes it easier to manualize cognitive therapy protocols. This, in turn, makes it easier to do research on cognitive therapy than on other forms of therapy where both the interventions and the goals of therapy are more ambiguous. The technical focus has also played an important role in demystifying psychotherapy and contributed to the climate of accountability that has gradually been developing in the psychotherapy field.

On the negative side, however, the technical focus of cognitive therapy can also lead therapists to rely excessively on techniques without understanding their underlying process. Without this understanding, the clinician becomes only a technician—effective in some contexts, but not in others—and unable to identify those factors that make the difference. Such technicians tend to confuse the surface aspects of what works with the underlying essence, and they lack the flexibility and adaptability to respond creatively to the demands of new clinical situations.

To counteract this imbalance, we emphasize the underlying process through which change takes place. By distinguishing between therapeutic interventions and the underlying mechanisms through which they operate, it becomes possible to experiment with different ways of activating the same change mechanisms. In this book we focus on three specific change mechanisms:

1. decentering—experiencing one's own role in constructing reality
2. experiential disconfirmation—disconfirming dysfunctional beliefs about the self, and others, through new experiences
3. accessing action-disposition information—discovering aspects of one's own inner experience that have previously been out of awareness

All three mechanisms involve the acquisition of new experience. As we will argue, change requires more than conceptual understanding or rational analysis; it means experiencing the self, and others, in new ways. These three mechanisms can be activated through exploring either events in the patient's life outside therapy or the therapeutic relationship itself. Ultimately, however, the therapeutic relationship will mediate whatever change takes place. A therapist who attempts to challenge a patient's belief that others are critical, but does it in a critical way, will ultimately confirm that belief, as will the therapist who is overly active in challenging a patient's belief that he or she is helpless.

Human beings and the events in which they participate are in a constant state of flux. Life is process. In an attempt to find security in the midst of groundlessness, there is a strong tendency to impose structure upon this flux. People view both themselves and others through concepts, and treat these concepts as real. By reifying things in this way, they blind themselves to the ever-changing nature of the underlying reality. As we shall see, developing rigid concepts of self and others is a central source of psychological dysfunction. Moreover, therapists who reify theoretical constructs and formulations of their patients, blind themselves to the ever-changing reality of both their patients' and their own experiences. *Nonreification*, or not mistaking static constructs for the underlying dynamic reality, is thus a central therapeutic principle in the current approach. It is vital for the therapist to track changes in therapy process as they take place.

Therapy process can be thought of as a series of events unfolding over time at three levels:

1. fluctuations in the moment-to-moment state of the patient's phenomenological world
2. fluctuations in the moment-to-moment state of the therapeutic relationship
3. fluctuations in the therapist's inner experience.

These levels are interdependent. Thus, shifts in the patient's psychological state are always taking place in the context of fluctuations in the therapeutic relationship, and vice versa. Similarly, fluctuations in the therapist's inner experience always take place in the context of the relationship as it unfolds, and influence this unfolding.

Of particular importance in our approach is the process of tracking one's own inner experience as the therapist. As we shall see, the therapist's inner experiences can provide important clues about the patient's interpersonal and cognitive style. Moreover, fluctuations in the therapist's inner experience provide important information about the quality of the therapeutic relationship as it fluctuates, which, in turn, can provide important clues about the patient's inner experience.

The Nature of Reality

Traditional cognitive therapy has assumed that the therapist's task is to help the patient develop a more accurate or objective view of reality by relying on such tools as logic and empirical evidence. The underlying assumption is that psychological problems result from distortions of reality, and that it is the correction of these distortions that promotes change. Recently these assumptions have been questioned by critics within the cognitive therapy community (for example, Guidano 1987; Mahoney 1988; Safran and Greenberg 1986). Given the growing evidence that logical computation is only a small component of our complex information-processing system (Greenberg and Safran 1987), we are convinced that a position that equates psychological health solely with rationality is clearly untenable. Moreover, the growing empirical evidence suggesting that in many circumstances depressed individuals are actually more accurate in their perceptions and judgments than nondepressed individuals (Taylor and Brown 1988) challenges the criterion of objectivity as the hallmark of mental health. Finally, in light of developments in epistemology, neuroscience, and cognitive development (Mahoney 1985), it is difficult to support the rationalist assumption that the function of the brain is merely to mirror reality accurately and that adaptive behavior is then guided by this reflection.

An alternative perspective, which is more consistent with the approach to be outlined here, is held by constructivists like Guidano (1987), Guidano and Liotti (1983), and Mahoney (1990). In theory and in therapy, the constructivists take a more evolutionary developmental approach than the rationalists. Rather than emphasizing the accurate perception of physical absolutes, they stress the active "construction" of reality. In therapy, they focus on the "self's" process of maturation through progressive differentiation.

More important than purely philosophical reasons for abandoning the perspective that therapy involves the correction of cognitive distortions are the therapeutic implications of such a position. As Coyne and Gotlib (1983) have argued from an interpersonal perspective, when the patient lives in a dysfunctional interpersonal situation, the assumption that depression results from cognitive distortions can have potentially pernicious effects because it can lead the therapist into condoning an unhealthy status quo. Moreover, a perspective that views psychological problems as resulting from cognitive distortions encounters the unanswerable question of who ultimately will decide what constitutes a distortion. Traditionally, cognitive therapists deal with this issue by saying that the ultimate criterion is what works for the patient, but this sidesteps the issue. Thus far, many cognitive therapists have failed to take a stand on the vital question of who is the final arbiter of the patient's reality—patient or therapist. Perhaps the clearest position comes from the experiential tradition, which has always emphasized that only the patient can be the expert on his or her reality (Perls 1973; Rice 1974; Rogers 1961).

The only way for therapists truly to accept patients as the final arbiters of their own reality is to be genuinely open to the possibility that the patient knows something about reality that the therapist does not. If therapists believe this, then there is as much possibility that their own models of the world will be changed as a result of a patient's therapy as there is that a patient's will be. Instead of socializing patients into the therapist's view of reality, this stance allows therapists to become available to patients in such a way that helps each patient discover his or her own reality creatively and constructively.

In this way the patient and the therapist are viewed as two actively construing human beings who have their respective constructions of reality that overlap in some respects and differ in others. Therapy is conceived of as a dialectical process in which the influence is bidirectional in nature, and the result of a successful therapy is often change in both patient and therapist. To experience a patient as he or she is at any given moment, the therapist must ultimately be able to let go of preconceptions about that patient; in so doing, the therapist may well change. Thus, as Jung (1963) suggested, therapy is an opportunity for both patient and therapist to grow.

Metatheory

In understanding the process of change, it is important to distinguish between clinical theory, which attempts to clarify the mechanisms through which specific interventions work, and metatheory, which provides a higher level theory of human functioning. Whereas some theorists advocate focusing on what actually takes place in therapy rather than on developing higher level models of human functioning, our view is that both levels of theoretical analysis are necessary.

Although many cognitive therapists are turning to information-processing theory for this kind of framework, we believe that as a comprehensive model of human functioning its value is limited. An adequate theoretical model must be able to clarify not only how information is processed, but also the ways in which affective, cognitive, and behavioral processes develop and interact in an interpersonal context. The metatheory articulated here is both interpersonal and cognitive: interpersonal, because it starts with the fundamental assumption that human beings are by nature interpersonal creatures, and that this has profound implications for human development, clinical problems, and psychotherapy; cognitive, because its emphasis is on the way people construct representations of their experience.

We have attempted to integrate developments from cognitive theory, interpersonal theory, attachment theory, and emotion theory that are both consistent with current empirical evidence and clinically useful. The metatheoretical framework we articulate should, however, be regarded as preliminary. It will be important for this framework to be refined as new theoretical and empirical developments emerge.

Supportive versus Insight-Oriented Therapy

One criticism often leveled at cognitive-behavior therapy is that it is a supportive and surface-oriented, rather than true insight-oriented, therapy (Wolberg 1988). To determine whether this assertion has substance, we will review the distinction between these two forms of therapy.

The traditional distinction between supportive and insight-oriented therapies derives from a classical psychoanalytic model of human functioning that is far from universal. In this view, the task of supportive psychotherapy consists of strengthening mental functions that are "acutely or chronically inadequate to cope with the demands of the external world and of the patient's inner psychological world" (Werman 1984, p. 5). The task of the supportive psychotherapist as it is traditionally viewed is to help patients distinguish between realistic and distorted perceptions of a situation, to help them clarify constructive alternative approaches or solutions to problem situations, and to

10

provide the support and reassurance necessary to modulate anxiety so that patients can function adequately.

In contrast, the task of the insight-oriented psychotherapist is to help patients to become aware of ego/alien or warded-off impulses and desires, to reduce or modify the defenses that keep these impulses out of their consciousness, and to gain insight into the historical or genetic events that contributed to the development of their neurotic conflicts.

By these criteria, traditional cognitive therapy as described in writings by Aaron Beck and coworkers (1979) is, indeed, closer to supportive psychotherapy than to insight-oriented psychotherapy. First, the former focuses extensively on the use of cognitive procedures designed explicitly to help patients test their perceptions and distinguish between accurate and distorted perceptions of reality. Second, not only does it explicitly reject classical psychoanalytic concepts of neurotic conflict, but the analysis of defenses and the uncovering of warded-off impulses play no role.

The distinction between insight-oriented and supportive psychotherapy is, however, not as clear-cut as it initially appears. First, much of what goes on in those forms of psychotherapy that are supposedly insight-oriented is directed toward distinguishing between adaptive and maladaptive appraisals of reality—a focus usually associated with supportive psychotherapy. Thus, the psychoanalytic practice of analyzing the transference relationship helps patients distinguish between reality and reality as they construe it. This is particularly true in neo-Freudian and interpersonal approaches, where the emphasis has shifted from the development of insight into the historical causes of the current problem toward providing corrective emotional experience. Clearly, the meaning of the concept of insight itself is being questioned.

Second, as Lester Luborsky (1984) argues, good therapy involves a sensible and fluctuating balance between supportive aspects of the therapy, which help modulate the patient's anxiety level by bolstering the therapeutic alliance, and more insight-oriented aspects of the therapy, which involve exploring psychological and affective processes that the patient may not currently be aware of.

Although the boundary between supportive and insight-oriented psychotherapy is thus not clear-cut, it nevertheless remains true that the exploration of warded-off impulses, and the defenses that exclude them from awareness, play no role in traditional cognitive therapy.

Our approach, however, *does* concern itself with the defensive exclusion of information from awareness. While contemporary cognitive theorists and therapists reject the classical psychoanalytic conceptualization of the unconscious and the associated drive metapsychology, compelling evidence from experimental cognitive psychology suggests that different forms of information processing do take place outside awareness (Erdelyi 1974; Shevrin and Dickman 1980). This realization has led some cognitive therapists to a growing recognition that there is a role for the construct of the unconscious in cognitive theory (Meichenbaum and Gilmore 1984; Safran and Greenberg 1987).

To clarify the role that the defensive exclusion of information from awareness plays in the clinical situation, our approach draws on developments in information-processing theory, emotion theory, and developmental psychology. The conceptualization of emotion, which is increasingly accepted by more cognitive-oriented theorists and researchers, views it as a form of internally generated information about "action disposition" (Greenberg and Safran 1987; Frijda 1988; Lang 1983; Leventhal 1984). In human functioning, emotion motivates adaptive behavior, providing people with information about their preparedness to act in certain ways.

Problems can emerge, however, when people fail fully to synthesize potentially adaptive action disposition information. For example, the person who fails to synthesize action-disposition information consistent with loneliness may fail to engage in intimacy-seeking behaviors that could potentially lead to important interpersonal relationships. The person who fails to synthesize potentially adaptive action-disposition information consistent with anger may fail to protect himself or herself from destructive interpersonal situations.

Interactions with significant others play a central role in influencing emotional development. One learns to attend selectively to different kinds of emotional experience and then to integrate them into an overall sense of self. Through interactions with significant others one develops tacit rules that guide the processing of affective information. From the interpersonally oriented cognitive perspective described here, a central premise is that these tacit rules can become a dysfunctional attitude that is just as important to identify and challenge as the dysfunctional attitudes targeted in the typical cognitive approaches described by Beck and colleagues (1979).

Short-Term versus Long-Term Therapy

There has been a growing movement toward the development of short-term therapeutic approaches. This trend is consistent with the increased climate of accountability which has emerged in the last ten years. At the same time, however, there is a growing recognition among cognitive therapists that not all problems are amenable to change through short-term therapy. This is becoming particularly evident as cognitive therapists turn their attention to patients who have more entrenched cognitive and interpersonal styles. The interest in longer term approaches has also been influenced by theoretical developments that emphasize the importance of modifying core cognitive structures (Guidano and Liotti 1983; Mahoney 1982; Safran, Vallis et al. 1986).

The approach outlined in this book can be employed in either long-term or short-term formats. Although there are differences between the scope and nature of the changes that one may expect to take place in long-term and short-term approaches, in our view there is an important respect in which the goal is the same. Ultimately it is vital for the patient to have a constructive interpersonal experience. Using a short-term approach with patients who do not have the particular characteristics that will allow them to benefit from it, increases the possibility of treatment failure and of a nonconstructive interpersonal experience that will reduce the patient's receptiveness to future therapeutic interventions. It thus becomes critical to have some means of assessing patients' suitability for short-term therapy—a topic we will explore later.

Psychotherapy Integration

There are two ways in which different psychotherapy systems capture different aspects of human functioning and clinical reality. First, they focus on and describe different phenomena. For example, the behavioral focus on the generalization of treatment gains and out-of-session events has contributed to the understanding of the principles underlying the maintenance of change. In contrast, the traditional psychodynamic focus on the unconscious has contributed to the understanding of an important aspect of psychological functioning generally ignored by behaviorists.

Second, different psychotherapy systems bring different conceptual lenses to bear on the same phenomenon. Thus, for example, the psychodynamic focus on transference emphasizes the role of the past in shaping current relationships. In contrast, the client-centered tradition emphasizes the real nature of the therapeutic relationship.

The integration of different psychotherapy systems thus increases the possibility of understanding and working with important clinical phenomena by broadening the range of the phenomena actually examined and by providing multiple perspectives on the same phenomenon.

The advantage of providing multiple perspectives on the same phenomenon has an analogy in quantum physics; there it is recognized that reality can never be apprehended in an absolute sense and that different perspectives are necessary if one is to capture different and seemingly contradictory features of a phenomenon. To portray light's properties, for example, contemporary physicists accept the notion that light has the characteristics of both a particle and a wave. They recognize, however, that these concepts are only approximations of reality, and that the limitations of logical and conceptual processes require that different and sometimes contradictory conceptual lenses be brought to bear on the same phenomenon.

When we consider what has happened historically in psychotherapy, we find that different traditions have become orthodoxies, each with its defining rules or conditions for charter membership. For example, one rule for membership in the behavioral school has been the belief that the transference relationship either does not exist or is unimportant. One rule for membership in the psychodynamic school has been the belief that active prescriptions will always obstruct the therapy process.

Ironically, the conceptual and technical constraints, and the clearly delineated boundaries of each system, increase the possibility that the system will become more and more specialized and expert in its focus, just as people who are blind develop heightened abilities in other sensory modalities. But despite these heightened abilities, the blind will remain handicapped, and the psychotherapy system with delineated boundaries will retain its limitations.

For these reasons, it is important to synthesize different psychotherapy approaches. Of course, eliminating all boundaries between different psychotherapy systems is not desirable because it would impede the specialization that *is* facilitated by having clearly delineated boundaries. Moreover, there is some value in having "true believers" who adhere to different schools of psychotherapy: an emotional attachment to a system can provide incentive and motivation to develop it to its full potential.

As more theorists from different traditions become interested in psychotherapy integration, it is important to distinguish between genuinely new therapy concepts and strategies and the mere translation of ideas from one language into another, thereby "reinventing the wheel." In one sense, it is impossible to reinvent the wheel or *merely* to translate from one language into another. Just as there is no such thing as an exact translation from Russian into English, it is unlikely that one can achieve an exact translation of a concept from one psychotherapy tradition into another. Nevertheless, the possibility of developing a genuinely new synthesis is heightened if we are able to engage in an explicit and critical analysis of the similarities and differences between concepts and interventions from different traditions. This kind of analysis is, thus, an important feature of our book.

Another feature is the extensive use of psychotherapy transcripts. Approaches that sound similar at a conceptual level can be dramatically different in practice. Because an understanding of the process of change and the subtleties of the interpersonal transactions between therapists and patients is pivotal in our approach, transcripts are analyzed in detail to examine what actually takes place in therapy.

We regard our approach—and this book—as a snapshot of a continuing attempt to understand how change takes place. Although our conceptual structure is based on the integration of cognitive and interpersonal approaches, it is important to acknowledge the impact other psychotherapy traditions have had on our perspective—in particular, the experiential traditions of client-centered therapy and gestalt therapy. Our strong emphasis on examining the subtleties of the patient's phenomenology in all of its idiosyncratic detail is client-centered, as is the emphasis on helping the patient understand and reveal the true nature of his or her own experience without imposing the therapist's preconceptions on that experience.

This emphasis is consistent with both the cognitive focus on understanding the patient's process of constructing reality and with Sullivan's (1953) lifelong concern about the dangers of reification in psychotherapy theory and practice. Other important influences from the gestalt therapy tradition are the focus on the here and now, on the process rather than the product, and on the acceptance by both patient and therapist of what *is* rather than of what could or should be.

The Plan of the Book

In chapter 2, we review the cognitive-behavioral literature on the therapeutic relationship. The purpose of this chapter is to clarify the value of integrating cognitive and interpersonal perspectives and to provide a survey of current cognitive perspectives on this theme in order to establish a point of departure for subsequent developments.

In chapter 3, we review both theoretical and empirical literature on the therapeutic relationship in the general psychotherapy field, present empirical evidence on the pivotal role that the therapeutic relationship plays in psychotherapy, and begin to show how it may relate to the technical aspects of therapy.

In chapter 4, we review empirical and theoretical literature relevant to developing a systematic, integrative framework for guiding the use of the relationship in cognitive therapy. This literature is culled from a number of different psychology subdisciplines, including information-processing theory, the ecological approach to perception, developmental psychology, attachment theory, and emotion theory. This chapter provides the theoretical foundation for the rest of the book.

In chapter 5, we focus on the assessment of cognitive and interpersonal processes, guided by an integrative cognitive-interpersonal framework. This chapter emphasizes the importance of participant observation by the therapist and provides guidelines for dealing with problems that emerge in the assessment process.

Chapter 6 focuses on the activation of change through the exploration of out-of-session events. Two different change mechanisms are examined: (1) experiential disconfirmation and (2) decentering. This chapter offers a basic conceptualization of how these change mechanisms operate, provides guidelines for intervening in different contexts, and highlights the role of the therapeutic relationship in mediating the change process.

Chapter 7 explores the activation of experiential disconfirmation and decentering through the exploration of the therapeutic relationship. This chapter places particular emphasis on the role of therapeutic metacommunication in activating these processes and also stresses the importance of working through ruptures in the therapeutic alliance.

Chapter 8 examines the change mechanism of accessing action-disposition information. Here we propose that gaining access to affective information that has not been fully synthesized can play an important role in modifying the patient's sense of self and that the therapeutic relationship plays a critical role in mediating this process.

Chapter 9 explores a number of clinical issues that are highlighted when cognitive and interpersonal approaches are integrated. These include such considerations as: how to maintain a therapeutic focus, calibrating the activity level of the therapist, offering the therapeutic rationale to the patient, and dealing with termination.

Chapter 10 provides an outline of the procedure we have developed for evaluating the suitability of patients for treatment with short-term or time-limited therapy.

Chapter 11 summarizes the distinguishing principles of our approach and outlines relevant research directions.

Finally, the appendices contain an interview manual and specific rating scales for judging patient suitability for short-term treatment as well as forms for monitoring whether therapy is being conducted in a manner consistent with the principles outlined in this book.

CHAPTER 2

The Cognitive-Behavioral Perspective on the Therapeutic Relationship

In this chapter we explore the practical and theoretical reasons for expanding the cognitive-behavioral approach by incorporating aspects of interpersonal theory. We also review the cognitive-behavioral literature that deals with the relationship aspect of therapy.

Treatment Efficacy

Although the outcome literature on cognitive-behavioral treatment is promising, there is still much room for improvement. The most solid, consistent body of experimental evidence supporting the efficacy of cognitive-behavioral procedures comes from research on the cognitive therapy of depression. There are now about ten well-designed, controlled outcome studies demonstrating that cognitive therapy is as effective or more effective than antidepressant medication (Hollon and Najavits 1988; Hollon and Beck 1986). Yet, despite this impressive body of evidence, cognitive therapy is not effective for all patients. In the treatment of adult unipolar depression, psychotherapy, in general, is found to be superior to drug therapy (Steinbrueck, Maxwell, and Howard 1983), but meta-analytic studies comparing the effectiveness of cognitive therapy to systematic desensitization have provided only limited support for the superiority of specifically cognitive methods (Berman, Miller, and Massman 1985; Shapiro and Shapiro 1982).

Furthermore, the recently completed National Institute of Mental Health collaborative study on the treatment of depression found that although both psychological treatments were as effective as medication in the treatment of moderately depressed patients, in the treatment of severely depressed patients cognitive therapy was not significantly more effective than the placebo condition. In contrast, both antidepressant medication and interpersonal therapy were significantly more effective in the treatment of severely depressed patients than the placebo condition (Elkin et al. 1986).

As Donald Kiesler (1966) noted more than two decades ago, we must avoid subscribing to uniformity myths about patients and treatment procedures. Although cognitive therapy in its current form is effective for many patients, it is not effective for all. Even in outcome studies with the most impressive results (for example, Beck, Hollon et al. 1985; Murphy et al. 1984), 25 percent to 30 percent of depressed patients treated with cognitive therapy had not shown clinical improvement by the time of termination. When we add the additional 25 percent of all patients who drop out of therapy before the completion of treatment (Beck, Hollon et al. 1985; Murphy et al. 1984), we find a sizable number excluded from the benefits of this approach. These patients are typically thought of as treatment resistant. In the next section we examine the various ways in which the problem of treatment resistance has been conceptualized from a cognitive-behavioral perspective.

Therapeutic Resistance

Cognitive-behavioral theory has traditionally rejected the psychodynamic concept of patient resistance and chosen instead to conceptualize the problem as one of treatment noncompliance. One reason for this shift in conceptualization is articulated by Arnold Lazarus and Allen Fay (1982), who argue that the psychodynamic concept of resistance is all too frequently a rationalization for treatment failure rather than a helpful explanation.

Other cognitive behaviorists, such as G. T. Wilson (1984), attack the psychodynamic conceptualization of resistance on the grounds that it is motivationally based. According to Wilson, the hypothesis that a patient resists a particular interpretation because it is threatening to the ego is simply unparsimonious. He argues that it is more reasonable to attempt to explain "mental phenomena in simple, nonmotivational terms in contrast to less parsimonious, motivational (typically psychodynamic) constructs" (p. 332). Wilson (1984) follows R. Nisbett and L. Ross (1980) in arguing that the difficulty in gaining access to

19

certain kinds of cognitive material is better accounted for by the inherent limitations of human cognitive machinery than by motivational constructs. He suggests dealing with resistance by foreseeing difficulties that particular patients may have with specific behavioral techniques, and then working with the patient to develop strategies to prepare for such eventualities. This approach is reminiscent of G. A. Marlatt and G. R. Gordon's (1980) relapse prevention approach in the treatment of alcoholism.

In keeping with Wilson's suggestions, many behaviorists and cognitive behavior therapists advocate dealing with the problem of noncompliance by giving patients an adequate rationale for the treatment and for assigned homework and by developing all homework assignments in collaboration with the patient (Beck, Rush et al. 1979; Beck and Emery 1985; Lazarus and Fay 1982; Meichenbaum and Gilmore 1982).

M. R. Goldfried (1982) maintains that resistance may reflect one or more of the following variables: the direct sampling of the patient's presenting problem itself; the patient's other problems; pessimism about changing; fear of changing; minimal motivation to change; psychological reactance; overburdening the patient with too many homework assignments; and interfering contingencies in the patient's environment.

Lazarus and Fay (1982) identify four types of resistance in therapy: resistance as a function of the patient's individual characteristics; resistance as a product of the patient's interpersonal relationships (systems or family processes); resistance as a function of the therapist (or the relationship); and resistance as a function of the state of the art. They also note that one of the major forms of resistance in cognitive-behavioral therapy is the failure to carry out homework assignments. According to them, if a homework assignment is not completed, the therapist should consider such questions as: Was the homework assignment incorrect or irrelevant? Was it too threatening? Does the patient not appreciate the value of and rationale behind homework exercises? Is the therapeutic relationship at fault? Is someone in the patient's network undermining or sabotaging therapy, or is the patient receiving too many secondary gains to relinquish his or her maladaptive behavior?

D. Meichenbaum and J. B. Gilmore (1982) emphasize the importance of patients' initial expectations of psychotherapy and of the therapist's understanding of the role these expectations play in cre-

learn to cope with panic, patients rated therapists' encouragement and sympathy to be more important than the practicing component of the treatment. More recently, J. B. Persons and D. D. Burns (1985) found that patients' assessments of the quality of the therapeutic relationship were significantly related to mood changes in cognitive therapy.

The empirical evidence has thus been consistent in implicating the therapeutic relationship as an important variable in the change process, even though cognitive-behavioral theory has not consistently done so.

Facilitating the Social Influence Process

A central and enduring theme in the cognitive-behavioral literature on the therapeutic relationship has been to conceptualize therapy as a process of social influence that can be facilitated by increasing the therapist's attractiveness (Goldstein, Heller, and Sechrest 1966; Lazarus 1971; Wilson and Evans 1977). Personal qualities of the therapist such as empathy, warmth, and self-disclosure are often viewed as exerting a positive influence on the therapeutic process by increasing the possibility that patients will comply with therapeutic tasks. It is interesting to note that in contrast to the client-centered tradition in which empathy and warmth are seen as essential in facilitating self-acceptance in the patient, the behavioral tradition tends to see these qualities as instrumental in increasing the social attractiveness and consequent social influence of the therapist.

Behavior therapists and cognitive behavior therapists have reacted by arguing that a good therapeutic relationship may be necessary but certainly not sufficient for good therapy outcome. For example, Edna Foa and colleagues (1983) maintain that "The personal qualities of the therapist, which appear to be essential to the outcome of psychotherapy, have less impact on the more precisely formulated techniques of behavioral therapy. It is likely that the more powerful the therapeutic procedure employed the less potent will be the effect of the therapist" (p. 15). L. Krasner (1962) characterized the early behavior therapist as a social reinforcement machine who was able to elicit new, adaptive behavior from the patient, a characterization subsequently rejected by many because of its dehumanizing connotations and its conceptual simplicity.

G. T. Wilson and I. M. Evans (1977), for example, point out that social reinforcement does not take place at an automatic level, and that all social reinforcement processes are subject to the interpretation of the individual whose behaviors are being reinforced. As they point out: "Whether a patient emits the targeted behavior or engages in counter-control actions will depend on a number of complex, interacting factors, including the situation or context, the nature of the incentive, personal characteristics of both therapist and patient, and so on" (p. 550). Nevertheless, they still see social reinforcement processes as one of the central processes through which the therapeutic relationship plays a role in behavior therapy.

Positive Therapeutic Expectancies

Another aspect of the therapeutic relationship focused on by behavioral and cognitive-behaviorally oriented therapists has been its role in developing positive therapeutic expectancies. A. P. Goldstein and coworkers (1966), for example, argued that a useful way of increasing the patient's expectations of success in therapy is to provide the patient with a convincing conceptualization of the specific problem and a convincing rationale for the specific treatment employed. Goldfried and G. C. Davison (1976) also emphasize the importance of conveying a convincing rationale. In particular, they suggest the use of "advance organizers," or conceptual seeds of important aspects of the therapeutic rationale that will be introduced later. Thus, for example, they suggest introducing concepts such as "past learning," "learned fears," and "models for imitation" early in the course of therapy. Similarly, Goldfried and Davison (1976) emphasize the importance of increasing the patient's expectations of treatment efficacy by such procedures as alluding to similar problems that patients who have achieved success have had, suggesting relevant literature, and emphasizing the difference between previous therapeutic experiences that have failed and the current therapy experience. Wilson and Evans (1977) maintain that "Anyone watching behavior therapists at work will notice systematic attempts to increase expectancies in the clients" (p. 554).

The Therapist as Role Model

The focus here has tended to be on the role that modeling can play in techniques such as participant modeling (Bandura 1971) and assertion training (Alberti and Emmons 1974). T. J. D'Zurilla and M. R. Goldfried (1971) emphasize the usefulness to patients of learning to imitate appropriate models when learning problem-solving strategies. Mahoney (1974) maintains it can be useful for the therapist to "think out loud" to give patients a good model of the kind of cognitive-mediational skills that can be used in dealing with difficult situations.

In the foregoing approaches, the emphasis is on the intentional use of oneself as a model for dealing with specific problem situations. Some cognitive-behavior therapists (for example, Mahoney 1974) stress the importance of presenting the patient with a coping model rather than a mastery model because, they caution, if therapists present themselves as perfectly adjusted people rather than as human beings with flaws, patients may have more difficulty emulating them.

Collaborative Empiricism

A. T. Beck and his colleagues (Beck, Rush et al. 1979; Beck and Emery 1985; Beck and Young 1985) have not focused extensively on the role of the therapeutic relationship in cognitive therapy, but they have always emphasized the importance of "collaborative empiricism," the need for therapists to develop collaborative relationships with patients to help them *discover* those perceptions that are inconsistent with reality, rather than attempting to persuade patients of the irrationality or biased nature of their perceptions.

In developing a good therapeutic collaboration, Beck and J. E. Young (1985) maintain that therapists should be genuinely warm, empathic, open, and concerned, and not play the role of "absolute expert." They should take care not to seem critical or disapproving, and strive for a confident, professional manner, which can help inspire confidence and counteract the initial hopelessness a patient may have. Part of the process of developing a good collaborative relationship, they point out, involves working together with the patient to set therapeutic goals, determine priorities, and set an agenda for each session.

Obtaining regular feedback from the patient, Beck and G. Emery (1985) also note, is useful in establishing a good collaborative relationship. Such feedback will help the therapist determine whether the patient is complying with the therapist's assertions or instructions only because of fear of rejection. They suggest as well that it is important to give an adequate rationale for a treatment procedure, so the patient can understand and actively collaborate in the treatment process.

In-Session Behavior as a Problem Sample

In contrast to the psychodynamic tradition, behavioral and cognitive-behaviorally oriented therapists have de-emphasized the importance of the transference relationship in the psychotherapy process. The traditional cognitive-behavioral position on this issue has been that the therapeutic cultivation and management of the transference relationship has little impact upon the patient's everyday life. As Albert Bandura (1969) stated: "Whatever the patients may reenact with the psychotherapist, relatively few beneficial effects of these reenactments trickle down to daily interpersonal living. Most likely the artificial relationship provides substitute gratifications for those lacking in the patient's natural relationships instead of serving as a major vehicle for personality change" (p. 79).

More recently, however, some cognitive behaviorists have begun taking a less hardline position. Goldfried and Davison (1976) and Goldfried (1982), for example, recommend that therapists consider problematic in-session behavior exhibited by patients as a sample of the problem behavior that brings them into therapy in the first place. Influenced explicitly by the work of Sullivan (1953), they suggest that the patient's behavior in-session can be treated as a sample of the patient's problem behavior and that the therapeutic interaction can thus be useful for assessment purposes. According to them, behaviorally oriented therapists can use their own feelings for and reactions to the patient as a means of pinpointing and identifying patient behaviors that are likely to be problematic in interpersonal situations.

D. G. Arnkoff (1983) argues that there are three ways in which a focus on in-session therapeutic interactions can be useful. First, she argues that therapeutic interactions can provide the therapist with first-hand observations of the patient's current functioning. Second, she maintains that focusing on the therapeutic relationship can be emotionally riveting to the patient. Third, she argues that to the extent that the patient's current problems are reenacted in the therapeutic relationship, the patient can make discoveries and try out new behaviors that will generalize outside of therapy.

In discussing similarities and differences between psychodynamic and cognitive-behavioral perspectives, Arnkoff (1983) makes the following distinctions: the cognitive-behavioral perspective places less emphasis on past history than does the psychodynamic perspective, and, the focus in cognitive therapy is more present-oriented; cognitive-behavior therapy focuses on dysfunctional cognitions and behavioral deficits and excesses, whereas psychodynamic therapy focuses on psychosexual conflicts and motivational states; transference issues are more central to psychodynamic therapy than to cognitive therapy; cognitive therapists may treat transference issues as distortions in the patient's perception of the therapist, but it is not assumed that changes in the patient's perception as a result of addressing these distortions will necessarily generalize to out-of-session perceptions and behaviors.

N. S. Jacobson (1989) also says that important dysfunctional beliefs that influence the patient's everyday life are likely to influence the therapeutic relationship and points to the need for exploring and challenging these beliefs as they emerge in the therapeutic relationship.

As this brief review indicates, cognitive therapists in recent years have become increasingly interested in the therapeutic relationship as an arena for exploring and modifying dysfunctional behaviors and beliefs. Yet as Jacobson (1989) maintains, "Although psychoanalytic theorists and therapists have been writing about the healing potential of the therapist-client relationship for decades, it has only recently crept into the cognitive-behavioral literature" (p. 89).

Developing a Systematic Cognitive Approach to the Therapeutic Relationship

M. J. Lambert (1983), in his review of the perspective that different therapy traditions adopt on the therapeutic relationship, remarks that "Cognitive behavioral theories . . . have mentioned the therapist/ patient relationship only in passing and only as part of the administrative functions of the therapist, not as an integrated facet of the theory of change" (p. 4). As our review of the relevant literature to this point indicates, this assessment of the situation is not completely accurate because, in recent years, increasing attention has been devoted to the topic of the therapeutic relationship by cognitive therapists.

There are, however, two considerations that we believe warrant further attention. The first is whether there is an adequate, overall conceptual framework in cognitive therapy for understanding the relationship between specific technical factors and the generic therapeutic relationship. The second is whether adequate attention has been paid to specifying the moment-by-moment, or step-by-step considerations in the therapeutic process through which relationship and technical factors interrelate.

In discussing the first issue, Paul Wachtel (1982) maintains that although cognitive-behavior therapists may recognize the importance of the therapeutic relationship, they do not have a systematic theoretical framework for integrating relationship and technical factors. He suggests that without this integrative, theoretical framework, cognitive therapists are, for example, more likely to assume, mistakenly, that a warm, supportive therapeutic stance is appropriate for all patients. Wachtel maintains that cognitive-behavioral theories do not focus as much on the idiosyncratic learning histories of specific patients as psychodynamic theories do and are thus less likely to understand how a particular patient may view a particular therapeutic stance. He also points out that behavior therapy is based on theories that "are essentially content-free, theories concerned with basic processes, with *how* but not particularly with *what* is learned or thought or found reinforcing. Consequently, since these theories do not guide them in this respect, behavior therapists have tended to base their content assumptions on general cultural assumptions" (p. 597).

Wilson (1984), in responding to this criticism, maintains that cognitive therapists *are* sensitive to subtle interactional factors that indicate whether a particular relationship stance is appropriate for a specific patient. He maintains that cognitive-behavior therapists learn a variety of nonspecific therapy skills that come not from the findings of experimental psychology, but rather from their own social learning histories and life experiences, and from clinical supervision. He maintains that although cognitive therapists discuss the process of clinical supervision less than psychodynamic therapists do, in cognitive-behavioral supervision there is still a focus on what he refers to as "the nonspecifics of therapy."

If Wilson is correct, and cognitive therapists learn the appropriate therapy "nonspecifics" in clinical supervision, then why are these "nonspecifics" not spoken of in greater detail in the cognitive-behavioral literature? Would it not make sense to develop a systematic theoretical framework so we can begin the process of empirically investigating these variables?

A similar point is made by A. A. Sweet (1984). After reviewing a number of empirical studies demonstrating the importance of the therapeutic relationship in cognitive-behavioral therapy, he argues that it is surprising that cognitive-behaviorally oriented researchers have not done systematic research on how relationship factors contribute to therapy outcome. He suggests that researchers need to answer such questions as: "What style of data gathering, non-verbal behavior, technique presentation, or the assigning of homework tasks will lead to maximum results? What kinds of clients will respond best to a particular technique? Which persons will terminate prematurely and how does one keep these people in treatment?" (p. 265). He also suggests that it is important to begin investigating and operationalizing the therapeutic behaviors of therapists who naturally form good relationships with patients. He concludes that "The appropriate management of the relationship is a skill that involves accurate assessment and careful implementation. This is perhaps the most difficult skill to teach, but because it interacts with techniques, learning to use it correctly is critical" (p. 266).

G. E. Swan and M. L. MacDonald's (1978) finding that relationship-enhancement methods are the treatment procedures most frequently reported as being used by behavior therapists, raises the questions of what exactly the relationship enhancement methods being employed are, and what kind of conceptual framework is guiding their implementation.

A book edited by Foa and P. M. G. Emmelkamp (1983) attempted to have contributors specify some of the subtle interactional processes that are important in effective cognitive-behavioral treatment. Writings of this kind, however, have been relatively rare in the cognitive-behavioral literature. We would argue that it is not sufficient to include a few pages on the relationship in a book on cognitive therapy or, as Wilson (1984) suggests, to *assume* that therapists will learn these skills in clinical supervision even if they are not discussed extensively in written material. Specifying the subtleties of relationship skills is only part of the battle. Just as important is the task of developing an integrative theoretical model that clarifies the relationship between specific and nonspecific factors and facilitates the process of intervening.

CHAPTER 3

Technical and Relationship Factors in Therapy

Technical versus Relationship Factors

The separation of therapy into specific and nonspecific factors has a long history in psychotherapy research. The term "specific" is generally applied to those technical factors believed to be specific to a particular form of psychotherapy, whereas "nonspecific" applies to factors common to all forms of psychotherapy. These factors are usually seen as qualities of the relationship between the therapist and patient that contribute to change such as warmth, empathy, acceptance, and the expectation that treatment will help. The term "nonspecific factor" is also sometimes used interchangeably with the concept of placebo effect.

On the basis of their comprehensive review of psychotherapy research findings, Lambert (1986) and Lambert, D. A. Shapiro, and A. E. Bergin (1986) estimate that only 15 percent of the variance in outcome findings can be attributed to specific technical factors, whereas up to 45 percent of the variance can be attributed to nonspecific factors.

J. D. Frank (1973; 1979; 1982) has been one of the more important proponents of the common-factors perspective. He argues that therapeutic change can be attributed predominantly to factors common to different forms of psychotherapy, including the presence of a trusting relationship, a convincing rationale, and faith that the treatment will help. Faith is seen as the factor that helps reverse the patient's demoralized feelings.

Because these factors can be present in other normal relationships and social institutions, ranging from the relationship between close friends to religious institutions, some have argued that there is nothing unique about psychotherapy and that it is pointless to do research on and develop new therapeutic mechanisms of change.

Stephen Butler and Hans Strupp (1986) address this issue by challenging the traditional distinction between specific and nonspecific factors in psychotherapy. They argue that this distinction is based on the inappropriate assumption that psychotherapy is analogous to medical treatment. Unlike treatment through medication, wherein biological action is distinguishable in theory from the symbolic meaning of the treatment, psychotherapeutic techniques are intrinsically linked to the interpersonal context in which they take place. Thus, they argue that "the complexity and subtlety of psychotherapeutic processes cannot be reduced to a set of disembodied techniques because techniques gain their meaning and, in turn, their effectiveness from the particular interaction of the individuals involved" (p. 33).

Butler and Strupp point out that the impact of the therapist's behavior upon the patient must finally be understood in terms of the patient's perception of the behavior, and that this perception is ultimately determined by the patient's unique learning history. They argue further that the particular meaning the patient attributes to the therapist's behavior will determine not only the patient's response, but whether the event will lead to new learning or to confirming the patient's maladaptive perceptions and interpersonal patterns.

This mistaken separation of therapy into specific and nonspecific factors is partly responsible for the difficulty involved in demonstrating the superiority of one form of psychotherapy over another, or the superiority of so-called "active treatments" over a "placebo effect." As others have argued, the construct of the placebo, although appropriate in the context of pharmacological investigations in which biochemical mechanisms of change can be contrasted with psychosocial mechanisms, is inappropriate in the context of psychotherapy, wherein all mechanisms are psychosocial in nature.

Predicting Individual Differences

Although research has consistently failed to demonstrate the superiority of one brand of psychotherapy over others, it would be a mistake to assume that all patients do equally well in psychotherapy. As Bergin (1970) argued, research comparing group averages obscures the fact that in any treatment group, some patients do extremely well, some moderately well, some remain unchanged, and some deteriorate. Great individual differences in treatment outcome combined with the failure to demonstrate consistent differences among treatments has led psychotherapy researchers to attempt to identify variables that will predict treatment outcome.

Initial attempts in this direction, which focused on patient characteristics identified prior to treatment, were disappointing. Lester Luborsky and coworkers (1980), for example, in an attempt to predict therapy outcome with data from the Penn Psychotherapy Project, found that the success of predictive measures based on pre-treatment information was generally insignificant, and that the best of them predicted only 5 percent to 10 percent of the outcome variance. This led Luborsky to speculate that the crucial predictive factors may not be apparent until the patient and therapist have had a chance to interact (Luborsky et al. 1980). The assessment of different psychotherapy-process characteristics and aspects of the therapist-patient interaction has shown more promise.

The Therapeutic Alliance

The construct of the therapeutic alliance has its origin in the psychoanalytic literature, but in recent years researchers and theorists from different psychotherapy traditions have begun to explore its potential value as a generic psychotherapy construct. Josef Breuer and Sigmund Freud ([1895] 1955) originally spoke about the patient as an active collaborator in treatment, but did not, at first, focus extensively on the importance of the therapeutic alliance in psychoanalysis. By 1912, however, Freud ([1912] 1958) more clearly emphasized the importance of friendliness and affection between the patient and therapist in psychoanalysis.

Richard Sterba (1934) is often credited with playing an important role in the development of interest in the therapeutic alliance in psychoanalysis. He emphasized that positive identification with the therapist may at times motivate the patient to work toward the accomplishment of therapeutic tasks. Freud (1940) echoed these sentiments when he described the analyst and patient as banding together against the patient's symptoms in a "pact" based on free exploration by the patient, and discretion and competent understanding by the therapist.

While the above contributions can be taken as important precursors of the therapeutic alliance construct, E. Zetzel (1956) is often seen as having begun the current trend in psychoanalysis to distinguish between the "real" aspects of the relationship between the therapist and the patient and its "transferential" aspects. According to R. R. Greenson (1967), the development of a therapeutic alliance depends upon the ability of the patient and the therapist to develop a real and nondistorted collaboration with each other based upon authentic liking, trust, and respect. He maintained that this aspect of the therapeutic relationship exists in parallel to the distorted or transferential aspect of the therapeutic relationship and that it forms the basis for developing the working alliance.

Although the therapeutic alliance has clearly been an important construct in the psychoanalytic literature for some time, it was not until the late 1970s that the therapeutic alliance began to attract the attention and interest of psychotherapy theorists and researchers.

In an influential article, E. S. Bordin (1979) partitioned the therapeutic alliance into three components: tasks, bonds, and goals. He suggests that different psychotherapies can be distinguished on the basis of these components, and that the strength of the therapeutic alliance is dependent upon the degree of agreement between the therapist and patient about the goals of therapy, the tasks of therapy, and on the strength of the bond between the therapist and patient.

The goals of psychotherapy are the general objectives toward which the psychotherapy is directed. For example, psychoanalysis assumes that the problems that bring people into therapy are a function of an underlying core of feelings, attitudes, and beliefs. The objective of psychoanalysis is to modify this underlying core rather than to remove symptoms. In contrast, the goal of traditional behavior therapy is much more likely to consist of eliminating the symptoms, rather than modifying the underlying core.

The tasks of psychotherapy consist of the specific activities (either overt or covert) the patient is required to engage in to benefit from the treatment. For example, classical psychoanalysis requires the patient to free associate by attending to the flow of inner experience and by attempting to report on that flow without censoring it. An example of an important task in cognitive-behavior therapy would consist of completing an active behavioral assignment between therapy sessions.

The bond component of the therapeutic alliance refers to the nature of the relationship between the therapist and patient. Bordin (1979) argues that different forms of psychotherapy make different demands upon the relationship. For example, the kind of bond necessary to encourage the patient to engage in a behavioral assignment is in all probability different in quality (although not necessarily in strength) from the kind of bond requiring the client to disclose intimate material to the therapist. The kind of bond necessary for a strategic therapy is likely to be very different than the kind of bond necessary for client-centered therapy.

In recent years, a number of therapeutic-alliance measures have been developed (for example, Luborsky et al. 1983; Gomes-Schwartz 1978; Marmar et al. 1986; Horvath and Greenberg 1986; Allen et al. 1984) that have reasonable psychometric properties and good predictive validity. D. E. Orlinsky and R. I. Howard (1986), in their comprehensive review of the research relating psychotherapy process variables to psychotherapy outcome, estimate that up to 80 percent of research relevant to the predictive value of the therapeutic alliance has produced significantly positive results. They also conclude that the perspective (therapist, patient, or third party) from which different aspects of the therapeutic relationship are measured, makes an important difference. It is particularly striking that when assessed from the patient perspective the evidence indicates that variables such as therapist empathy are consistently related to outcome; this is far less the case when measured from the perspectives of the therapist and a third party. In contrast, the research demonstrates that variables such as patient warmth and investment in the therapeutic process, and mutual or reciprocal affirmation between patient and therapist, are consistently predictive of outcome even when rated by third-party observers.

These findings suggest that although the quality of the therapeutic interaction and aspects of the patient's behavior that are relevant to outcome are observable to third-party raters, the important qualities of the therapist are in the eyes of the patient. It is, thus, the patient's perception of the meaning of the therapist's behavior that is a critical determinant of whether psychotherapy will be effective.

Therapist Competence

In contrast to the consistent failure to demonstrate that one form of psychotherapy is superior to other forms, empirical results are beginning to emerge that indicate that certain psychotherapists are consistently more effective than others (Ricks 1974; Piper et al. 1984).

Luborsky and coworkers (1986) re-analyzed the data from four major psychotherapy outcome studies to evaluate the impact of the therapist variable on outcome. They found that the size of the therapist effects in these studies overshadowed any differences due to treatment effects.

Although little other research has been done to evaluate the role of therapist effects, this work is consistent with evidence emerging from earlier research demonstrating that the personality of the therapist can play an important role in contributing to change, and that therapists who are assessed as having healthier personalities, both on objective measurements and peer ratings, have better therapeutic results than those who are not (Beutler, Crago, and Arrizmendi 1986).

Such evidence may lead some to conclude that if personality is more important than technique, research aimed at developing new techniques or trying to understand the mechanisms by which psychotherapy operates is futile. An even more pessimistic conclusion would hold that lay people with the appropriate personalities presumably can be just as effective as well-trained psychotherapists.

These positions reflect the assumption that one can treat the therapeutic techniques and the person that administers them as independent entities. As Butler and Strupp (1986) argue, however, it is more valid to conceptualize therapeutic technique and the person administering the techniques as inseparable parts of an organic whole.

An interesting study by Luborsky and coworkers (1985) is particularly relevant here. This study compared cognitive therapy plus drug counseling, psychodynamic therapy plus drug counseling, and drug counseling alone as treatments for drug dependency. Although they found that the three treatments were equally effective, significant differences emerged in the effectiveness of the individual therapists. The most significant variable distinguishing successful from unsuccessful therapists was the ability to form a good therapeutic alliance with patients. This, in turn, was mediated by therapist qualities like personal adjustment and interest in helping. These findings point to the inseparability of therapy technique, the personal qualities of the therapist, and the therapeutic relationship.

Although the quality of the therapeutic alliance as assessed early in therapy is predictive of outcome, poor therapeutic alliances are not irreversible. For example, Luborsky and coworkers (1983) found that early positive signs in the therapeutic alliance have considerable consistency from early to late sessions and are good predictors of outcome, but early negative signs of the helping alliance are not always negative predictors of outcome. They thus suggest that evidence about positive and negative signs of the therapeutic alliance are consistent with the observation about love relationships: "yes" means "yes," but "no" means "maybe."

Because the quality of the therapeutic alliance appears to be so important to therapy outcome, it is useful to have some idea of factors that may potentially sustain therapeutic alliances or improve upon them. Strupp (1980), in his intensive analysis of the data from the Vanderbilt I Study, found that a major characteristic of poor-outcome cases was a tendency for therapists to respond to patient negativism and hostility with counter-hostility.

S. A. Foreman and C. R. Marmar (1985) studied six patients assessed by the second session of time-limited psychodynamic therapy as having established poor therapeutic alliances. Of these six, three showed improved alliances and good outcome by the end of treatment, while three continued to have poor alliances throughout therapy and were low-outcome patients. The therapist actions that most strongly discriminated between the two groups were: addressing the patient's defenses; addressing the patient's guilt and expectations of punishment; addressing the patient's problematic feelings in relation to the therapist; and linking the problematic feelings in relation to the therapist with the patient's defenses.

While these two studies are preliminary, they point to some factors potentially responsible for maintaining poor therapeutic alliances as well as those that may contribute to improvement. Given the apparent centrality of the alliance to the therapeutic process, it would seem important for any fully adequate approach to therapy to focus on this topic in greater detail.

Implications for Cognitive Therapy

Both theoretical and empirical developments in the psychotherapy field are increasingly pointing to the pivotal role of the therapeutic relationship in the change process, and cognitive therapists are beginning to pay greater attention to the role of the therapeutic relationship in treatment. Systematic research and theoretical development on the topic are, however, lacking.

There are few empirical studies examining the therapeutic alliance as a possible predictor of treatment efficacy in cognitive therapy, and there has been a tendency in the cognitive-behavioral literature to conceive of the patient/therapist working relationship and the specific therapy procedures as independent, theoretically separable components of the treatment. J. B. Persons and D. D. Burns (1985), for example, maintain that "In contrast with most other psychotherapies, the nature or quality of the patient/therapist relationship in cognitive therapy is seen as important but not central to the treatment or its outcome (Beck, Rush et al. 1979). The active ingredient in the treatment, and the mechanism underlying the change in mood, is hypothesized to be the patient's decreased belief in his automatic thoughts, and the therapist's energies accordingly are directed primarily toward that end. A good working relationship is conceptualized as necessary but not sufficient for effective cognitive therapy" (p. 540). They conclude that relationship and technical factors play additive and independent roles in the change process.

As we have argued earlier, however, it may be possible to separate technical and relationship factors empirically, but it is not meaningful to do so on theoretical grounds. As the literature reviewed in this chapter suggests, the therapeutic alliance is not a static, unchanging entity but a fluctuating, dynamic aspect of the therapeutic relationship, mediated in an ongoing fashion by the *patient's perception* of the meaning of the therapist's actions.

It would thus seem that any "technical" intervention that the therapist makes will inevitably have an impact upon the therapeutic alliance. Conversely, any so-called "relationship enhancement" intervention is, in reality, a technical intervention that shapes the patient's perception of the meaning of the therapist's actions, thereby providing information relevant to his or her beliefs about other people. If we can begin to view "relationship interventions" from this cognitive perspective, the possibility of developing a refined understanding of factors that promote or retard the development of the therapeutic alliance begins to emerge.

Because cognitive therapy concerns itself explicitly with understanding and modifying perceptions, there is certainly no reason, in theory, for cognitive therapists to avoid investigating the relationship between the patient's perceptions and the therapeutic alliance. To do this, however, requires developing an understanding of the patient's characteristic way of construing events by identifying both the specific, interpersonal patterns that tend to be linked to this construal style and the events that take place in the therapeutic interaction.

An interesting example of such an attempt can be found in an article by A. Ryle (1979), who speaks of "dilemmas, snags, and traps" that constitute different kinds of impasses in psychotherapy. He defines traps as resulting from relating to others in an "either/or" and "if/then" fashion. An example of relating to the therapist in an "either/or" fashion is one where the patient appears to have the option of being either unduly accommodating toward others or unreasonably angry and aggressive. This kind of either/or dilemma can arise when a patient initially feels unduly accommodating to others, but then starts to feel abused and invaded by them, and as a result becomes irritable and angry. This reaction leads the patient to feel guilty and then, in response to the guilt, to become overly accommodating. Because the patient has only the alternatives of being unduly accommodating or unreasonably angry, he or she cannot escape from the cycle, which then creates an obstacle to therapy: the patient does not have the option of forming the kind of role relationship with the therapist that would lead to change. This example shows how problems in the therapeutic relationship can be linked to the patient's fundamental beliefs about interpersonal relationships and illuminates the integral link between modifying these beliefs and resolving the impasse in the therapeutic relationship.

A related approach can be found in the work of M. J. Horowitz (1979) and Horowitz and Marmar (1985) who introduce the concept of role-relationship models as a way of analyzing factors to see whether an adequate therapeutic relationship can be established. According to Horowitz and Marmar (1985): "Any individual patient can be described in terms of varied role-relationship models that he or she may use to organize expectations and intentions as they take place in psychotherapy" (p. 575). Certain kinds of role-relationship models facilitate the development of the therapeutic alliance; others are problematic.

Following Ryle's (1979) lead, Horowitz and Marmar (1985) list some dilemmas that recurrently emerge as obstacles to achieving an appropriate role-relationship model. Three examples are: (1) patients who are frightened about their own inner experience, but see it as an intrusion or invasion of privacy if the therapist tries to structure the communication of this experience; (2) patients so depressed or demoralized that very little of their effort works in therapy, but who experience the therapist as uncaring or naïvely optimistic about their ability to change if the therapist tries to address this attitude; and (3) patients who tend to act out and who increase their rebellion when the therapist addresses this pattern because they take the therapist's remarks as criticism.

While Ryle (1979) tends to specify each horn of the dilemma from the patient's viewpoint, Horowitz and Marmar (1985) attempt to specify standard therapist/patient interactional patterns that can lead to impasses in therapy. Both approaches are potentially useful. It would seem, however, that a comprehensive understanding of typical therapist/patient impasse patterns would involve both an understanding of the interpersonal patterns and the characteristic construal styles that lead to them.

The specific types of patient/therapist impasse patterns that Horowitz and Marmar (1985) describe can be viewed as the result of interaction between types of patient construal and the demands of the psychotherapy situation, or what L. N. Rice and L. S. Greenberg (1984) refer to as the specific-therapy "task environment." A task environment consisting of a challenge to the patient's cognitive distortions will interact in a specific and predictable way with patients who view significant others as critical and invalidating. For example, the task environment that consists of helping a patient experience warded-off affect may interact, specifically and predictably, with those patients who view significant others as intrusive or who believe their own feelings and ideas are overly chaotic and potentially disruptive to interpersonal relationships.

Cognitive therapy's focus on understanding the patient's current phenomenology is in some ways well suited to clarifying the nature of such therapeutic dilemmas. However, to pursue this line of investigation we need a better understanding of the way cognitive and interpersonal factors interact. What is the relationship between characteristic cognitive construal styles and redundant interpersonal patterns that are likely to emerge both in everyday life and the therapeutic relationship? How can the therapist use this kind of knowledge to facilitate the development of the therapeutic alliance? These are the questions that an integrated, cognitive-interpersonal perspective should be able to address, and that will be explored in the following chapters.

By analyzing problems in the therapeutic alliance through the interaction of the patient's typical construal style and the therapist's behavior, a possibility of "unpacking" the concept of the therapeutic alliance emerges (Safran 1990a; 1990b; Safran, Crocker, et al. in press), one that can potentially provide new insights into facilitating the alliance and resolving impasses in the therapeutic relationship that impede treatment.

The Therapist's Role
in the Therapeutic Interaction

Although cognitive therapy writings have increasingly emphasized the importance of relationship factors, little attention has been paid to the role of the therapist's feelings, thoughts, and reactions. The tendency is to assume that therapists will apply—optimally—whatever interventions are appropriate without their personal feelings interfering in any way. Perhaps it is assumed, as Wilson (1984) suggests, that therapists learn to deal therapeutically with their own feelings and reactions through their own personal experiences or that clinical supervision teaches them these skills. Given the importance of this variable, however, these are dangerous assumptions to make.

Traditions in which the therapist's feelings are seen as an important source of information relevant to understanding the patient, such as some of the psychodynamic and interpersonal approaches, pay the greatest attention to this variable. Strupp (1980) pointed out the difficulty in harnessing negative feelings in therapists so that they can contribute to the therapeutic interaction rather than obstruct it. After comparing the course of therapy for high-outcome and low-outcome cases in the Vanderbilt Psychotherapy Project, he made the following observations:

> thus major deterrents to the formation of a good working alliance are not only the patient's characterological distortions and maladaptive defenses but—at least equally important—the therapist's personal reactions . . . traditionally these reactions have been considered under the heading of countertransference.
>
> It is becoming increasingly clear, however, that this conception is too narrow. The plain fact is that any therapist—indeed any human being—cannot remain immune from negative (angry) reactions to the suppressed and repressed rage regularly encountered in patients with moderate to severe disturbances. As soon as one enters the inner world of such a person through a therapeutic relationship, one is faced with the inescapable necessity of dealing with one's own response to the patient's tendency to make the therapist a partner in his difficulties via the transference. In the Vanderbilt Project, therapists—even highly experienced ones and those who had undergone a personal analysis—tended to respond to such patients with counter-hostility that not uncommonly took the form of coldness, distancing, and other forms of rejection. Needless to

say, to the patient such responses became self-fulfilling prophecies leading to a dissolution of the therapeutic relationship, early termination, and poor outcome. In our study we failed to encounter a single instance in which a difficult patient's hostility and negativism were successfully confronted or resolved. Admittedly, this may be due to peculiarities of our therapist sample and the brevity of therapy; however, a more likely possibility is that therapists' negative responses to difficult patients are far more common and far more intractable than had been generally recognized. (P. 953)

Although Strupp made these observations in the context of psychodynamic therapy, there is no reason to assume that cognitive therapists are any more immune to countertherapeutic reactions and feelings than their psychoanalytic colleagues. Whether or not the central focus of the therapy is on the therapeutic relationship, it would seem vital to have an integrated theoretical perspective that (1) accounts for the role a therapist's feelings and reactions play in the interpersonal system created by the therapist and patient and (2) clearly articulates technical prescriptions for using a therapist's feelings and reactions in the service of therapy rather than allowing them to become obstacles to therapy. Incorporating this perspective into an integrative theoretical framework would permit us to analyze the therapeutic alliance as a function of continuing transaction at both cognitive and interpersonal levels. Such a framework for understanding therapy processes must be formulated in the context of an even broader perspective: the understanding of the relationship between cognitive and interpersonal processes in human development and everyday functioning.

CHAPTER 4

A Theoretical Model
for Integration

Cognitive versus Interpersonal Processes

Since the late 1960s, increased attention to the role of cognition in the etiology and treatment of emotional disorders has sparked a prodigious research effort that has yielded an impressive literature on cognitive processes. Although attesting to the popularity of the cognitive model among psychopathology researchers, this literature has produced its share of controversies (Segal and Shaw 1986a; 1986b).

One debate that has intensified in recent years concerns the relative importance of cognitive versus interpersonal processes in the etiology and treatment of emotional disorders. Much of this controversy has revolved around the cognitive model of depression and has far-reaching implications. One of the more enduring criticisms leveled at cognitive models of depression has been that cognitive therapists pay insufficient attention to the environmental difficulties faced by depressed persons, and then fail to understand why their efforts to cope with stressors are often unproductive (Coyne and Gotlib 1983; 1986; Krantz, 1985). These writers also point to the literature on social factors in depression, which suggests that the interpersonal aspects of this disorder are related to its maintenance and to the patient's eventual recovery (Brown and Harris 1978; Weissman and Paykel 1974). Research has demonstrated, for example, that the lack of a confiding relationship with the marital partner contributes to the patient's vulnerability to depression (Brown and Harris 1978), and that angry criticism from a spouse (Hooley, Orley, and Teasdale 1986), or an increase in the rate of marital arguments, frequently precedes the onset of a depressive episode (Weissman and Paykel 1974).

Studies examining both the behavior of depressed persons engaged in social interaction and the responses of other people to them support the idea that depressed persons demonstrate an interpersonal style that is markedly different from that of nondepressed persons. I. H. Gotlib and R. F. Asarnow (1979) found them to be less skilled in solving interpersonal problems. In conversations with others, depressed persons frequently focus on themselves and speak in negative tones with the goal of communicating self-devaluation, sadness, and helplessness (Biglan et al. 1985).

Their marital functioning has also received scrutiny. In a sample of twenty depressed persons interacting with their spouses and opposite-sex strangers, M. Hinchcliffe, D. Hooper, and F. J. Roberts (1978) found that compared to the interactions of control subjects (nondepressed surgical patients), couples with a depressed spouse showed greater conflict, tension, and negative expression. M. Hautzinger, M. Linden, and N. Hoffman (1982) found similar results in their study of twenty-six couples seeking marital therapy. Among the thirteen couples where one spouse was depressed, communication patterns were more disturbed than were those in couples without a depressed partner.

Hostility is also a common factor in such patterns of interaction. H. Arkowitz, S. Holliday, and M. Hutter (1982) found that following interactions with their wives, husbands of depressed women reported feeling more hostile than did husbands of psychiatric and nonpsychiatric controls. J. Kahn, J. C. Coyne, and G. Margolin (1985) also reported that following marital interactions, couples with a depressed spouse were sadder, angrier, and saw each other as more negative, hostile, and detached than did nondepressed couples.

Living with a depressed person can take its toll on the partner. Coyne and colleagues (1987) found that up to 40 percent of survey respondents living with a depressed person were distressed enough to meet referral criteria for therapeutic intervention. They point out that clinical depression often signals the presence of a more generally dysfunctional interpersonal context and that what cognitive therapists identify as distortions in thinking ought to be more properly seen as features of the depressed patients' exchange with the environments they live in. Their cognitions may be negative because they are reflections of interpersonal realities. The danger here is that an inaccuracy in the cognitive model of depression—the assumption that depressives distort information negatively—will lead to clinical abuse wherein therapists challenge or intervene in the perceptions that patients present rather than try to discover whether the circumstances that patients live in cause these construals.

Coyne and Gotlib (1986) suggest that either cognitive modeling of depressive processes be abandoned in favor of descriptions of the circumstances of depressed people's lives, or that cognitive therapy be eschewed in favor of systemic approaches. In our view, this solution replaces one theoretical imbalance with another. Others (for example, Bedrosian 1981; Gotlib and Colby 1987; Krantz 1985; Meddin 1982) have suggested that techniques from both cognitive and systemic or interpersonal approaches be combined. The problem with this solution, however, is that it can lead to an uninformed eclecticism rather than a genuinely integrative theoretical perspective.

The debate over the relative importance of cognitive versus interpersonal factors parallels the debate over the relative importance of specific versus nonspecific factors in the change process. It assumes that cognitive and interpersonal processes are theoretically separable. We argue that cognitive and interpersonal levels are completely interdependent; they are two sides of the same coin. What is required is an integrative theoretical model that clarifies the nature of this interdependence. Such a model can be useful in shedding light on our understanding of the development of emotional disorders, and on the relationship between specific and nonspecific change factors in therapy.

Experimental Cognitive Psychology

Despite the increasing popularity of cognitively oriented theorizing in psychotherapy, there is no single, uniform, cognitive theory of personality development, psychopathology, and change, only a host of differing cognitive concepts, many of which appear to be independent and lacking in cohesion (Greenberg and Safran 1980; 1981).

To find an encompassing, theoretical underpinning for their work, researchers and theorists in cognitive therapy are more and more turning to experimental cognitive psychology (for example, Goldfried and Robins 1983; Hollon and Kriss 1984; Ingram and Kendall 1986; Segal 1988; Williams et al. 1988). Their hope is to develop cognitive models of emotional disorders by accumulating findings from empirical research and employing rigorous methodologies originating in the cognitive sciences.

Indeed, it is easy to find examples of concepts derived from experimental cognitive psychology that have been applied to the analysis of specific disorders (for example, anxiety: Mathews and Macleod 1985; depression: Segal et al. 1988; Segal and Vella in press) and used to describe the process of change in cognitive therapy (Ingram and Hollon 1986; Winfrey and Goldfried 1986).

Because the enthusiasm of cognitive therapists for experimental cognitive psychology shows no sign of abating, we believe it is important to evaluate some of its strengths and weaknesses. In this section, we will argue that despite its virtues as a scientific paradigm, cognitive psychology—particularly the information-processing approach—has shortcomings as a broad theoretical framework for understanding the relationship between cognitive and interpersonal realms in human development and the process of change.

To find the foundation for such a model we will first examine the strengths and weaknesses of contemporary cognitive theory. We will then examine the ways in which we might incorporate theory and research from such areas as developmental psychology, emotion theory, and attachment theory into an expanded cognitive model, one that views cognition, emotion, and action as integrated aspects of a biological organism that develops and functions in an interpersonal context.

Since the 1950s, when cognitive challenges to the more firmly ensconced behaviorist traditions could no longer be ignored, it has been clear that simple associationist accounts of the chaining between a stimulus and a response could not possibly account for the complexity and hierarchical organization of serially ordered behavior. Nor did these accounts adequately describe how behavioral sequences come to be planned and organized (Gardner 1985). The alternative that cognitive scientists proposed was to develop models of human thought that would allow them to analyze the process by which stimuli are converted into behavior and to engage in empirically derived research that would avoid the pitfalls encountered by introspectionists in earlier attempts to grapple with these same problems.

A key feature of the cognitive sciences, according to Howard Gardner (1985), is an emphasis on mental representation as an explanatory construct: environmental features are coded and manipulated in imagination and the results of these computations are then acted upon. Two other features are an emphasis on the computer as a metaphor for understanding and modeling cognitive processes and an inter-disciplinary approach, which draws on information from philosophy, linguistics, anthropology, neuroscience, artificial intelligence, and psychology.

As outlined by R. Lachman and J. Lachman (1986), information-processing approaches in clinical psychology can be traced to two emphases in the cognitive science tradition. The first is the formalist approach, which is closely linked to work in artificial intelligence and places a premium on the detailed development of computer simulations of mental processes. This work is aimed at theory development that spans both cognitive psychology and artificial intelligence and often relies on simulations or modeling of processes studied through computer programs.

The second is the neofunctionalist approach, which can be described as systematic research programs aimed at explicating the micro-organization underlying particular cognitive tasks. The interest here is to discover which variables influence cognitive performance and to try to construct appropriate mathematical models for conveying the detail of this performance. Within this tradition, classic paradigms include the use of verbal reports on imagery states, decision process analysis, and employing established procedures of memory measurement. This approach, in particular, emphasizes the use of laboratory studies of human performance and has, thereby, contributed to the increasing use of these tasks and procedures in the study of clinical problems.

Information-processing approaches have contributed to what has been a revolution in the information sciences. Psychology has also benefited from them through the detailed analysis of specific cognitive activities and the consequent modeling of these activities through verifiable programs and procedures, which have been hailed as a step forward from earlier introspectionist accounts of phenomena such as mental imagery, cognitive plans, and reconstructive memory. An additional benefit is that the scientific application of cognitive science methods to certain problems can provide a blueprint for their eventual solution, a "path" that can be traced backwards by other experimenters to establish its validity.

Taking the phenomenon of information processing that is out of awareness as an example, Meichenbaum and Gilmore (1984) point out that even if cognitive science findings show increasing convergence toward earlier mentalistic constructs, such as the unconscious, it is important that these conclusions be arrived at through the path of rigorous experimental research. Cognitive and other therapeutic approaches can benefit from the precision and rigor of cognitive science methods because these methods can be used to evaluate important theoretical constructs in addition to providing a way of productively reformulating those constructs that lack support. Understandably, the application of these tools to the investigation of clinical phenomena holds great appeal for those interested in approaching the study of psychotherapy scientifically.

Problems with the Information-Processing Approach

The information-processing approach clearly has its strengths, but as U. Neisser (1976; 1980; 1982) has argued, it has important limitations that need to be considered in evaluating its potential contributions. He points out that because the narrow laboratory tasks commonly employed in information-processing research lack ecological validity, the results often cannot be generalized to real-world situations.

Neisser (1982) has consistently argued that this lack of ecological validity restricts the ultimate value of cognitive theory. Citing the research on memory as an example of the problem, he argues that: "the results of 100 years of the psychological study of memory are somewhat discouraging. We have established firm empirical generalizations, but most of them are so obvious that every ten-year-old knows them anyway. We have made discoveries, but they are only marginally about memory; and in many cases we do not know what to do with them, and wear them out with endless experimental variations. We have an intellectually impressive group of theories, but history offers little confidence that they will provide any meaningful insight into natural behavior" (p. 11–12).

Neisser's criticism is, in part, a methodological objection that, in theory, one should be able to satisfy by designing experimental tasks that are more ecologically valid (for example, interacting with people rather than reacting to a written stimulus). The criticism about ecological validity, however, extends beyond this methodological point to a more fundamental concern.

The computer metaphor has shaped the information-processing approach, and has provided a way of thinking about human psychological processes that helped free experimental psychologists from the shackles of radical behaviorism, and made unobservable psychological processes accessible for experimental purposes. Such analogies are tremendously important in scientific inquiry because they open up ways of thinking about processes that are not clearly understood and guide experimental psychologists in selecting research questions and developing theories. As with any analogy, however, the computer metaphor has limitations. Although there are some similarities between computers and human psychological processes, there are also significant differences.

Critics of the information-processing approach argue that there is a tendency in this paradigm to conceptualize human beings as disembodied, competing machines that neither feel nor act. They question whether it is possible to understand how cognition functions outside the context of action and emotion (Safran and Greenberg 1986; 1987).

To quote R. Shaw and J. Bransford (1977), in pursuing the person/computer analogy, cognitive psychologists "tend to forget that humans and animals are active, investigatory creatures driven by definite intents through complex, changing environments which are replete with meaning at a variety of levels of analysis. Thus we feel no tinge of theoretical compunction in blindly comparing such active, knowledge-seeking beings with unconscious, static machines that lack a whit of natural motivation. Unlike humans and animals, who perceptually mine the world for information on a need-to-know basis, artificial systems can soak up information passively by being spoon-fed batches of alphanumeric characters that have been conceptually predigested by human programers . . . in such a sterile model of man, perceiving becomes a passive process and knowing a purposeless one, and as for action (that is, purposive behavior) it remains nonexistent" (p. 3).

Computers perform various activities because they are programmed to process information that way. In computers, motivational questions are irrelevant. In human beings, they are paramount. Why people do certain things and act the way they do are questions of central significance in everyday life and certainly in psychotherapy. The information-processing approach, influenced as it has been by the computer metaphor, was never intended to deal with motivational questions.

Neisser (1967) recognized this in his seminal work on cognitive psychology where he stated that: "Although cognitive psychology is concerned with all human activity rather than some fraction of it, the concern is from a particular point of view. Other viewpoints are equally legitimate and necessary. Dynamic psychology, which begins with motives rather than with sensory input, is a case in point.

Instead of asking how a man's actions and experiences result from what he saw, remembered, or believed, the dynamic psychologist asks how it followed from the subject's goals, needs, or instincts. Both questions can be asked about any activity, whether it be normal or abnormal, spontaneous or induced, overt or covert, waking or dreaming'' (p. 4).

Thus, there was a clear recognition early on that information-processing theory cannot provide a comprehensive perspective on human functioning. Although cognitive therapy's initial development was largely independent of cognitive psychology, this neglect of motivational issues also has been and continues to be characteristic of cognitive-therapy theory as cognitive therapists turn to cognitive psychology for an integrative metatheoretical framework.

The Concept of Motivation

Although cognitive-behavioral theory consistently eschews motivational concepts, there is little written in the cognitive-behavioral literature that explicitly clarifies the reasons for this omission. Also, in any discussion about the concept of motivation, an important, complicating factor is the confusion about what the concept means.

Although an elaborate analysis of the concept of motivation is beyond the scope of the present work (but see Peters 1960 for an excellent philosophical analysis), it would seem useful to distinguish between two different usages of the term that are often confused in practice. The first context in which the concept of motivation is applied is when an individual's specific actions are being assessed because there has been a breakdown in conventional expectations (Peters 1960).

To use Peters's example, when the question "Why did Jones cross the street?" is asked, a satisfactory answer well might be "To buy some tobacco." On the other hand, "To buy some tobacco" would be an odd answer to the question "Why did Jones crawl across the street?" In the second situation, then, unless Jones was able to offer an answer consistent with a rule-following, purposive model of man, it would be reasonable to inquire about his true motive. Thus, the first context in which the concept of motivation is evoked is when a person's behavior departs from conventional expectations and the reasons offered for that departure are not convincing.

In psychotherapy, for example, motivational questions are often asked when patients arrive late for a session and do not offer a reason for their tardiness that makes sense in terms of a rational, purposive model of behavior. The therapist, then, may begin to speculate about the patient's motivations. Cognitive-behavioral theorists may prefer to avoid dealing with the topic of motivation because of an understandable wish to take their patients' explanations at face value and a justifiable reluctance to make assumptions about their "true" motives.

The concept of motivation, however, is also employed to provide a general explanatory model for human action. In this second context, the questions are: What factors are responsible for the organization of human behavior? What are the various forces, goals, and needs that shape the organization of human behavior? This second context often interacts with the first context. When an individual's behavior departs from conventional norms and we are not satisfied with the explanation in terms of a rational, rule-following model, we turn for guidance to a general theory of motivation to answer the question.

Information-Processing Theory versus Drive Metapsychology

Unlike traditional cognitive theory, motivational questions lie at the heart of classical psychoanalytic theory. Here, the motivational theory is drive metapsychology. Another reason that behavioral and cognitive-behavioral theorists avoid motivational theorizing is that they object to such aspects of drive metapsychology as Freud's psychosexual model, the theory of infantile sexuality, and the role that unconscious sexual and aggressive impulses are hypothesized to play in human behavior. Moreover, criticisms of drive metapsychology from within the psychoanalytic community and tensions between proponents and critics of drive metapsychology have been a central creative dialectic within the development of psychoanalytic theory (Greenberg and Mitchell 1983).

It may, thus, be instructive to examine the function that drive metapsychology was initially intended to perform within Freud's theoretical enterprise, and to look at the problems with it. Freud's drive theory and psychic energy model were developed to explain the way psychological and biological factors interact to organize human action.

As Greenberg and Mitchell (1983) state: "Freud's research took him into what he regarded as the 'depths' of human experience, the impulses that were manifestations of man's biological nature, demands generated by the body which provide the energy for, and the goals of, all mental activity'' (p. 3). His ideas about motivation reflected his early training in neurophysiology and his use of the concept of instinct was an attempt to link psychoanalysis with biology. Freud thus considered all aspects of human functioning, personality development, and psychopathology as derivatives or as a function of drive. He was convinced that we could never truly understand human beings unless we understood them as biological creatures, and that any psychology that failed to grasp this fundamental aspect of human functioning would be shallow.

Proponents of drive metapsychology are concerned that its abandonment would mean the abandonment of one, if not *the* most important, of Freud's insights: that human beings are not exclusively rational rule-following creatures, but rather biological organisms who are ruled by animal passions not always obvious to them. Their concern about the potential neglect of this human biological heritage in psychological theorizing is consonant with some of our criticisms of the information-processing paradigm.

Critics from within the psychoanalytic community have, however, identified problematic features within drive metatheory. First, the unit of analysis for Freud was the individual, rather than the individual in interaction with others (Eagle 1984; Greenberg and Mitchell 1983). People are not viewed as intrinsically social animals. Instead, society is imposed upon individuals who are already complete within themselves and who accept the protection of society at the cost of renouncing many of their most personal goals. In this model, it is possible to speak about the individual outside an interpersonal context.

The origin of all human activity can, thus, be ultimately traced to the demands of a biologically inherited instinctual drive whose origin is not influenced by social context. In this model, there is no inherent object, no preordained tie to the human environment.

Empirical evidence, however, suggests that to the contrary, human beings are innately interpersonal in nature. H. F. Harlow's (1958) classic studies, for example, showed that an infant monkey's attachment to its surrogate mother is not secondary to or derivative of a nonsocial instinctual drive (for example, hunger or thirst). Rather, such attachment seems to be based on an instinctive propensity for seeking what Harlow (1958) called contact comfort.

The research evidence also suggests that human infants are biologically biased to be sensitive to information transmitted by other human beings. For example, R. Fantz (1963) in a series of studies demonstrated that infants prefer looking at human faces than at other visual patterns. Other research (for example, Friedlander 1970) demonstrates that infants prefer the human voice to other sounds of the same pitch and loudness, and that infants gaze differently when scanning live human faces than when viewing geometric forms. When scanning human faces, they are less captured by single features or elements and scan the entire face more fluidly (Donee 1973). Infants also act differently when scanning new faces than when scanning inanimate patterns. When scanning new faces, they move their arms and legs and open and close their hands and feet in a smoother, more regulated, and less jerky fashion. They also emit more vocalizations (Brazelton, Koslowski, and Main 1974).

Further evidence indicates that two- to three-day-old infants can discriminate and imitate smiles, frowns, and surprised expressions seen on the faces of live human beings (Field et al. 1982). Evidence suggests, then, that infants appear to have a wired-in ability to detect and discriminate between facial features and the facial expressions associated with different emotions.

Finally, research on intersubjectivity, which can be defined as a "deliberately sought sharing of experiences about events and things" (Trevarthan and Hubley 1978), indicates that infants seek and are able to share a variety of subjective experiences with others before the development of verbal ability. One type of evidence indicates that at a very early age infants are able to share their mothers' focus of attention. For example, C. M. Murphy and D. J. Messer (1977) showed that nine-month-old infants detach their gaze from the pointing hand of the mother and focus upon the object to which she is pointing, suggesting that at this early age the infant can appreciate the subjective intention behind the mother's pointing gesture. Other research indicates that at an even earlier age infants are able to follow the mother's line of vision when she turns her head (Scaife and Bruner 1975).

Another line of research demonstrates that shortly after nine months, infants are able to understand and communicate intentions and expectations in a subtle form. For example, J. Dunn (1982) and Dunn and C. Kendrick (1979; 1982) have observed that young infants share jokes with slightly older children. A three-year-old and a one-year-old may suddenly burst into laughter over a private joke for which no one else can find the cause. Such events require the ability to understand and share the mental state and intentions of the other without direct verbal communication.

The accumulating evidence thus suggests that human beings are innately interpersonal creatures. The failure of drive theory to take this into account is thus problematic.

The second major concern about drive metapsychology is that it is a mechanistic theory and thus incompatible with a psychology of meaning. Freud's concepts of psychic energy, libidinal cathexis, and the constancy principle use physical and hydraulic metaphors. As M. M. Gill (1976) has noted, drive metapsychology is formulated within a natural science framework of force, energy, and structure that has no natural connection to psychological propositions dealing with intention and meaning. Drive metapsychology can be understood, in part, as an attempt to conceptualize the data of psychology in terms that were analogous to those that were current in contemporary physics and chemistry during Freud's day (Sulloway 1979). Freud, who was eager to frame his concepts in proper, acceptable scientific terms thus borrowed theoretical concepts developed by theorists in the natural sciences, such as G. T. Fechner, H. Helmholtz, and J. F. Herbart. This emulation of the natural sciences is not unlike the tendency of contemporary cognitive therapists to borrow from the developments in the more established cognitive sciences.

That Freud's thinking was inevitably colored by a now outdated scientific framework does not mean, however, that his desire to understand the link between biology and psychology was fundamentally misguided. As we have argued, one of the significant problems arising from the attempt of cognitive therapists to borrow a metatheoretical framework from cognitive psychology is the exclusion of considerations of our biological heritage and the resulting failure to deal with purposive or motivational aspects of behavior.

An Alternative Approach to Motivation

We have identified two major concerns about the incorporation of motivational concepts in psychotherapy theory. The first is clinical, that is, the potentially pernicious practice of discounting the patient's subjective experience and making assumptions about the patient's underlying motives. The second is theoretical, that is, problems with the motivational framework that originated in classical psychoanalytic theory. In recent years, however, new theoretical and empirical developments in two allied psychological areas have provided the foundation for an alternative way of conceptualizing motivational issues, one that is more consistent with both cognitive and interpersonal perspectives and is also nonmechanistic. The first area is attachment theory (Bowlby 1969; 1973), and the second consists of recent theoretical and empirical developments in emotion theory (Greenberg and Safran 1987; 1989; Izard 1971; Lazarus 1971; Leventhal 1984; Lang 1983; Safran and Greenberg, 1986; 1989).

For over two decades, J. Bowlby's (1969) work on attachment theory has had an impact on both theory and research in developmental psychology, but its impact on clinical theorizing and research has been more recent. With the increasing popularity of interpersonal and object-relations theory, however, some empirically minded psychoanalytic theorists have begun to turn to attachment theory and related empirical developments in an attempt to link current psychoanalytic thinking to empirically grounded concepts (for example, Eagle 1984; Stern 1985).

Cognitive therapists have been slower to show interest in the interpersonal perspective, but cognitive theorists such as Guidano and Liotti (Guidano and Liotti 1983; Guidano 1987; Liotti in press), Mahoney (1985), and C. Perris (1989), have begun recognizing the importance of understanding the development of cognitive processes within an interpersonal context and have also begun to make use of theoretical developments in attachment theory. Bowlby's general approach, which is grounded within both contemporary ethology and contemporary information processing and cybernetic thinking, can provide part of a comprehensive framework for conceptualizing motivational issues. Because of this, it provides a perspective on human motivation that confronts some of the important issues currently not dealt with in cognitive theory, but which are compatible with contemporary cognitive theorizing.

Action Patterns/Behavioral Systems

Building on concepts previously developed by ethologists, Bowlby (1969) suggests that it is conceptually useful to understand the structure underlying fundamental sequences of social behavior in terms of action patterns that have been wired into the human species through a process of natural selection. He makes a distinction between two kinds of biologically wired-in behavioral patterns: fixed-action patterns and set-goal patterns. Fixed-action patterns are highly stereotyped, structured patterns of movement that once initiated follow their typical course to completion. Action patterns of this type are far more common in species lower on the phylogenetic ladder and have been studied extensively by ethologists. Examples would be the mating behavior of the three-spined stickleback fish (Tinbergen 1953) or the courtship displays of the goldeneye ducks (Dane, Walcott, and Drury 1959).

Set-goal patterns are more complex, less stereotyped forms of wired-in action patterns and are more likely to be found in human beings and other higher species. In a set-goal pattern, the particular goal of the action pattern is biologically wired-in and the system continuously selects specific behaviors and combinations of behaviors from a large repertoire until that goal is attained. These set-goal patterns can be referred to as goal-corrected systems because the system selects specific behaviors in response to continuous feedback on the organism's progress in pursuing the goal. In more advanced species, and in human beings in particular, instinctive behavior thus functions to direct the organism toward biologically wired-in goals, but in a relatively flexible way. The more sophisticated the organism, the greater the role that cognitive processes play in organizing and coordinating different action sequences and behavioral systems in the pursuit of biologically wired-in goals.

Wired-in behavioral patterns can be conceptually organized into units of different sizes. Some are relatively small and discrete; for example, the smiling response of the six- to eight-week-old infant in response to human facial features (Spitz 1946). This relatively simple behavioral system is initiated by specific stimulus configurations and is typically activated and terminated over a fairly brief time period. Other behavioral systems are more complex and involve the coordination of a number of smaller, simpler behavioral units over an extended time.

One example of a more complex behavioral system would be attachment behavior. Others are: mating behavior, exploratory behavior, and parenting behavior. Because attachment behavior is of particular significance to the interpersonal perspective, we will consider it in greater detail.

Attachment

Attachment behavior is a set-goal pattern of fundamental significance in human beings (Ainsworth 1982; Bowlby 1969; 1973; 1980; Stern 1985; Sroufe 1979). It has the specific biological function of maintaining proximity between the infant and the primary caregiver. When the infant becomes separated from the primary caregiver, a number of specific, component, behavioral systems can be activated to reduce the distance between them or maintain their proximity. Some of these behaviors function by drawing the caregiver to the infant, for example, crying and smiling. Other behaviors function to bring the infant to the caregiver, for example, clinging and following (Bowlby 1963).

Like other wired-in behavioral patterns, attachment behavior plays a role in the survival of the species. In human beings and other higher species who are helpless at birth and completely dependent upon the primary caregiver for a long period after birth, attachment behaviors play an important role in ensuring infants' physical safety and satisfaction of their basic physical needs. Moreover, because human infants are very much dependent on adults for learning the basic life skills necessary for survival, the maintenance of proximity is important.

Clearly, attachment behavior plays a significant role in the development of the infant, yet it does not end with infancy, but rather continues in different forms throughout the lifespan. Maintaining proximity to other human beings has an important survival function in adults and was particularly important in the environment of evolutionary adaptedness for human beings, where interpersonal isolation exposed a human being to predators and other natural catastrophes.

Emotion and Behavioral Systems

In traditional cognitive-behavioral theory, emotion is regarded as a postcognitive phenomenon. In traditional cognitive-behavioral treatments of emotion the focus is on negative, affective states, such as anxiety and depression, and on developing techniques for controlling them. Little attempt is made to understand emotion as an integrated aspect of the human biological system with a particular role to play in human functioning. More recent treatments of emotion by cognitive theorists (Greenberg and Safran 1984; 1987; 1989; Safran and Greenberg 1986; 1987; in press; Guidano 1987; Guidano in press; Mahoney 1983) are remedying this neglect.

There is growing acceptance, bolstered by empirical evidence, that emotion has an intrinsic connection to action dispositions or to behavioral systems (Greenberg and Safran 1987; Safran and Greenberg 1986). Although this perspective on emotion was recognized by

Bowlby (1969) and some emotion theorists (for example, Arnold 1960; 1970; Izard 1971; Plutchik 1980; Tomkins 1962), it has been more fully articulated in recent years by a wide range of emotion theorists with greater grounding in contemporary cognitive information-processing theory (Buck 1980; Frijda 1988; Lang 1983; Leventhal 1984). This perspective attempts to integrate what we know about cognitive information-processing with a biological and evolutionary perspective on emotion and regards emotion as a biologically wired-in form of information about the self in interaction with the environment.

When behavioral systems of varying degrees of size and complexity are evoked by the right activating conditions, information about the organism's preparedness to act in a specific way is continuously processed subjectively through emotional experience. Specific emotional states are thus linked with specific action dispositions. Anger, for example, occurs in response to an event experienced as an assault and is associated with actions that are self-protective and retaliative. Fear is evoked by events appraised as dangerous and is linked to hypervigilance and flight. Love is linked to affiliative behaviors. The core of emotional experience thus consists of organized expressive-motor acts associated with behavioral systems that are biologically wired-in through a process of natural selection.

Emotion serves an important adaptive function because it provides us with a continuous readout of our system's preparedness to engage in certain types of behavior or to implement various behavioral systems (Leventhal 1984). This readout is subjected to a higher level of cognitive processing from which decisions are then made about which behavioral systems to implement and how to achieve coordination among these systems. Emotional processing thus provides a means of integrating and coordinating wired-in behavioral systems of varying degrees of complexity with higher level cortical processes and executive functions (Leventhal 1984; Greenberg and Safran 1987; Safran and Greenberg 1986). In addition to providing a readout of behavioral systems that are pressing for activation, emotion also provides a continuous readout of how well a set-goal behavioral system is proceeding to its goal once it has been activated.

Although the human organism's basic structure for emotional experience is genetically wired-in, the idiosyncratic quality of the individual's emotional experience evolves as a result of individual learning experiences as do differences in the conditions that will activate different behavioral systems. Emotion is thus a complex blend of biology and learning, wired-in action patterns and complex symbolic processes. It is beyond the scope of this book to speculate in detail about the ways in which this blending takes place, but interested readers are referred to other sources such as Greenberg and Safran (1987; 1989) and Safran and Greenberg (1986; in press).

The Coordination of Behavioral Systems

At times, it is inevitable that the organism or individual will encounter activating conditions that elicit conflicting behavioral systems or action dispositions. For example, an individual may be in the vicinity of a stimulus that would normally activate exploratory behavior, but appraises the immediate environment as dangerous. Or an individual encounters an activating condition that elicits both aggressive and attachment behaviors. The way the individual reconciles conflicting behavioral dispositions or behavioral systems plays a pivotal role in the development of personal identity.

As Sullivan (1953) theorized, there is a continuous tension between what he referred to as *satisfaction needs* and *security needs*. According to him, in the development of the human species, satisfaction needs are phylogenetically prior to security needs. They include such basic biological needs as hunger, sexual desire, and self-protection. Security needs are the wired-in propensity for interpersonal relatedness.

Although the particular ways in which these biologically wired-in behavioral systems ultimately come to be coordinated and expressed are determined by the individual's social learning experiences, these social learning experiences are themselves influenced by an innate propensity for maintaining interpersonal relatedness. Thus children learn to coordinate their affective and behavioral repertoire in the process of maintaining relatedness with attachment figures. For example, one child may learn to suppress the full activation of behavioral systems associated with dependency and to experience associated feelings as aversive. Another child, who learns that implementing behavioral systems that seek succorance along with playful, sexually toned behavior can lead to warm responses from others, may learn to act seductively as a way of maintaining interpersonal relatedness. In both examples, the attachment process mediates the coordination of behavioral systems in a particular configuration. Thus, it is through social learning experiences that the human organism's rudimentary, wired-in structures for behavior are filled in and elaborated on. Through a process of natural evolution and adaptation to its particular ecological niche, the human organism has so evolved that it is biologically programmed to undergo further programming through social-learning experiences.

The human infant's receptivity and sensitivity to the influence of attachment figures, although tremendously important for survival, ironically contain the seeds of pathological development. Whereas adaptive social-learning experiences provide the necessary opportunity for the infant to learn to elaborate, activate, and coordinate various behavioral structures in healthy and adaptive ways, maladaptive social-learning experiences do the opposite and contribute to the impoverishment of behavioral repertoires.

Throughout the individual's lifespan, the attachment system mediates the precise way in which other behavioral systems become elaborated, coordinated, and expressed. A primary way this mediation takes place is through influencing the choice of rules to follow in processing information from these other behavioral systems, information that is experienced subjectively in the form of emotion. The attachment system thus plays a central role in mediating emotional development which, in turn, functions as the primary motivational system in the human organism (Greenberg and Safran 1987).

A core feature of an individual's subjective experience of self is the particular pattern in which his or her behavioral systems and associated emotions become organized and structured through various learning experiences. Conversely, the sense of self can be thought of as a psychological structuring of internal experience that shapes future experiences and behaviors. For these reasons, a detailed understanding of how the self becomes structured is useful in understanding both normal and pathological development.

Development of the Self

The self is an invariant pattern of awarenesses through which psychological processes are organized (Stern 1985). It provides an organizing subjective experience that gives perception a sense of coherence and unity. Without an organizing sense of self, sensory experiences would be fragmented and incoherent, and little distinction would exist between self and others, or for that matter, self and the rest of the world. Furthermore, without a sense of self there would be no appreciation of the continuity of experience over time, and therefore no organizing structure for experience (Guidano 1987; Hartman and

Blankstein 1986; Markus 1977). For these reasons, if we are to understand the way cognitive processes are structured and organized and how they can best be changed, an understanding of the way the self develops would seem pivotal.

Because the capacity to detect invariants, and thus organize experience, is essential for survival purposes, the development of a sense of self plays a central role in cognitive development. D. N. Stern (1985) argues that there are four experiential invariants that are crucial to the core sense of the self. These are: agency, or authorship of action; self-coherence; self-affectivity; and self-history.

According to Stern (1985), agency or authorship of action is the most fundamental invariant of core self-experience and consists of the sense of volition that precedes a motor act and the sense of predictability and consequences that follow actions. Without this fundamental sense of agency, people could not learn to manipulate the world for survival purposes.

Self-coherence describes the organization of different sensory, motor, and conceptual experiences into a unitary sense of self and involves having a sense of being a nonfragmented, physical whole with boundaries and a locus of integrated action. Without this sense of self-coherence the individual's experiences would be fragmented and depersonalized.

Self-affectivity consists of the organization of experience into different feeling states, each with a characteristic and invariant constellation of internal events; the individual experiences a characteristic and invariant pattern of proprioceptive feedback and subjective experience for each emotional state. Self-affectivity, according to Stern (1985), is thus a higher order of self-invariance. R. N. Emde (1983) explains this by suggesting that because the basic structure for different emotional experiences is "wired-in" to the human organism and remains invariant over time, affective experience plays an important role in maintaining the continuity of selfhood, while the individual changes in other ways.

Finally, self-history provides a continuity to experience through time, without which learning would be nearly impossible. Although a sense of self-history is essential for learning or for experience to be organized over time, it is precisely this aspect of selfhood that allows dysfunctional learning to take place. By imposing a historical structure on experience, the contents of subjective awareness become entrenched and in this way resist or stand in the way of new learning.

What factors mediate the development of self-knowledge? One factor, hypothesized to be crucial by Sullivan (1953; 1956), is anxiety. He maintained that anxiety is a noxious tension inversely related to the experience of feeling good about one's self, and that this experience results from the failure to integrate interpersonal relationships. Sullivan did not offer a completely articulated explanation of the connection between anxiety and lack of integration of interpersonal relationships, but then he did not have the knowledge now available from theory and research on attachment behavior and emotional development. In light of such current developments, it now seems reasonable to regard anxiety as a biologically wired-in form of feedback on potential danger to the organism.

As Bowlby (1969) maintains, animals of every species are genetically biased to respond with anxiety to stimulus situations that serve as naturally occurring clues to events potentially dangerous to that species. Because maintaining proximity to other human beings plays such an important role in the survival of the human species (particularly in the helpless infant who depends upon the caretaker for moment-by-moment survival), it is not surprising that the perception of a potential disruption in an interpersonal relationship would automatically elicit an anxiety response in human beings.

It is thus reasonable to hypothesize that human beings are by nature perceptually attuned to detect any clues regarding the potential disintegration of interpersonal relationships and are programmed to respond with anxiety. Anxiety serves as a cue function in that behaviors and experiences that become associated with the disruption or disintegration of relationships with significant others also become identified as dangerous and subsequently trigger anxiety.

As Sullivan (1953; 1956) describes it, we come to experience certain personal characteristics belonging to the self through the reflected appraisals of others. Those characteristics that are valued by significant others become personified as the self (the "good me," in Sullivan's terms), and positively valued, whereas those experiences and characteristics that are associated with a moderate degree of disruption in significant interpersonal relationships (and thus a moderate degree of anxiety) still become personified as part of the self, but come to be viewed negatively. (Sullivan referred to these feelings, experiences, and characteristics as the "bad me.")

At the extreme end of the continuum are feelings, characteristics, and experiences that have in the past been associated with severe disruption in significant interpersonal relationships. Because of the intense anxiety associated with these experiences, the processing of information around them, both external (reactions of others) and internal (thoughts and feelings), is obstructed, and such information is not well coded in memory. For this reason, experiences and characteristics associated with extreme anxiety do not become well integrated in memory with other information, and do not become cognitively represented as part of the self. Thus, Sullivan (1953; 1956) referred to experiences and characteristics of this kind as the "not me."

Research on affect attunement (Stern 1985) sheds additional light on the way interactions with attachment figures may play a critical role in developing the individual's subjective sense of self. Affect attunement takes place when the infant's mother performs some behavior or communication that expresses the quality of an affective state the infant has experienced, without its being a direct imitation of the infant's behavior or vocalization. For example, a nine-month-old girl becomes very excited about a toy, lets out an exuberant "aah!", and looks at her mother. The mother responds by scrunching up her shoulders and shimmying her upper body in a way that mirrors the exuberance, or lyrical quality, of the little girl's vocalization. In another example, a nine-month-old boy rhythmically bangs his hand on a soft toy and his mother responds by saying "kaaaaab-bam, kaaaaab-bam," in rhythm to the infant's banging (Stern 1985).

As these examples illustrate, the mother seems to be responding to the infant in a way that appears to capture some inner affective state experienced by the infant. That the mother's behavior is not an exact imitation of the infant's behavior or vocalization suggests that she is attuned to the infant's inner subjective state through an empathic process, rather than merely imitating surface behavior.

Stern and colleagues (1985) also investigated what would happen if the mother were instructed to misattune her responses. Typically, when the mother attunes her response to the infant's affective experience, the infant responds by continuing his or her play or activity as if nothing had happened. When, however, mothers were instructed to modify their attunement response so as to create a mismatch to the infant's inner experience, it was found that, typically, the infants would note the discrepancy and stop their behavior as if surprised. When the mothers were, then, instructed to attune their responses as they normally would, the infants would also resume their normal behavior.

Finally, Stern (1985) and colleagues have found that when these affect attunement responses are videotaped and the mothers are subsequently asked about these affect attunements, they are often not fully aware of their behavior. When the behavior is brought to their attention, however, and they are asked their reasons for performing these attunements, typical responses are that they want to "be with" the infant, "to share" with the infant, "to participate" in the infant's experience, or to "join in" the infant's experience.

Research on affect attunement is intriguing, because it suggests another important process that may play a role in the infant's development of self: accurate affect attunement may help the infant come to recognize his or her own internal states of feeling as forms of human experience that can be shared with others. Conversely, feeling states that are misattuned to may never be fully experienced as communicable human experience. Thus, infants who have parents who consistently misattune to specific feeling states for various reasons (such as a lack of empathic ability, which could come from not fully experiencing similar affective states in themselves, or from feeling threatened by the infant's feelings) may never develop the relevant feelings or emotions as part of their communicable experience. *Associated experiences and behavioral systems may thus never be fully defined as part of the infants' sense of self,* and the pursuit of various important developmental goals (for example, intimacy, autonomy, and exploration) may be blocked.

Another line of developmental research provides further evidence of the ways that early relationships can influence the infant's developing sense of self. This research indicates that young infants "read" their mothers' affective states to get a second appraisal of how they should feel in ambiguous situations. When an infant is placed in an ambiguous situation (for example, lured by an attractive toy to crawl across a "visual cliff"), he or she will look toward the mother and read her face for affective content. If the mother has been instructed by the experimenter to smile, the infant will cross. If, however, the mother has been instructed to show facial fear, the infant retreats from the visual cliff and may become upset (Campos and Sternberg 1980; Emde and Sorce 1983; Emde et al. 1978; Klinnert 1978; Klinnert et al. 1983). Research of this kind supports Sullivan's (1953) contention that, prior to the development of verbal ability in the infant, subtle affective states are communicated between mothers and infants by what he designated as an empathic process. This evidence also has important implications because it suggests that attachment figures can subtly communicate approval and disapproval of affective states to the infant and that this nonverbal communication can have a significant impact on the kind of experiences the infant comes to define as an acceptable part of the self, or as a negative part of the self, or completely disowns.

A final line of relevant evidence comes from research on errors and repairs in affective communication in mother-infant dyads. In normal mother-infant dyads, the interaction frequently moves back and forth between periods of affective coordination in which the mother attunes to the child's affective experience and periods of miscoordinated states in which the mother misattunes to the infant's affective experience or responds in an affectively negative way (Tronick and Cohn 1989). When the infant encounters a misattunement or negative response to his or her affect, a secondary affective state results. For example, if the infant's appraisal is that the goal of pursuing autonomy is blocked and that the block can be overcome, he or she may respond with anger. If the infant's appraisal is that the goal of seeking intimacy is blocked and that the block cannot be overcome, he or she may respond with sadness.

In healthy mother-infant dyads, the mother accepts and empathizes with the secondary affective response and the affective communication becomes coordinated again. The infant then experiences a positive affective state. In dysfunctional dyads, the mother does not empathize with the secondary affective state, and the miscoordinated affective state continues (Tronick 1989).

In normal mother-infant dyads, the continuous oscillation between interactive miscoordination or error and interactive repair helps the infant develop expectations that disruptions in the relationship are remediable and that negative affective experience will be transformed into positive affective experience. Infants develop representations of themselves as effective and of caregivers as trustworthy, and are thus able to maintain interpersonal engagement in the face of stress.

In dysfunctional dyads, this kind of representation does not take place, and they are unable to maintain interpersonal engagement under stress. Furthermore, because of the threat to interpersonal relatedness, they may develop difficulty in experiencing the primary emotion that has been misattuned to, or the secondary emotion, or both (Tronick 1989). As we shall explore in chapter 7, this has important implications for problems in the alliance that are likely to emerge in therapy as well as for the processes involved in resolving them.

In summary, we postulate three possible interpersonal processes through which self-development is mediated: the empathic transmission of anxiety, affect attunement and misattunement, and "reading" the other's affective state. As we will see, these interpersonal pro-cesses mediate changes in the patient's sense of self in therapy as well. We hypothesize that these processes shape the development of all the experiential invariants of selfhood postulated by Stern (1985). The particular affective experiences that become represented as part of the self color the nature of the individual's self-affectivity. The indi-vidual's sense of self-agency is colored by the associated pattern of behavioral systems which become represented as within the possible realm of self-expression. Those that are so represented are experi-enced as intentional. Others are not.

Developmental interactions that help the individual to integrate both internal and external experiences fully help facilitate a coherent sense of self. Conversely, repeated experiences of intense anxiety or poor affect attunement can result in a fragmented sense of self. In more extreme cases, borderline states or multiple-personality syndromes may develop. Finally, repeated, similar experiences with significant others (for example, attuning to one type of emotion but not to another) result, over time, in a sense of continuity and a stable sense of self-history for the individual. This stable sense of self-history, as we shall see, tends to maintain itself through both cognitive and interpersonal processes.

Memory and Self-Knowledge

The memory system is the medium through which different aspects of self-experience (that is, agency, affectivity, coherence, and conti-nuity through time) become integrated into one organizing subjective perspective.

In recent years, the schema construct has come to assume a central role in memory theory (Alba and Hasher 1983; Hasher and Zacks 1979). A schema can be defined as a generic cognitive representation that the mind extracts in the course of its exposure to particular instances of a phenomenon (Bartlett 1932). This generic knowledge structure guides the processing of both information and action. Most workers in the field would agree that there is no unitary schema the-ory, but rather a range of empirical findings that are interpreted in relation to memory effects held to be consistent with Bartlett's initial propositions about schematic processing. The schema construct that has received the most attention in clinical theory and in social cog-nitive research is the self-schema, but although the same term is

65

employed in both literatures, there is an inconsistency in the way that it is used.

In social cognition literature, for example, the self-schema has traditionally been defined as "cognitive generalizations" about the self, derived from past experience, that organize and guide the processing of self-related information contained in an individual social experience (Markus 1977).

In the cognitive-behavioral literature, however, the tendency is to view the schema as a self-worth contingency (Kuiper and Olinger 1986). Beck and his associates have been the major proponents of this perspective (Beck 1967; Beck, Rush et al. 1979), and view the schema as a tacit rule that guides the process of self-evaluation. In Beck's model, the self-schema of the depressed individual is viewed as a rigid and dysfunctional attitude that functions as a contingency for evaluating one's self-worth. For example, the tacit rule or belief that "I have to be perfectly competent at everything I do to be worthwhile as a person" might be seen by Beck and associates as an important part of a particular depressed individual's self-schema.

This notion of schema as self-worth contingency has appeal from a clinical perspective because the processes governing the individual's subjective perception of worthiness are of obvious clinical import. From a conceptual viewpoint, however, it is unclear how this perspective applies to schema theory in cognitive psychology. Clearly, the theoretical link between the generic representation of experience and the rules for evaluating one's self needs to be illuminated (Safran 1986).

H. Markus's (1977) definition of the self-schema as a cognitive generalization about the self is more closely linked to schema research in cognitive psychology. However, the focus on the processing of static information (that is, adjectives) that has emerged out of the social cognition research on the self-schema has, as Markus and P. Nurius (1986) have pointed out, imposed a narrow focus on the investigation of self-knowledge.

How then are we to broaden our conceptualization of the schema in clinical theory in a way that permits us to deal with central motivational and self-evaluational concerns yet still be linked to and informed by cognitive theory and research? As a way of meeting those concerns, Safran (1986; 1990a; 1990b; Safran, Segal et al. in press) has proposed the notion of an *interpersonal schema* that can be defined as a generic representation of self-other interactions, which is abstracted from interpersonal experience.

From this perspective the focus is on the schematic processing of *events* in the real world, rather than on the processing of static adjectives or trait information. The processing of self-referent adjectives, although lending itself well to laboratory investigation, does not reflect the type of phenomenon that the schema concept was developed to account for. It is instructive to recall that Bartlett (1932) originally developed his approach to account for the way people deal with new events in the real world.

He thus investigated memory for narratives rather than isolated words, reasoning that this would provide a closer simulation of the type of memory process involved in everyday life. Although reading a narrative may be a more ecologically valid task than memorizing adjectives, it still has its limitations. In the real world, knowledge acquisition is an active process in which people walk around, act, handle things, and interact with other people (Gibson 1969; Neisser 1976).

Consider, for example, the kind of knowledge structure that would be required to play tennis, which is very much of a process where the individual is in constant dynamic interaction with the ball. The skilled tennis player does not learn fixed motor movements, and even if the ball arrives at a place where it has never been before he or she is better at hitting the ball than the unskilled tennis player. The tennis player requires generic knowledge rather than knowledge of specific instances or fixed motor movements.

This generic knowledge is more complex and elaborate than the knowledge structure required to appreciate a story, and *far* more complex and elaborate than the knowledge structure required to process isolated words. The generic knowledge structure for tennis would include, for example, general expectations about where the ball may land, if-then contingencies (if the ball lands in a certain place use a forehand, if it lands in another place use a backhand), knowledge of the self (what are one's strengths and weaknesses), general goals, and strategies. Presumably the knowledge structure relevant to processing information about the self would be even more complex.

Representation of Self/Other Interactions

If the self develops in an interpersonal context, it seems reasonable to hypothesize that the development of self-knowledge involves the cognitive representation of interpersonal events. As argued earlier, one of the survival-relevant events of greatest importance for the human infant involves the interaction with attachment figures. Bowlby (1969; 1980), in fact, theorizes that human infants develop internal working models of interactions with attachment figures that allow them to predict future interactions. According to Bowlby (1969), an internal working model of attachment relationships is organized out of the inner representation of experienced outcomes or plans that have particular relevance to attachment. The working model concept goes beyond the notion of internalizing a model of self or a model of the other, because its organizational structure consists of interactional units, rather than self-elements or attributes. This internal working model can be thought of as an interpersonal schema that allows the prediction (and shapes the processing) of new social interactions.

What kind of information would be coded in an interpersonal schema of this type? Just as in the tennis example described earlier, the relevant schematic principles would probably extend beyond information-processing biases such as selection, abstraction, or interpretation, to information about goals, action plans, and if-then contingencies relevant to maintaining relatedness. It may thus be useful to think of the schema of interest as being somewhat like a *program for maintaining relatedness* (Safran 1986). While the basic goal of maintaining interpersonal relatedness is hard-wired into the program, the specific plans, strategies, and principles employed to obtain this goal are soft-wired, or learned.

Viewing the interpersonal schema as analogous to a program for maintaining interpersonal relatedness illuminates the link between schema as generic cognitive representation and schema as self-worth contingency. In this way it helps to bridge the sometimes discrepant usages of this term in both the clinical and cognitive literatures. It maintains the important clinical notion of a connection between self-worth/self-esteem and performance according to standards and also supports the social-cognitive emphasis on abstract personal knowledge capable of continuously guiding behavior. In an interpersonal schema, the self-worth contingency functions as a *rule or a plan for maintaining relatedness*. This rule is abstracted from previous experiences with attachment figures, and reflects both the perception of self and the perception of others.

The concept of the interpersonal schema also helps clarify the relationship between self-perception and the perception of others, because it proposes that perception of self and other is intrinsically interactional. In the realm of social perception, the unit of interest is *both* the representation of self and the representation of other. For example, an individual who perceives himself or herself as unlovable is particularly likely to perceive others in terms of rejection and hostility. The individual who views himself or herself as weak and needing care may be predisposed to perceive others with certain characteristics (warmth or maturity) as caregivers.

Hypothesized Memory Processes

There appears to be general agreement in the field that different episodes of lived experience (including various attributes like sensations, perceptions, actions, thoughts, affects, and goals) occurring in some temporal, physical, or causal relationship to one another become coded together as a unit in memory (Shank and Abelson 1977; Stern 1985; Tulving 1972). A memory episode is thus defined as an experiential unit coded as a whole.

Once a specific kind of episode has occurred a number of times (for example, the infant suckling at the mother's breast), the infant will form a generalized memory for such episodes. While some future breast-suckling episodes are sufficiently distinct from the generalized episode to be coded as separate episodic memories, others are sufficiently similar to be assimilated into the existing generalized memory. K. Nelson and J. M. Greundel (1981) refer to this kind of generalized memory as a Generalized Event Structure (GES). Stern (1985) refers to these generalized memories as representations of interactions that have been generalized (RIGs). According to him, these RIGs should be thought of as prototypes of abstractions rather than precise representations of specific events.

What is the conceptual relationship between Bowlby's (1969) working model, Stern's (1985) RIG, and the interpersonal schema? The working model and the RIG can be thought of as interpersonal schemas at different levels of abstraction and generality. It may be useful, as Neisser (1976) suggests, to think of schemas of different orders of abstractness and generality as being embedded within one another, and as functioning hierarchically. Bowlby's (1969) working model can thus be thought of as a higher order, fairly general interpersonal schema that has a number of more specific interpersonal schemas, or RIGs, embedded within it.

The growing evidence that people have multiple working models (Bretherton 1985) can also be understood in this way. One may have different interpersonal schemas for people who play different roles in one's life (for example, authority figures, prototypical lovers), and these lower level schemas may all be embedded within a higher level, more abstract and generalized interpersonal schema.

Another important question concerns the form in which interpersonal schemas are coded. Information relevant to attachment behavior, in all likelihood, has an important affective component (Bowlby 1969; Greenberg and Safran 1987; Stern 1985). It is thus hypothesized that, in part, interpersonal schemas are coded in affective or expressive-motor form (Bucci 1985; Greenberg and Safran 1987; Safran 1990a; Safran and Greenberg 1987). That is, the relevant interpersonal information may be partly coded in the form of procedural knowledge that people experience as a currently felt sense when they encounter certain activating conditions.

For example, people who have consistently been misattuned to or who have encountered anxiety when they feel hurt or sad may develop a generalized visceral memory of this kind of experience. In future interpersonal encounters, when they feel hurt, they may automatically generate a visceral memory of being misattuned to or rejected and then respond to this visceral memory with anger, even when other people are capable of being appropriately responsive to their sadness.

If, however, as H. Leventhal (1984) suggests, the emotional synthesis process takes place at both expressive-motor and conceptual levels, then the relevant information would be at least partly coded in conceptual/propositional form as well. It may thus be useful to conceptualize interpersonal schemas as cognitive-affective schemas that are coded at both conceptual and expressive-motor levels. While some aspects of an individual's interpersonal schema may be readily accessible in conceptual/linguistic form, other aspects may be more difficult to reach symbolically. In theory, it would be both possible and important to reach the expressive-motor level in therapy by working with patients in an emotionally alive fashion. Once this has taken place, the possibility exists of forming a conceptual representation of information coded at the expressive-motor level (Greenberg and Safran 1987; Safran and Greenberg 1987).

Interpersonal Schemas and the Management of Anxiety

From an interpersonal perspective, one's self-esteem and fundamental sense of security in the world are a function of one's sense of potential interpersonal relatedness. Conversely, one experiences anxiety when this sense of security or interpersonal relatedness is threatened (Sullivan 1953). Once this anxiety alerts one to the real or fantasized potential of an interpersonal relationship's disintegration, there are three primary operations that can re-establish one's self-esteem and sense of relatedness: implementing an action, processing external information selectively, and processing internal information selectively.

One's choice of operations will be determined by one's interpersonal schema. For example, when anxious, a person whose parents prized intelligence may attempt to demonstrate his or her intelligence. Another person, whose parents were entertained by their child's wit, may deal with anxiety by being entertaining. Someone who has learned that interpersonal relatedness is contingent on being agreeable may not fully pay attention to feedback from others that he or she is quarrelsome, and someone who learns that sadness is a threat to interpersonal relatedness may fail to pay attention to internally generated expressive-motor information conveying sadness.

Sullivan (1953) employed the term "security operations" to refer to psychological and behavioral maneuvers that function to reduce anxiety by re-establishing a sense of interpersonal security. While the concept of security operations has its origins in the psychoanalytic notion of defense mechanisms, there are important differences. The first difference is that the concept of security operations reflects an interpersonal perspective on human motivation.

Sullivan believed that security operations function to manage anxiety stemming from an expected disintegration of interpersonal relationships. The particular conditions that will elicit such anxiety are thus learned. In contrast, there is less room for learning in the classical psychoanalytic notion of defense mechanisms. Classical psychoanalytic theory holds that libidinal impulses are intrinsically threatening to the reality-oriented ego, reflecting Freud's belief that the individual and society are inevitably at odds, unlike interpersonal theory which holds that human beings have an innate propensity for interpersonal relatedness.

A second important difference is that the concept of security operations reflects Sullivan's scrupulous attempt to avoid the dangers of reification in his writing. The concept of security operations does not depend upon hypothetical constructs such as id and ego, which have a tendency to become reified. Instead the emphasis is on the process of what Sullivan referred to as "selective inattention," a phenomenon that has received considerable experimental documentation in recent years (Dixon 1981; Erdelyi 1985; Shevrin and Dickman 1980).

The concept of security operations also avoids reification in another way: It does not use a pre-existing classification scheme of defense mechanisms consisting of terms like projection, intellectualization, and reaction formation. This has important clinical implications. Although the use of a taxonomy of defense mechanisms has the same kind of heuristic value as any taxonomy, it creates problems. When therapists reify whatever operation the patient is engaging in with a pre-established classification scheme, it prevents them from fully exploring and understanding the subtleties of the particular operation the patient is engaging in. It is entirely possible for two patients to be engaged in a process classified as intellectualizing and to be doing it in very different ways.

It is important to recognize that the particular operations patients engage in to re-establish their subjective sense of interpersonal relatedness are intrinsic to who they are as people and to how they construe themselves in interaction with others. By understanding these operations as intrinsic, therapists can use them as windows into their patients' interpersonal schemas. For example, a patient who is engaging in the process of intellectualizing may believe that his or her value as a person consists of being smart and so deals with anxiety by attempting to speak intelligently. By treating this operation as intrinsic to the patient rather than as an obstacle to be eliminated, a door opens to a further understanding of who the patient is.

The Cognitive-Interpersonal Cycle

A fundamental observation from an interpersonal perspective is that there is considerable redundancy in the interpersonal patterns that characterize an individual's experience. In fact, Sullivan defined personality as "that relatively enduring pattern of recurrent interpersonal situations which characterize the human life" (1953, p. 111). A central problem becomes one of understanding how it is that these characteristic interpersonal patterns, or what Sullivan referred to as "me-you patterns," become established and maintain themselves.

Interpersonal theory postulates that "maladaptive behavior persists over lengthy periods, because it is based on perceptions, expectations or constructions of the characteristics of other people that tend to be confirmed by the interpersonal consequences of the behavior emitted" (Carson 1982). This was referred to as the "theorem of reciprocal emotions" by Sullivan (1953) and as the "principle of reciprocal interpersonal relations" by Timothy Leary (1957). Here, the basic premise is that expectations function as self-fulfilling prophecies that influence the environment.

People develop interpersonal schemas that are adaptive in a developmental context because the schemas permit the prediction of interactions with attachment figures. Unfortunately, these interpersonal schemas often fail to adapt to new circumstances because they continue to shape interactions. For example, people who anticipate hostility from others selectively interpret neutral behavior as hostile, respond to expected and perceived hostility with their own hostility, and thus elicit hostility from others. This evoked anger, in turn, confirms their expectations of hostility, thus maintaining their interpersonal expectations and perpetuating the cognitive-interpersonal cycle.

This type of cognitive-interpersonal cycle, or what Karen Horney (1950) referred to as a vicious cycle, has been well described by a number of theorists (Carson 1982; Kiesler 1982a; 1988; Luborsky 1984; Wachtel 1977). In contrast to an exclusively cognitive focus that emphasizes the way that people actively construe their environment, this perspective emphasizes that, as Strupp and Binder (1984) have stated it, people both *construe* and *construct* their environments.

There are a number of different types of dysfunctional cognitive-interpersonal cycles. In some cases the individual consistently responds in a maladaptive fashion because of his or her dysfunctional expectations about the interpersonal behavior of others. For example, the individual who anticipates that other people will be aggressive, as a result constantly acts in a self-protective, aggressive fashion. Another example would be the individual who anticipates that others are untrustworthy, and as a result is suspicious or has difficulty trusting other people.

Other cognitive-interpersonal cycles are shaped by the security operations described earlier. For example, people who manage anxiety by speaking intelligently may distance others by being pedantic. Those who believe that feelings of sadness or anger are unacceptable may present themselves in such an emotionally flattened manner that it is difficult to get close to them, thereby confirming their belief that these feelings are unacceptable.

Psychologically healthy people tend to have interpersonal schemas that predict interpersonal relatedness as reasonably attainable and that allow them to feel and act in a wide range of ways without jeopardizing interpersonal relatedness. In contrast, people who are less psychologically healthy expect interpersonal relatedness to be difficult to obtain and believe that a wide range of feelings and actions present potential threats to interpersonal relatedness. There is thus a continuum of psychological health. At the lower end of the continuum, one has extremely negative expectations about the possibility of interpersonal relatedness and believes that the contingencies for maintaining interpersonal relatedness are extremely narrow and rigid. Such people disown large parts of their internal experience (emotions and associated action dispositions) and have a highly restrictive sense of how they must "be" to maintain relatedness. At the upper end of the continuum, one has generally positive expectations about interpersonal relatedness, and as a result of supportive and consistent developmental experiences learns to integrate a wide range of different internal experiences into one's sense of self.

Traditional cognitive therapy postulates that psychopathology or psychological ill health is associated with rigid, dysfunctional attitudes or contingencies of self-esteem (Beck, Rush et al. 1979). Because traditional cognitive therapy does not, however, emphasize the importance of processing internally generated action-disposition information, it does not deal with the implications for psychopathology or therapy of failing to process this information.

To the extent that one has positive expectations about interpersonal relatedness, is able to process a range of emotions, and is able to act in a wide range of ways, one will tend to exhibit a wide range of interpersonal patterns depending upon the demands of the particular situation and the nature of the person one is interacting with. In contrast, the individual with rigid expectations of other people and a highly restrictive sense of how he or she must be to maintain interpersonal relatedness will be characterized by rigid, restrictive, stereotypic interpersonal patterns.

For example, a man who learns that feeling "needy" is a sign of weakness that leads to rejection may have difficulty experiencing and expressing vulnerable feelings. He thus presents himself as intellectualized and detached, appearing to take a philosophical view of his relationships. Because of his emotional unavailability, significant others may react distantly, thus confirming his dysfunctional beliefs about self and others.

A woman who learns that acts of self-assertion disrupt interpersonal relatedness has difficulty processing angry feelings and consistently behaves submissively. Because she expects others to reject her if she asserts herself, she tends to construe their behavior in a schema-consistent way, which further amplifies her attempts to behave submissively. This, in turn, pulls for dominant behavior from others, which reinforces her sense of self as submissive and others as dominant.

A central hypothesis in interpersonal theory is that interpersonal exchanges are governed by the principle of *complementarity* (Kiesler 1982b; 1983; 1988). This principle states that specific, interpersonal behaviors tend, predictably, to pull for other specific, interpersonal behaviors. Drawing on communication theory (for example, Danziger 1976), Kiesler (1988) theorizes that dyadic communication not only conveys information, but also defines the relationship between the participants. If one person acts in a dominant way it is a bid to define the relationship in a certain way, that is, the self as dominant and the other as submissive. It is always a statement about the relationship, because one's self can only be defined in relation to the other. The other can either accept the definition of the relationship offered or contest it by acting in a noncomplementary fashion. When an individual exerts a very strong pull for complementary behavior, however, it is difficult not to respond accordingly.

A large proportion of interpersonal communication takes place at a nonverbal or paralinguistic level (Ekman 1972; Kiesler 1982a); people may, for example, communicate submissiveness by a cringing quality in posture, a self-demeaning voice tone, and a lack of eye contact, or they may communicate hostility or competitiveness by very direct eye contact, a tilt of the nose, and a clenching of the jaw. Because of the subtlety of nonverbal communication, people are often unaware of what they are responding to when someone pulls them to act in a complementary way, which makes it difficult, if not impossible, for them to give feedback even if they were so inclined.

For these reasons, those who are psychologically maladjusted experience a much greater redundancy in characteristic interpersonal patterns than psychologically healthy individuals. They live in an interpersonal world of their own making and rarely have the opportunity to encounter an interpersonal experience that can provide schema-disconfirming evidence. Moreover, even in those situations where they are exposed to disconfirming information, they will tend to assimilate the new information into the old schema.

As P. L. Wachtel (1977) points out, there is irony in these maladaptive, cognitive-interpersonal cycles in that they are typically perpetuated and maintained by one's attempt to deal with the problem as one sees it. For example, one who hides sad feelings because of fear of alienating others ends up alienating others precisely because one hides vulnerable feelings. One who expects others to be hostile ends up eliciting hostility by the attempt to deal with the expected hostility. As system/strategic theorists maintain, the attempted solution is the problem (Haley 1963; Watzlawick, Weakland, and Fisch 1974).

The situation becomes further complicated because people with emotional problems often present messages at verbal and nonverbal levels that are incongruent or even two incongruent messages at the nonverbal level. Consider this example: A male patient consistently interacts with people with a condescending smile on his face that leads others to react with a feeling of irritation they are unable to pinpoint. This irritation, however, leaks through into their interactions with him and contributes to his feeling a resentment he has difficulty understanding but which he continues to leak out nonverbally in paralinguistic communication, which others, then, interpret as condescension and aloofness.

This kind of incongruent communication takes place when people have difficulty fully owning or processing certain feelings and action dispositions because their interpersonal schema predicts that they will be threatening to interpersonal relatedness. Thus, for example, one who has learned that anger threatens interpersonal relatedness may not synthesize this emotional experience into awareness, and yet nevertheless experiences it and communicates it on a nonverbal level.

In such situations, the people who interact with one may respond to such nonverbal information without awareness and be unable to communicate the reasons for their reactions. Moreover, patients may be totally unaware of the action-disposition information they are communicating and thus be completely mystified by the confused and irritating responses they elicit from others. This has important implications for the therapeutic process, as we will see later.

PART II

PRACTICE

CHAPTER 5

Assessment

Assessing Core Cognitive Processes

In recent years a number of cognitive-behavioral theorists have begun to distinguish what are designated as core cognitive processes from those deemed peripheral (Arnkoff 1980; Guidano and Liotti 1983; Mahoney 1982; Meichenbaum and Gilmore 1984; Safran, Vallis, et al. 1986). Although the definition of core cognitive processes varies from theorist to theorist, there is general agreement that they play a central role in organizing the individual's cognitive and behavioral processes and must ultimately be modified if therapeutic changes are to endure. Clearly, then, it is vital for cognitive therapists to have a way of identifying these core cognitive processes accurately. The perspective we have outlined suggests that one's core cognitive processes are associated with one's interpersonal schema. It also suggests that they are embedded within a distinctive cognitive-interpersonal cycle that maintains itself.

Because of the subtlety of these cognitive-interpersonal cycles it is difficult, if not impossible, to assess accurately either the cognitive or the interpersonal aspect of the patient's problem out of the context of the other. To begin this assessment process, it is useful to have a sample of the relevant cognitive-interpersonal cycle to work with. Although it is possible to obtain useful information by having the patient recount problematic events that have taken place between sessions, the patient's reconstruction of an event may depart significantly from actuality. Moreover, many of the most important cognitive processes will be relatively inaccessible unless the relevant cognitive-interpersonal cycle is actually taking place. For this reason, group therapy or marital therapy can be useful in providing opportunities for the relevant cognitive-interpersonal cycles to be enacted in the therapist's office. As these cycles are being enacted the therapist can stop at various points to explore the patient's cognitive processes.

In the absence of a group therapy situation, or in the absence of having a patient's significant others in the room, the therapeutic interaction itself can provide a useful sample of the relevant cognitive-interpersonal cycle. Of course, therapists must remember that they contribute significantly to any interaction with a patient, and that there is no guarantee the interactional pattern occurring in therapy is similar to other interactions in the patient's life. The likelihood that the interpersonal pattern emerging in therapy will be similar to the patient's other interpersonal patterns will, however, increase as the degree of both the patient's maladjustment and the associated strength of his or her interpersonal pull increases (Kiesler 1982b). Also, therapists must remember to use therapeutic interaction *only* to generate hypotheses and explore the patient's characteristic construal style; they must never make categorical inferences about the patient's interpersonal style and cognitive processes.

Participant-Observation

How can the therapist use the therapeutic interaction for assessment purposes? The most important principle here is to follow Sullivan's (1953) dictum that the therapist assume the stance of participant-observer, that is, one that allows oneself to feel the patient's interpersonal pull and to observe the interaction one participates in with the patient. Only then can the therapist pinpoint in greater detail the behaviors and communications that create the pull the therapist experiences and explore the cognitive processes linked to the patient's interpersonal style.

To the extent that the patient exerts a strong pull for a complementary response, the same response will be evoked in the therapist as in other people. The therapeutic tasks are twofold. First, to generate therapeutic hypotheses, one must be able to attend to one's own feelings and action tendencies while participating in the interaction with the patient. Second, one must find some way of unhooking from this interaction to avoid perpetuating the dysfunctional interpersonal cycle characteristic of the patient and becoming yet another person who confirms the patient's dysfunctional interpersonal schema.

This process of unhooking oneself from the patient's interpersonal pull and metacommunicating with the patient about the shared interaction is essential to all interpersonal or interpersonally oriented forms of psychotherapy. One of the best attempts at operationalizing this process in a systematic fashion is provided by D. J. Kiesler (1982b; 1986; 1988). Kiesler (1988) identifies a process-stage model for metacommunication consisting of two distinct stages: a hooked stage and an unhooked stage. In the engaged or hooked stage, the patient's behavior forces or pulls the therapist into a narrow and restricted range of responses. The pull for complementary responses to the patient's own behavior is greatest at this point and the therapist is pushed into a position that is supportive and nonthreatening to the patient's self-definition.

In the disengaged or unhooked stage, the first therapeutic task is to notice, attend to, and try to label whatever is being pulled from the therapist by the patient. At this point, important cues are the repetitive patterns of the therapist's internal responses or the feeling that whatever is going on with the patient is recurrent or cyclical. The second step in the disengagement process involves discontinuing the complementary responses, and the third step is working with the patient to help interrupt his or her characteristic response-evoking style. In the final step, the therapist speaks directly to the patient about their interaction, making specific reference (metacommunicating with the patient) to the therapist's distinctive response to specific patient behaviors.

Interpersonal Markers

As Kiesler (1988) points out, an important part of the metacommunication process involves pinpointing specific instances of the patient's actions that appear to be associated with or linked to the feelings and action tendencies evoked in the therapist. These actions range from overt behaviors to subtle paralinguistic and nonverbal communications and body posture.

Identifying these actions and communications serves some important functions. First, as Kiesler (1988) points out, if a particular type of behavior or style of communicating is alienating other people, it is important for the patient to become aware of it. Kiesler (1988) describes the situation in which the patient often responds to things the therapist says with long silent pauses interspersed with quick smiles that flash on and off. The therapist in Kiesler's (1988) example infers that the patient thinks that the therapist's comment is stupid, but later it emerges that the patient was feeling stupid about himself. If, as Kiesler points out, this kind of interaction occurs repeatedly with other people (spouse, parents, friends), patients must first become aware of the messages they are communicating before they can begin changing their behavior.

For therapists, the identification of relevant patient actions and communications is also vital for other reasons. First, the very process of identifying and labeling the relevant interpersonal behavior facilitates the therapist's process of unhooking. By pinpointing the often subtle behaviors that are evoking their own emotional response, therapists can begin to understand their own reactions as being evoked by a particular stimulus and thus begin the process of decentering themselves from these emotions. Moreover, once the patient's relevant acts and communications have been identified, the therapist can be ready for them when they recur rather than reacting automatically. Second, the patient acts and communications that have been identified are important cues for probing accompanying cognitive processes. As Safran (1984a; 1990b) has suggested, these acts and communications can be thought of as *interpersonal markers*.

An interpersonal marker provides a clear indication of an appropriate juncture for cognitive and emotional exploration. These interpersonal markers can be thought of as windows into understanding the entire cognitive-interpersonal cycle. Interpersonal markers initiate the entire problematic interpersonal cycle because they are typically the behaviors and communications to which other people in the patient's environment respond in a negative complementary way. They are thus the interface between the patient's interpersonal schema and dysfunctional cycles. Not only do they mark the beginning of a dysfunctional interpersonal cycle characteristic of the patient, they are also linked to the patient's core cognitive processes.

Interpersonal markers provide useful cues to the therapist for exploring the patient's cognitive and emotional processes because those internal processes most problematic for the patient frequently occur in association with the interpersonal markers that play a central role in the patient's dysfunctional cognitive-interpersonal cycle. The patient's core cognitive processes are thus likely to be most accessible when the patient is exhibiting the interpersonal marker.

For example, the therapist becomes aware of feeling bored and disengaged. Then, through the process of participant observation, the therapist notices that these feelings become particularly intense when the patient speaks in an even, deadened voice tone. Next, by exploring the patient's experience at these times the therapist discovers the patient's concern about showing strong feelings to the therapist.

In another example, the therapist becomes aware of an angry, competitive feeling toward the patient. Further assessment reveals that these feelings appear to be explained by a particularly intense stare that the patient directs at the therapist along with a clenched jaw. Exploration of the patient's experience at these markers begins to reveal feelings of anger toward the therapist, combined with a fear of expressing them directly.

Once important interpersonal markers have been identified, the therapist can assign the patient the task of monitoring them between sessions, a process that helps patients to de-automate their habitual behavior and provides them with cues for exploring and challenging relevant cognitive/affective processes on their own (Safran 1984a).

The Inner Discipline of the Therapist

The first step in the unhooking or disengagement process is to become aware of one's own feelings and action tendencies toward the patient. As Kiesler (1988) states: "Since the therapist cannot *not* be pulled in by the patient, the therapist of necessity experiences feelings and other engagements with the patient *before* he or she ever notices or labels them. *The first essential step in this disengagement process, then, is that the therapist notice, attend to, and subsequently label the engagements being pulled from him or her from a given patient.* Until the therapist notices what is happening internally, he or she is caught in the patient's transactional game" (p. 38).

The ability to become fully aware of one's own feelings and action tendencies while in interaction with the patient is thus a prerequisite for effective therapy.

Just as the patient who has a rigid self-concept and believes that he or she *must* be a certain way in order to maintain interpersonal relatedness has difficulty becoming fully aware of inner experiences, the therapist who has a rigid self-concept will have difficulty becoming aware of certain feelings the patient evokes. For example, therapists who believe that it is wrong for a therapist to feel attracted to patients may have difficulty acknowledging such feelings when they emerge in therapy. Therapists who believe that they should always be warm, supportive, and empathic with patients will have difficulty acknowledging angry feelings toward patients. Therapists who make rigid demands on themselves to be unfailingly competent will have difficulty acknowledging feelings of powerlessness and helplessness with patients.

To the extent that therapists are not comfortable with such experiences, they will become hooked by interactions with specific patients and will not be able to assume the stance of the participant-observer and disengage when it is necessary. Obviously, an intellectual understanding of the importance of the stance of participant-observation will not suffice. To be a participant-observer, the therapist must have a sufficiently flexible self-concept to be able to acknowledge and accept his or her own feelings in the therapeutic interaction. The skill that must be acquired is thus not a technical skill that can be learned through practice alone. Rather, it is an inner discipline that can only be developed through personal growth.

Psychotherapy supervision must thus focus on the process of helping therapists become aware of and accept their own feelings as much as it does on the process of developing specific technical skills. It is useful for therapists to work with supervisors or colleagues to explore the feelings and action tendencies they are not fully aware of. By probing for feelings and reactions at strategic points in a supportive and accepting way, the supervisor or colleague can facilitate awareness. In addition, therapists should practice the discipline of observing their own feelings and personal reactions nonjudgmentally.

The therapist's personal qualities play an important role in therapy in yet another way. Therapists who have difficulty accepting certain feelings and experiences in themselves will have difficulty empathizing with these experiences in their patients, just as parents who have difficulty accepting certain feelings in themselves may have difficulty attuning to those feelings in the infant. For example, therapists who have difficulty accepting their own needs for nurturance and support will find it hard to empathize with and enter into the phenomenological world of dependent patients. Therapists who are afraid of their own sad feelings will have difficulty empathizing and accepting their patients' sad feelings. Such therapists will tend to pressure the patient *not* to be where he or she is or *not* to experience what he or she is fully experiencing, rather than trying to understand and empathize with the patient's current experience.

When therapists feel discomfort with an emotion such as sadness their anxiety will be communicated to patients, who may then have difficulty in fully articulating and experiencing their own feelings of sadness.

Still another way in which the inability of therapists to accept fully their own feelings obstructs the therapeutic process is that feelings that they do not recognize or express explicitly will, nevertheless, "leak out" and be expressed nonverbally and indirectly through their interventions.

Empathy

The cognitive perspective on empathy has traditionally been that an empathic relationship is necessary to establish the type of collaborative relationship that makes cognitive interventions work (Beck, Rush et al. 1979). There is a tendency to think of empathy as a simple reflection of the patient's feelings. Empathy, however, does not consist of merely reflecting the surface aspects of the patient's communications. It involves a process of immersing oneself in the patient's inner world so as to articulate tacit experience (Gendlin 1962; Rice 1974; Rogers 1951; 1961). Because cognition and affect are inseparable, empathy is simultaneously a cognitive and affective process. The therapist must not only get the "idea" of patients' inner experiences, but also the "feel" for subtle nuances of those experiences, which the patients may not have articulated for themselves. Empathy thus involves a process of affect attunement.

A problem often encountered in cognitive-behavioral writings is thinking of empathy and cognitive exploration as independent activities. This separation parallels the traditional distinction between specific and nonspecific factors in psychology in the sense that empathy is thought of as a nonspecific relationship factor and cognitive exploration is thought of as an intervention specific to cognitive therapy.

Empathy and cognitive exploration are, however, *completely interdependent*. The process of exploring the patient's phenomenological world is in part an empathic process. Empathy should not involve attempting to reassure patients that they are being heard and understood. Instead, it should involve the therapist's continuing attempt to understand the patients' inner experiences. Thus, empathy involves a therapist's disciplined stance in trying to walk in the patients' shoes so as to understand the subtleties of their phenomenological world.

The therapist must constantly ask: "What is my patient experiencing now? How does he or she really experience or see things in this moment? What would it be like to be in my patient's position right now?"

The failure to understand the true nature of empathy can result in the therapist providing a false empathic response. Often therapists, because they believe they should be understanding and empathic, will attempt to convey understanding when, in reality, they are not empathically immersed in the patient's inner world. This false empathy does not facilitate the therapeutic process, it interferes with it. At some level, patients will know that their inner experience is not truly understood by the therapist, but they will often have difficulty communicating this to the therapist because, first, they themselves are often unable to articulate their inner experience explicity to themselves, and, second, they will not wish to threaten the relationship with the therapist by suggesting that they feel misunderstood. Nevertheless, at some level, they will feel that something is wrong. When this occurs, a pseudo-intimacy or pseudo-alliance is created, in which therapists pretend that they understand and patients pretend to feel understood. As a result, patients become further alienated from their therapist and from themselves.

In addition to resulting in a pseudo-alliance, assuring patients that they are being understood when one is not feeling empathic can obscure a very important piece of information. If a therapist is having difficulty empathizing with the patient's experience, there may be reasons for it. One possibility is that the therapist's own issues are creating an obstacle, but a second possibility is that something is going on inside the patient. A patient who is currently divorced from his or her authentic, inner experience will have difficulty communicating it to the therapist.

The quality of the therapeutic relationship always mediates the patient's ability to explore his or her own inner world and fluctuations in the ability to do so must always be understood in terms of the context of the immediate relationship. Bearing this in mind, however, it is useful for the therapist to distinguish among different kinds of emotional expression and to clarify their relationship to authentic inner experience as Greenberg and Safran (1987) have done.

Primary emotion is a direct reflection of an authentic, organismically experienced response to the current situation. This emotional experience carries a tacit meaning that may not be well articulated for the individual, but which nevertheless says something important about one's current appraisal of the situation and preparedness for action. It is this kind of primary, authentic emotional experience that therapists must empathize with if they are to help patients articulate their internal experiences and come to fully accept themselves.

A reactive emotion involves a secondary emotional reaction to an underlying cognitive or emotional experience. There are two major subtypes of reactive emotional experience. One involves a negative self-critical response to an underlying feeling or construal and is likely to occur in a situation where the patient has learned that the experience or expression of a particular emotion is threatening to interpersonal relatedness. For example, a patient feels angry and then becomes self-critical for feeling angry. In this example, the depressed feeling associated with the self-criticism is a reactive emotion.

A second sub-type of reactive emotion is referred to by Safran and Greenberg (1988) as a "security operation emotion." Here the person who experiences the primary emotion as potentially threatening to interpersonal relatedness responds with another emotion that temporarily reduces anxiety or increases self-esteem. For example, a person who is feeling vulnerable responds by expressing anger. This expression of anger helps the person feel, temporarily, more in control. Here, it would be a mistake for the therapist to empathize with the feeling of anger, because it is the underlying feeling of vulnerability that is primary.

Greenberg and Safran (1987) refer to another category of emotional experience as "instrumental emotion." Instrumental emotions are learned repertoires that have interpersonal functions. For example, one who has learned that crying can elicit interpersonal support or nurturance may cry rather than express needs directly or express the underlying primary emotion threatening interpersonal relatedness. For example, a male patient who appeared to be extremely angry at his girlfriend would cry when he spoke about her, rather than express his anger. The therapist felt that he should feel empathic toward his patient, but for some reason could not. When listening to the audiotape of the session in supervision, the attempt to convey an empathic response to his patient sounded hollow.

In this situation, the therapist's failure to relate to the patient's crying empathically provided an important piece of information. It reflected the fact that the patient's expressed emotion was not an accurate reflection of his authentic, underlying emotional experience. It was thus important for the therapist to attempt to understand what the underlying emotional experience and the obstacles that prevented the patient from directly experiencing and expressing that emotion were.

The Alliance Rupture
as a Focus for Exploration

An alliance rupture can be defined as a point in the interaction between therapist and patient when the quality of the therapeutic alliance is strained or impaired. Alliance ruptures vary in terms of intensity, severity, and duration. They range from simple misunderstandings, quickly and easily resolved within a few moments, to more chronic problems in the therapeutic alliance which may extend over the course of one or more sessions, or over the course of the entire therapy.

It is common in cognitive-behavioral writings to conceptualize the therapeutic alliance as a static entity which either does or does not exist. The assumption is that if there is an adequate therapeutic alliance then therapy can proceed, while if the quality of the therapeutic alliance is not adequate then therapy will not be successful. Rather than thinking of the therapeutic alliance in all or nothing terms, however, it is far more useful for the therapist to think of the therapeutic alliance as a quality of the relationship that continuously fluctuates.

The therapist should, at all times, be sensitive to the quality of the therapeutic alliance and aware of these fluctuations. Problems in the therapeutic alliance are always a result of an interaction among the patient, the therapist, and the particular approach or intervention the therapist employs. Different kinds of therapy and different kinds of therapeutic intervention are likely to lead to different kinds of alliance ruptures. For example, the neutral stance of the classical psychoanalyst is likely to lead to an alliance rupture in which the patient views the therapist as being withholding. In contrast, cognitive therapy interventions that involve challenging can create alliance ruptures in which the patient feels criticized and invalidated.

There is always an interaction among the particular intervention, the manner in which it is employed, and the particular sensitivities of the patient. For example, the cognitive therapist who challenges the patient's automatic thoughts in a sensitive and empathic way may not induce an alliance rupture, particularly if the patient is not overly sensitive to the possibility of invalidation. In contrast, the patient who is particularly concerned about being invalidated may perceive a challenging intervention as invalidating, even if the therapist intervenes sensitively.

Because of the role of the patient's sensitivities, ruptures in the therapeutic alliance may provide important information for the therapist about particular sensitivities. A rupture in the therapeutic alliance can function as a useful window into the patient's subjective world, or "role-relationship model," to use Horowitz and Marmar's (1985) terminology. For this reason, the presence of an alliance rupture is not an unfortunate occurrence to be eliminated as soon as possible. It functions as an ideal juncture for clarifying the nature of the patient's particular sensitivities and interpersonal schema. Moreover, as we will explore in chapter 7, the process of healing a rupture in the therapeutic alliance can be an extremely potent change event.

In any cognitive therapy that employs interventions to challenge the patient's automatic thoughts or dysfunctional beliefs, this juncture is particularly at risk for alliance ruptures. Thus, a therapist who is challenging or questioning the patient's automatic thoughts should be particularly alert to the possibility that the intervention is not working. At the first sign that the patient does not appear to be open to an alternative construction of reality, the therapist should stop in the midst of the intervention and begin to explore precisely what is going on for the patient at that moment.

By exploring the patient's experience at that moment, the therapist may find that the patient is closed to an alternative construction of reality because of the feeling of being criticized or invalidated by the therapist. If the therapist is then able to unhook from the interaction and explore that patient's feelings empathically, he or she may help the patient explore and eventually challenge core cognitive processes. On the other hand, the therapist who remains hooked and continues to challenge the patient's belief may confirm the patient's dysfunctional belief that he or she is not respected by others.

When there is a good therapeutic alliance there is an empathic resonance between therapist and patient. The therapist walks in the patient's shoes, feels affected emotionally by what the patient says, and finds that the patient responds to the therapist's empathic comments in ways that acknowledge the feeling of being understood. The therapist and patient thus respond to each other as if they were dancing. The patient says something and then waits for the therapist's response, the therapist speaks and then is open to the patient's response. The patient's comments appear to flow directly in response to the therapist's comments and questions. There is thus a sense of building or creating something together.

In contrast, when there are problems in the therapeutic alliance, there is a lack of empathic resonance between the therapist and patient. The therapist has difficulty identifying with the patient. Or the therapist may feel that he or she understands the patient, attempts to communicate this understanding, and finds that the patient does not feel understood. There is no interactional synchrony between them. Rather than interacting openly and receptively, they tend to talk over each other. Thus, the patient may interrupt the therapist continually, or the therapist may feel that to be understood, it is necessary to interrupt the patient.

Seven common indications of alliance problems are (Safran, Crocker et al. in press):

1. the patient directly communicates negative or skeptical sentiments;
2. the patient indirectly communicates negative sentiments through sarcasm;
3. the patient alludes to problems in the therapeutic relationship by speaking about thematically similar relationships;
4. the patient and therapist disagree about the goals or tasks of therapy;
5. the patient complies or acquiesces;
6. the patient does not respond to an intervention;
7. the patient activates security operations.

Understanding the Patient's Interpersonal Schema

Our emphasis on the importance of understanding the patient's interpersonal schema parallels, in some ways, the perspective advocated by various psychodynamically oriented theorists. For example, brief-term therapists such as D. H. Malan (1976) and P. E. Sifneos (1979) advocate developing formulations of the patient's core conflict as soon as possible. Strupp and Binder (1984) suggest that it is important to develop a formulation of the patient's dynamic focus early in the therapy. Luborsky (1984) emphasizes the importance of assessing the patient's core conflictual relationship theme.

While we agree with these theorists about the importance of developing some conceptualization of themes that are central for the patient, we also wish to emphasize the importance of fully exploring the patient's current phenomenology instead of making assumptions about it based upon a formulation. Although this may seem a truism, once therapists have developed a clear-cut formulation of the patient's core issues, they often tend to assimilate the phenomenology into this formulation instead of exploring and understanding the patient's ongoing construal process.

The therapist's understanding of the patient's relationship to the therapist must never be determined by the therapist's ideas about the patient's relationships with parents or other significant figures in the patient's life. Historical information of this kind should function as background information which will inevitably influence what is salient for the therapist in the patient's presentation. If therapists assume that they understand a patient's immediate inner experience on the basis of historical information, they are in danger of missing what is truly going on for the patient here and now.

Some cognitive therapists tend to fit the patient's construal processes into ready-made categories (overgeneralization, selective abstraction, negative self-statements) rather than attempt to understand the idiosyncratic nature of the patient's phenomenology at a given time. The clinician can develop a useful framework by identifying various dysfunctional cognitive styles in advance. To offset the danger of reification, however, it is necessary to conduct disciplined, continual phenomenological exploration.

How can the therapist generate hypotheses and therapeutic strategies, yet still be open to whatever emerges in the moment? Research on the simulation of expert systems is revealing here (Dreyfus and Dreyfus 1986). Consider the example of the skilled chess player. The difference between an expert chess player and a novice is that the novice uses a sequential reasoning process to anticipate different moves his or her opponent could make and to consider alternative responses. Research with expert chess players, however, indicates that they operate on the basis of holistic pattern analysis rather than through sequential, linear reasoning. An expert chess player has stored in memory a wealth of information about various moves, countermoves, and previous games, as well as about the specific opponent. This information operates as background; it is there at a tacit rather than an explicit level. It is in the context of this background, however, that an immediate holistic perception emerges and the expert chess player literally sees different patterns inherent in his or her opponent's moves without having to compute them logically. The tacit background information *frees the expert chess player's attention so that he or she can be maximally open to the possibilities of the moment.*

Similarly, a skilled clinician can draw upon a wealth of experience about human interactions and therapy process, based on previous experiences with other patients and on prior knowledge about the patient. This information, however, functions as the ground from which current patterns are perceived holistically. Thus, the expert clinician does not impose theories on the patient derived from previous experiences with similar phenomena, but literally perceives new patterns in what is immediately taking place.

We thus discourage therapists from developing detailed and elaborate formulations in advance. These formulations, although impressive at first, often blind the clinician to new developments that are immediately taking place. The more sophisticated and elaborated the formulation, the more likely the clinician will be attached to it and less open to new developments of the moment that are incompatible with that formulation.

Instead, early on in therapy, the therapist should develop a very general formulation about the patient's core cognitive processes, keep it at a fairly informal level, and revise it in an ongoing fashion in response to new, emerging information. In some ways this state of mind is similar to what Freud described as free-floating or evenly-suspended attention, or as Reik (1948) has described it, listening with the third ear.

It is also similar to the kind of intuitive mind cultivated in the Taoist tradition. As Allan Watts (1957) explains, Taoist philosophy has great respect for the natural or intuitive mind as opposed to the reflecting or contrived mind. From this perspective, the psychological state appropriate for creativity and living is one of openness and receptivity to the patterns of the moment rather than that of attempting to impose one's will upon it. This basic philosophy is expressed well in the use of the I-Ching, the traditional Chinese oracle, which expresses the essence of the Taoist philosophy. The person who is using the I-Ching throws coins to discover a pattern that is a reflection of the moment in which they are thrown. The idea is that by considering the pattern in a receptive state of mind, one may be receptive to patterns of change and forces inherent in the moment. Only by deciphering the patterns of the moment and responding to the precise configuration of that moment can one act in harmony with the Tao or the principles of the universe.

The principle involved in this kind of receptive, open state of mind is what is referred to as *wu-wei*, which means "nonaction," not in the sense of passivity, but in not trying to make things happen in a way that is insensitive to the configuration of the moment. The basic idea is that if one is able to suspend one's attempt to force things to happen, and can be receptive to the patterns of the moment, one will be able to respond to them completely, spontaneously, and creatively.

Another principle in Taoist philosophy is *te*, which is translated as virtue. *Te* is not virtue in the conventional Western sense, rather it is the effectiveness or power that arises from acting intuitively and spontaneously in response to the moment. This kind of spontaneous, creative ingenuity is a guiding principle in many Asian arts and in superior work. The principle of *te* stipulates that although the artist requires technical skills, these skills are instrumental and secondary and should become background: one's superior work is the result of a creative accident that comes about when one responds, in a nondeliberate and noncontrived way, to the moment. Similarly, the formal knowledge and technical skill of the therapist should be the background, or the soil in which the seed of spontaneous and nondeliberate acts, completely responsive to the moment of the therapeutic interaction, can germinate.

Assessing the Cognitive-Interpersonal Cycle

The following transcript, which illustrates the assessment of a patient's cognitive-interpersonal cycle, is extracted from a session with a 30-year-old male patient who was hospitalized for severe depression. This patient's interpersonal style is particularly striking for its bitter, sarcastic wit, which shapes his interactions with the therapist and with other people. As the transcript opens, the patient is discussing his anger at hospital professionals who, he feels, have been treating him incompetently.

PATIENT: I'm not having a very good time on the medication they're giving me, which is really rotten, and I've been taking codeine to alleviate the suffering. I feel like shit—not that I would know how that feels—but I would assume that's what shit feels like. I'm really down on myself, very negative, really mad, really mad at one doctor in particular. They leave you on the medication that they're trying you on for as long as possible, in the hope that all the side effects will eventually go away, regardless of how much suffering is going on. I have headaches as well—and that's treated with additional drugs. I've been walking around the last four or five days like an absolute zombie and feeling really terrible. Had the drapes closed in my room—feeling noncommunicative and pretty awful.

THERAPIST: It sounds like it's been a really rough week for you.

PATIENT: Yeah. And because I wasn't totally capable of expressing myself, one of the nurses, who is particularly assertive, yesterday went up to the resident and said, "What do you think you're doing?" He gave me my medication this morning to see if I would get a headache, and naturally I have a headache. And now he's going to hold my lunchtime medication, which is awful big of him.

THERAPIST: So, finally some action is being taken, but you're saying "It's awful big of him." You're saying it's—like too little too late—in a way?

PATIENT: It's too late. It's too late. When I was on the previous medication, which was Parnate, they had me on it for four weeks and my blood pressure was averaging about 70 over 54—which is a very low blood pressure. You know, sort of holding on to objects and very dizzy and very light-headed, and it's not a pleasant experience to go through. But I survived it, thinking it would go away. And then they decided—no—it wouldn't go away. And they changed medications. I appreciate the need for trial and error, but—mind you, as it was pointed out to me, they know what they're doing. And I'm a sick person.

THERAPIST: Who points that out?

PATIENT: The doctors point that out, you know, in a very polite way. "These side effects very often disappear, and one must be patient," and you know, "Certainly, we realize you must be very frustrated and you want something that is going to work right away. But, you must be patient, and sometimes, these drugs will have side effects for a couple of weeks, and that the side effects in time will disappear. But, you must be patient."

THERAPIST: Uh-huh.

PATIENT: So, I'm practicing the patience of Job. We all know how his story turned out, don't we? Not good.

THERAPIST: Uh-huh. So, you're not feeling very patient. You're trying to practice patience, but you—

PATIENT: I'm a very patient man, basically. But, it is hard to be patient when you're feeling pain. It's not easy.

THERAPIST: Yeah, it sounds like your patience is really running thin—being stretched to the limit.

PATIENT: And—I always go back to my old Catholic training, you know. All pain is to be offered up, you know, and you offer up your pain and you absolve all these souls in Purgatory. I don't know why that stuff comes back to me, but it does. So I've phoned my mother and informed her that there is no one left in Purgatory, so this has to stop. You had to be there to appreciate it.

THERAPIST: Okay, so you're suffering a lot of pain, and it sounds like, on the one hand, you're trying to endure the pain and be patient, and you go back to memories from your childhood, about examples of people who endured pain, but on the other hand—

PATIENT: Yeah, I must admit when you used the word *martyr*, two weeks ago, it brought back things from boyhood.

THERAPIST: Uh-huh, but it sounds like you're getting pretty pissed off as well.

PATIENT: Me? No. I never get pissed off, I never yell. Never (said with emphasis). The only thing—the only good that came out of this was when I had the resident in my room yesterday, and I was speaking to him finally about this headache, and how it couldn't go on any longer, I gave him my warts.

THERAPIST: You gave him your—

PATIENT: My—the warts on my foot. I felt he could handle them.

THERAPIST: So, you're saying you took a dig at him.

PATIENT: Took a dig at him all right. Yeah. And he told me he didn't do warts. So it was lost.

THERAPIST: Uh-huh. So you took a jab at him, but he didn't even get it, is that what you're saying?

PATIENT: It went over his head. Either that or his body language was so protected that he didn't even register it. He may have gotten it on his way home on the subway. This man is closed, closed.

THERAPIST: I'm struck with how bitter and angry you sound to me right now.

PATIENT: Sorry. I hate being—I hate sounding bitter. I'm too young to be bitter. Bitter is something that comes with old age.

THERAPIST: Yeah, but I'm wondering what you're really experiencing right now.

PATIENT: Me? I'm just tired. I'm—I'm in pain and I'm tired. I'm tired of the fact that when they want to try you on a medication, you have to be on it for three or four weeks. In both previous instances, I've had to suffer like hell, to prove to them that it's not working. And I'm more depressed and feeling more suicidal. And then they say, "Oh, this medication is not working." You know, well, I could have told you that two weeks ago.

In this segment, the patient begins to display a sample of his interpersonal style—an agile, caustic wit, which when combined with his frustration and bitterness can be turned on those who have hurt or offended him, as in the case of the psychiatric resident. In an attempt to help the patient explore the feelings associated with his actions, the therapist relays his perception of the patient's anger and bitterness. This intervention, however, has an unexpected effect. The patient denies feeling bitter. The therapist senses a slight strain in the alliance and in the next segment begins to explore how his comment affected the patient.

THERAPIST: Uh-huh. I'm wondering what happens for you when I tell you that my experience of you, is that you're sounding really bitter right now. I mean what happens for you when I say that?
PATIENT: It feels like it's a negative dig.
THERAPIST: It feels like I'm taking a dig at you?
PATIENT: Uh-huh. But, not one that's meant to hurt.
THERAPIST: But, does it?
PATIENT: Coming from you? No, it doesn't hurt, but it's still a dig. Because I've separated you—you're separated in my mind in the role that you play—in that I can't take anything you say personally to rip me to shreds. Maybe it's a protection. What's the word I want? A defense mechanism, perhaps?
THERAPIST: Uh-huh.
PATIENT: Maybe I'm not going to take your comment about bitterness in the same way I would take it from my—my mother, or my brother or my sister. From you it's a more professional kind of thing—therefore, it's not going to tear my heart quite as severely. But, I accept it the same way as being truthful. Do you understand what I'm saying?
THERAPIST: Not completely. I understand parts of it, I think.
PATIENT: You can't tear out my heart. You know, if my mother said that, it would tear my heart. You can't do that, but you're still

registered as being truthful—not like if it were coming from her, or my father or someone else.

THERAPIST: Okay, so I understand that it doesn't tear at you as much as it might if it had come from somebody else. When I said it, I hadn't meant it as a dig. And I'm wondering, first of all, if it doesn't connect with your experience at all? You don't experience yourself as being bitter right now?

PATIENT: I'm not sure.

In the response to his inquiry, the therapist discovers that being bitter has a negative connotation for the patient, who consequently experiences the therapist's comment as a criticism (although he appears to have some difficulty acknowledging that he was hurt by the comment). Note that the patient says it would "tear his heart" if his mother gave him feedback of this type. The vividness and poignancy of this expression gives some indication of how negatively he regards the characteristic of bitterness.

Because he views such feelings as so unacceptable, it may be difficult for this patient to acknowledge and explore *any* feelings of bitterness. This could potentially present a dilemma in terms of change, because the first step in the change process involves acknowledging whatever feelings one has. Feelings of bitterness often reflect a mixture of anger, frustration, and resignation. The resignation often comes from giving up in fear of the consequences of expressing anger more directly.

In the next segment, the patient's beliefs about the consequences of being angry and bitter are explored.

PATIENT: I'm afraid to be bitter. Too risky around here. I find that I have to be really careful what I say and mask a lot of what I feel, because I'm afraid of getting turfed out, or you know, denied treatment.

THERAPIST: Uh-huh.

PATIENT: When I'm with my doctor I sit like this. My hands are folded in my lap, and I try to be very congenial. I say, "Yes, of course." I'm usually positive, and try to ask intelligent questions. Or I'll use some reflective questioning with him, which I enjoy immensely. And that's about the size of it. And then they always draw the meeting to some kind of conclusion by their—their care plan for the following week. And I regurgitate it back to them, and they feel heard—and that's the end of it.

THERAPIST: What about here?

PATIENT: With you?

THERAPIST: Yeah, do you experience some of the——?

PATIENT: No. I don't sit like that all the time. Here we go through a lot of stuff. In my relationship—in talking to you, there's not the same kind of sterility. I don't know—I feel more comfortable here. Initially I felt the need to be more guarded. Now, I feel less guarded. With the doctors who are in the other part of the hospital, I feel the need to be very guarded. If that makes any sense.

THERAPIST: You're saying that with certain people you feel sort of a need to be cautious because——

PATIENT: You're more likely to get in trouble if you make a sarcastic remark with them.

THERAPIST: Have you ever gotten in trouble for——

PATIENT: I got into trouble once with a nurse for making a sarcastic remark. She couldn't figure out how to take my blood pressure, so I showed her and asked her what year she went to nursing school. She was so offended. But I mean, is it my problem, if I tend to say things to them that are beyond their—beyond their scope?

THERAPIST: As a way of taking a dig at them, or——

PATIENT: Well, sometimes. It depends who it is.

Here the patient is able to explore his fears of being directly angry with other people, but denies that this is a problem in the current situation. At this point in the therapeutic relationship it may be too risky for the patient openly to acknowledge and explore feelings of anger and his fear of the consequences. This segment also captures the flavor of the patient's interpersonal style in greater depth. A certain caustic, superior, or arrogant tone continues to emerge ("Is it my problem, if I tend to say things to them that are beyond their scope?") The transcript now skips to a later phase in the session in which the patient speaks about his feelings of depression.

PATIENT: I feel heavy and ugly and horrible. And when I was in the shower this morning, I felt as though I couldn't get the heaviness away, but it was guilt. I looked into the mirror this morning to shave and thought, "Oh, God!" It's like seeing the world with very different colored glasses, and they're certainly not rose-colored glasses. It's all directed toward me.

THERAPIST: Directed toward you?

PATIENT: Yeah, yeah.

THERAPIST: What is directed toward you?

PATIENT: A lot of negative, negative, rotten stuff.

THERAPIST: Right now, as we sit here, do you have this experience of directing negative stuff toward yourself?

PATIENT: Uh-huh. When I saw your red socks, I thought, "Is that ever nice, nice red socks." You know, I immediately turned it on myself and thought, "You're so stupid and ugly, you could never, ever do anything like that."

THERAPIST: Hmm——

PATIENT: Like this morning on the ward, they showed us a wonderful film about how twelve to fifteen percent of depressed people become suicides. I wanted to start a pool with all the depressed people in the room. Somebody had an immense chance there of profit. No one would cooperate.

THERAPIST: I'm really struck with what I'm hearing. What I understand is that you're really feeling a lot of despair right now, but then—you keep making humorous comments as well at the same time, so it keeps kind of taking me unexpectedly.

PATIENT: That's my M.O.

THERAPIST: M.O.?

PATIENT: Modus operandi.

THERAPIST: You're too fast for me. It keeps me off balance in a way.

At this point, the therapist identifies a subtle feeling that has been on the edge of his awareness throughout the session, but that he has not been able to articulate until now. It is a sense of being slightly off balance—of never knowing quite what to expect. One might hypothesize that it is not unlike the feeling that some of the other staff members (the resident or the nurse) experience with the patient more intensely. Although the patient is not currently turning his wit on the therapist, the therapist may be indirectly feeling some impact from the latter's caustic humor and arrogant manner. Were the therapist not to identify these feelings in himself, he might unwittingly participate in a dysfunctional interpersonal cycle in which he acts out of the feeling of being frustrated or threatened by the patient. In fact, it is possible that the somewhat poorly timed intervention, in which the therapist commented on the patient's bitterness, stemmed partly from the therapist's own discomfort.

PATIENT: (Laughing) Unintentional.

THERAPIST: Yeah, maybe it is unintentional, but——

PATIENT: It keeps you from hitting on the real stuff? It's too difficult to talk about. With my previous therapist that was my standard procedure. I figured if the therapist was any good she would get beyond it and get to the meat of the matter. If she wasn't—as the last one wasn't—she would tell me I was her most entertaining patient, and spend the hour on the broadloom killing herself laughing, and meantime, I'm—you know, saying stuff that hurts, but then backing up.

THERAPIST: Uh-huh. Yeah. So, is there some of this going on now?

PATIENT: Sure, but it's—it's a conditioned response. It happens and I don't have control over it. I don't know. I'm sorry.

THERAPIST: What would happen right now if I did get beyond that humor into some of your painful experience?

PATIENT: That remains to be seen, you know. It would be depressing, upsetting. It could be constructive. It might be quite difficult.

THERAPIST: Difficult in what way?

PATIENT: 'Cause nobody has done that.

THERAPIST: So that it would be difficult for me to get beyond it?

PATIENT: Not difficult for you, but—just that it's never been done. It might be hard. I'm not saying I won't cooperate at all. I would cooperate the best I could in trying.

THERAPIST: Well, what I would ask of you, actually, and it's not so much a matter of cooperation as it is a matter of just trying to stay in awareness—you're saying that a lot of it is automatic for you right now, right?

PATIENT: It's reflex.

THERAPIST: It's reflex. So that when you're being humorous, if you can just be aware for a moment of what you're doing and what you're experiencing under the humor.

PATIENT: Okay. (Long pause.)

THERAPIST: What are you feeling now? What are you experiencing?

PATIENT: Actually, I was thinking about the potential of being left naked without my one-liners. What a terrifying thought that is! Because to me that's really ugly.

THERAPIST: Without the one-liners, you're saying, what's underneath is really ugly.

PATIENT: Yeah.

THERAPIST: If that were stripped away——

PATIENT: Without that—that safety net out there, it would be very difficult.

THERAPIST: So you say it's a kind of a safety net. Kind of a protection in a way, huh?

PATIENT: Sure, absolutely.

In this segment, a characteristic cognitive-interpersonal cycle for this patient begins to be fleshed out in greater detail. The patient appears to be emotionally isolated, pained, angry, and bitter. He is concerned that if he lets people see his anger they will reject him, and that if they see the pain underneath, they will be repulsed. He believes that he must hide his true feelings and cooperate with people to maintain relatedness. This theme emerges in the therapeutic relationship as well ("I'm not saying I won't cooperate at all").

His caustic humor and lively intellect protect him—but also alienate him from people and keep him isolated. He appears to experience a mixture of scorn and contempt for those who cannot keep up with him, in addition to the pain of emotional isolation. Many of his interpersonal encounters thus result in bitter, hollow victories in which he maintains some respect for himself at the cost of continued loneliness.

To avoid perpetuating this dysfunctional interpersonal cycle, the therapist must begin to identify his own feelings of discomfort with the patient and then pinpoint the interpersonal marker, the sarcastic wit, they are associated with—not an easy task here when the cycle is not being enacted intensely. In situations of this kind, it is particularly important for therapists to be attuned to subtle feelings or action tendencies they may be experiencing.

General Considerations
Relevant to Cognitive Assessment

To this point, we have focused on the role of participant observation in assessing the patient's cognitive-interpersonal cycle so as to emphasize the interpersonal context of cognitive assessment and establish a basic, orienting foundation. Although we have stressed the use of the therapeutic relationship in facilitating this process, we do not mean to imply that the patient's recollection of out-of-session events—an important traditional source of information in cognitive therapy—should be neglected, and we will now examine some of the more general considerations of cognitive assessment in the context of both in-session material and out-of-session material.

In speaking about various techniques that can be employed to challenge dysfunctional thinking, many cognitive-behavioral writings take for granted that the relevant cognitive processes are available in the first place. There may be situations in which the patient has ready access to the relevant construal processes at the beginning of therapy, but there are also many situations in which gaining access to the relevant cognitive processes is a difficult and painstaking activity (Safran and Greenberg 1982a). Because practically oriented cognitive therapy writings typically emphasize the challenging aspect of the change process and de-emphasize the exploratory phase, we will try to redress this imbalance by exploring some of the practical considerations relevant to gaining access to cognitive processes.

Concreteness and Specificity

The first general principle is that whenever possible the therapist should always encourage the patient to provide specific, concrete examples of the problem being described. Generalized abstract problem descriptions should always be converted into concrete, specific examples. Moreover, the more recent the example, the better.

Once the patient has described the general outlines of a specific situation, the therapist can ask for a picture of the situation in specific detail, as full and vivid a picture as possible. In this way, the patient reconstructs the situation in minute detail, describing relevant visual and auditory cues. By furnishing as many contextual cues as possible the patient is able to reconstruct the situation in a way that increases his or her ability to gain access to the construal of the situation by reconstructing it. Rice (1984) has made a convincing argument for the value of this kind of vivid reconstruction in accessing subjective construals that would otherwise be unavailable and refers to this approach as "systematic, evocative unfolding."

The patient can be instructed to slow down a description of the situation, and essentially "walk through it" as if it were taking place in the present. The therapist can stop the patient at various points that seem particularly relevant and probe for feelings, thoughts, and reactions that the patient is experiencing. Greenberg and Safran (1980; 1981) and Toukmanian (1986), using Shiffrin and Schneider's (1977) distinction between automatic and controlled processing, have described this as a process of de-automization through which the therapist helps the patient slow down or de-automate an habitual mode of perceptual processing and begin to attend to minute details that might otherwise escape awareness.

In this way, the therapist can help reconstruct the relevant scene and the patient's reactions to it. In Rice's (1984) approach the therapist systematically moves back and forth between aspects of the stimulus situation that are particularly salient for the patient and the patient's personal reaction in response to these aspects. We have found that this kind of oscillation can be particularly helpful in assessing cognitive processes that might otherwise be difficult to access.

It is also particularly useful to oscillate between the patient's feelings and the patient's thoughts. Thus, for example, the therapist might say "What do you feel as you describe the situation?" or "Can you get in touch with what you are feeling as you describe the situation?" If the patient is able to gain access to the reaction at a more affective level, he or she is also often able to grasp associated thoughts (Safran and Greenberg 1982a; 1982b; 1986).

For example, a male patient describes the difficulty he has in speaking in front of groups of people. The therapist asks him to recall the last time this happened and the patient says that two days earlier when he was sitting in a class at the university he experienced intense anxiety while he was thinking about stating his view of the topic then under discussion. The therapist asks the patient to describe the situation in detail.

THERAPIST: Can you remember where you were sitting in the classroom?

PATIENT: I was sitting near the back of the classroom in the right-hand corner.

THERAPIST: Can you recall what you were looking at? Describe it as if it is taking place right now.

PATIENT: Well, I'm sitting in the back right-hand corner of the classroom and I'm looking around at other members of the classroom.

THERAPIST: And what do you see?

PATIENT: Well—I see the professor, standing there and looking expectantly at people and I see the faces of various people—and one in particular—this guy who I never thought of as being particularly smart—and I am waiting to see what he's going to say.

THERAPIST: And what are you experiencing as this is happening? Can you get in contact with your feelings?

PATIENT: Yeah—kind of—I feel kind of tense.

THERAPIST: Can you actually feel that tension right now?

PATIENT: Yes—kind of.

THERAPIST: Where do you feel it?

PATIENT: I feel it in my stomach. It's kind of like somebody pressing on my stomach.

THERAPIST: Now go back to the situation. What happens then? What stands out for you?

PATIENT: Well, this guy starts to talk and he actually sounds quite intelligent.

THERAPIST: Can you actually picture him or hear what he is saying as you describe this?

PATIENT: Yes. I can actually see him sitting there talking—and then I'm looking at his face.

THERAPIST: Can you describe what you see?

PATIENT: Well, he has a beard and dark eyes and he looks very calm and poised.

THERAPIST: And what's going on for you as you describe this?

PATIENT: I'm feeling more and more uncomfortable.

THERAPIST: And what's going through your mind?

PATIENT: I'm thinking, "He seems so calm and self-possessed and everybody likes him. And I'm feeling so tense. And I'll sound so awkward when I talk." And I imagine the things I'm going to say will sound so simple and obvious.

By helping the patient reconstruct the problem situation in this way, the therapist can find possible contextual cues for gaining access to cognitive processes that might otherwise be difficult to reach. By checking periodically to see if the patient is re-experiencing the relevant feelings, the therapist can evaluate whether the task is proceeding optimally or whether the patient is having difficulty re-creating the situation. If the patient is not re-experiencing the relevant feelings, it may be that he or she is having difficulty with some aspect of the reconstruction and the therapist can help find out what the problem is.

One of the most common problems in this process arises when patients have a hard time reporting a subjective construal because it is experienced as a threat to their self-esteem. For example, in the foregoing situation, should the patient have difficulty re-experiencing or reporting his true feelings and thoughts about the situation, it might be because comparing himself with other people in the class seems petty to him. Patients often feel that it is petty, childish, or immature to see things the way they do. There is thus a disjunction between their rational appraisal of the situation and their more primary or intuitive appraisal (Safran and Greenberg 1982a). In situations of this kind it is vital to explore the underlying intuitive appraisal rather than support the patient's own tendency to avoid such exploration through rational reappraisal.

Awareness and Interpersonal Context

Awareness of internal experience and communication of that experience to others are interdependent processes, because the process of communicating helps one construct reality. Reality is thus essentially interpersonal. As Stern (1985) argues, those affects that are not responded to empathically by the infant's mother may never become fully recognized by the individual. Similarly, many of our innermost thoughts may remain tacit until they are explicated through communication. The very process of communicating intuitive appraisals to the therapist that the patient has not communicated before may make the patient more fully conscious of them.

There is thus a continuum of self-awareness and public communicability. At one end are experiences patients have never communicated to anyone else and which they themselves are not fully aware of. At the other end are subjective construals patients are fully aware of and have communicated to others. Between the two ends of the continuum, however, are other possibilities. One possibility is that, to some degree, patients are aware of a certain subjective construal but are too ashamed to report this to other people or to the therapist. In this situation, the act of reporting it to an accepting therapist may be therapeutic in that patients may begin to feel more accepting of themselves. Another possibility is that the patients are generally aware of their internal experience, but the process of communicating helps them articulate it more fully.

Intervening When Automatic Thoughts Are Blocked

It should come as no surprise that there are often substantial barriers to gaining access to relevant cognitive processes, given the threat to interpersonal relatedness some patients experience when asked to relay experiences and perceptions. For this reason, unless patients have very clear access to dysfunctional cognitive processes, we are reluctant to challenge them in any way at the outset of therapy. Moreover, even when patients do appear to have clear access at the outset, we usually hesitate to challenge them until we understand them and know how they will view challenges.

At the beginning of therapy, in particular, it is important to avoid situations in which patients get the message that they are somehow to blame for having dysfunctional cognitive processes. This can only increase their natural reluctance to report experiences or subjective construals they feel ashamed of. Moreover, patients who are unsuccessful in their attempts to challenge their automatic thoughts, may become pessimistic about the therapeutic process. Warnings to the contrary, however, some patients are often eager to challenge their automatic thoughts immediately. Such patients often have a hard time seeing the process of becoming more aware of their subjective construals and automatic thoughts as being a part of the therapy process, and may make comments such as: "When does the therapy actually begin?"

Another reason patients often object to focusing on becoming aware of automatic thoughts instead of challenging them, is that they feel they are already aware of their negative, self-critical thinking. With these patients it is important to emphasize the difference between knowing one is self-critical and being fully aware of one's construal processes while they are taking place.

There are a number of procedures that can be useful in helping patients gain access to the relevant cognitive process. First, one can suggest that everybody has a more rational side and a more intuitive or experiential side and that the rational side often gets in the way of helping to see the intuitive side more fully. One can suggest that for the purposes of therapy it would be useful to put the rational part aside briefly to get a better look at the more intuitive side which it may be obscuring (Safran and Greenberg 1982b). Subsequently, when one sees the patient having difficulty, one can say something to the effect of: "That sounds like your rational side. What about the other side?"

A second useful procedure is to explore and challenge thoughts and beliefs that obstruct the access to more primary subjective construal processes. When patients have difficulty gaining access to automatic thoughts, one can focus on feelings and automatic thoughts relevant to the immediate interaction, which may be more salient for the patient and may also be impeding the full exploration of the problematic situation. Here, one can use a very general probe about the current, interpersonal situation such as: "How are you feeling about what's happening right now?"

It can also be useful to help patients distinguish between being aware of what they were thinking in the problem situation and reporting those thoughts to the therapist. One can say, for example, "You may not feel comfortable telling me the feelings and thoughts you're having, and it's okay if you don't. But, for your own information, check to see if you know what you *are* feeling and what's going through your mind."

By thus giving patients permission to keep the information private, one can decrease their anxiety about the immediate interpersonal encounter and help them free up their attention for the task of self-exploration. Once patients learn they have the right to withhold any information they wish, self-exploration will be easier for them. A common problem that therapists must always be alert to is that patients often feel they are bad patients when they do not report their inner experience and that the pressure to produce something for the therapist interferes with the task of self-exploration. Once patients feel relieved of the pressure to report their inner experiences and have been able to become aware of their inner thoughts, they can then make the decision about communicating them to the therapist at any particular point.

When one learns that a patient *is* aware of a subjective construal about a particular situation but does not feel comfortable discussing it, it is essential to emphasize to the patient that he or she will not be pressured into communicating this particular experience, and that the therapist is only interested in exploring the *obstacles* that make it difficult to communicate these feelings and thoughts.

For example, one might say: "I want you to know that whether you tell me is not important and that either telling me about it or not telling me about it are equally valid choices. It may be useful, however, for us to sort out the factors that might affect your choice so that you'll have more information to go on in deciding whether you want to tell me."

By explicitly emphasizing that any choice patients make is acceptable, one counters any implicit message patients might perceive as pressure to relay their automatic thoughts. Of course, the therapist must truly respect the patient's right not to disclose something at the present time and recognize that whether the patient does or does not disclose the particular feelings or thoughts are, indeed, equally valid choices. Thus, one's ability to respect the patient's privacy and right to make decisions must assume therapeutic priority over any immediate goal of gaining access to the patient's automatic thoughts. This kind of respect is an important learning experience for the patient, because many patients believe they do not have the right to refuse to share their experience when somebody asks them to.

Exploring what the patient perceives the risk of talking about an experience might be can be done with simple probes such as: "What do you imagine might happen if you were to tell me what's going on in your mind?" or "Are you aware of any fears you may have about what might happen if you were to tell me what is going on in your mind?" or "Can you get an image in your mind of how I might react if you were to tell me what is going on for you right now?"

Common concerns are the fear that the therapist would judge or ridicule the patient, or that the therapist would not overtly say anything negative or judgmental, but, inside, would feel judgmental, repulsed, or disgusted. Often, the very process of articulating these fears helps to free the patient from them sufficiently to disclose the withheld information.

If patients are able to articulate what they expect the risk would be in disclosing the relevant information, they are then in a better position to evaluate their willingness to take that risk. For example, a patient may believe that the therapist will find a particular automatic thought childish. In this situation, there are three possibilities for further progress. The first is that the therapist can help patients evaluate how likely it would be that the therapist would really think that they are childish and that patients will decide that it is relatively unlikely. The second possibility is that patients may decide that there is no guarantee that the therapist would not think them childish, but feel that it would not be catastrophic if he or she did. In this case, too, patients may decide that the risk is worth it.

The third possibility is that patients may decide that there is a considerable risk involved in disclosing the relevant information to the therapist, that it is highly likely that the therapist would be judgmental, and that this possibility seems catastrophic, and that these patients are not willing to take the risk at present.

If patients decide not to disclose the information to the therapist at the time, it is essential that they have the experience of directly taking responsibility for that decision, that is, the patients must have the experience of volition or intention: "I am *not willing* to take that risk right now" rather than "I *can't* get in touch with what I am thinking or feeling." Thus, even if patients do not disclose the information, therapeutic progress can take place *if* they take responsibility for their actions.

Patients leave that particular interaction with the therapist, learning that they communicated an *intentional* decision *not* to disclose something to the therapist, and that it was all right. Thus, there has been a process of self-affirmation and a move toward learning to make intentional decisions and taking increased responsibility for one's actions.

In this situation (as in others), learning about the self and others that comes from the immediate, interpersonal encounter with the therapist again takes priority over any therapeutic gain that it is presumed will emerge out of the original therapeutic target. In the long run, too, the therapist has increased the possibility that patients will feel confident enough to risk disclosing a particular piece of information to the therapist.

Emotional Immediacy

Cognitive therapists are becoming increasingly aware of the role of emotion in the change process and of the importance of understanding and working with material that is emotionally alive for the patient (Guidano 1987; Mahoney 1985; Young in press). We will not deal with this topic at a detailed theoretical level, because explorations of this issue can be found elsewhere (Greenberg and Safran 1987; 1989; Safran and Greenberg 1986; in press). We will, however, comment on it briefly from a technical viewpoint. As Greenberg and Safran (1987) have pointed out, in the therapeutic literature on emotion one of the biggest problems has been a failure to adopt a perspective that distinguishes among different kinds of emotional change processes in different contexts. There is thus a tendency for therapists to talk about helping patients "get in touch with their emotions," without being clear about why patients should, and to what end. As Greenberg and Safran (1987) have pointed out, however, there is a variety of different emotional change processes in psychotherapy that can be distinguished from one another.

Here, we will deal with one general category of affective change process, which has been referred to as accessing mood-congruent cognitions (Greenberg and Safran 1987; Safran and Greenberg 1982a). The basic principle underlying this process is that change in cognitive therapy is more likely to take place if the patient's cognitive processes are accessed and challenged in an emotionally immediate way (Safran and Greenberg 1986). The reasoning behind this principle can be understood, first, in terms of G. H. Bower's (1981) semantic network model of mood and memory. Bower's original theory was that emotion and cognition are linked together in semantic memory and that, as a result, memory retrieval should be enhanced when the individual is in an emotional state associated with that memory. Bower (1981) corroborated this hypothesis in a number of studies.

Subsequent investigations, however, have failed to replicate the mood-dependent memory effect consistently, and Bower and J. D. Mayer (1985) have reformulated the hypothesis, which Bower now calls causal-belongingness theory. The causal-belongingness hypothesis asserts that specific events become connected in memory with specific emotions only when one appraises the two as belonging together during the process of encoding. For example, if one experiences a rejection and feels sad, the rejection and the sadness will become linked in memory only if one appraises the sadness as being related to the rejection at the time of encoding.

Whether or not Bower's causal-belongingness hypothesis is ultimately borne out by the data, clinical experience suggests that negative self-critical cognitions are more accessible in therapy when the patient is in a mood similar to that experienced in the original situation. One of the reasons for the difference between clinical and laboratory contexts may be that two types of cognitive processes are involved. In the research typically employed to investigate the mood-dependent retrieval effect, the cognitive processes investigated involve episodic memories. In the clinical situation, the relevant cognitive process involves negative self-evaluations.

Rather than gaining access to a specific episodic memory, the cognitive therapist is typically attempting to tap into an ongoing constructive process. The relevant constructive process may be specific to the associated mood (sadness, anger, anxiety), but it is also possible that the specific thoughts that are accessible to the clinician are synthesized through an expressive motor base *in the moment*. We are always processing information to varying degrees at expressive motor, preconceptual, and conceptual levels (Leventhal 1979), and the therapeutic process of representing experience in verbal, conceptual form provides patients with the opportunity, first, to recognize the way they construe events at an implicit level and, second, to change that construal. Thus, automatic thoughts in cognitive therapy do not exist in the head waiting to spring forth like Athena, fully formed from Zeus's brow. They are synthesized in the moment. Their emotional immediacy comes from a constructive cognitive-affective process in which the expressive motor aspect of emotional experience plays an integral role.

Emotional immediacy in cognitive therapy may also be valuable because thoughts that are not affectively laden may be only a conceptual representation of an underlying information-processing activity that, in reality, is expressive-motor in nature. This conceptual representation can thus be split off from the underlying processing activity which, then, cannot be modified because it is not accessible (Foa and Kozak 1986; in press; Safran and Greenberg 1986; 1987).

Interpersonal schemas conceptualized as cognitive-affective structures rather than as purely cognitive structures are similar to the emotion schema described by Leventhal (1979). We hypothesize that they contain at least four components: specific images and episodic memories of events prototypical for the relevant cognitive-interpersonal cycle; associated expressive motor behaviors; autonomic arousal; and plans and if-then contingencies for maintaining interpersonal relatedness. Many rules for actions that maintain interpersonal relatedness are probably coded in motoric form. A certain interpersonal circumstance may thus automatically evoke a preparedness to act in a certain way.

If interpersonal schemas are, indeed, at least partly encoded in expressive-motor form, it stands to reason that the relevant schematic structure cannot be fully activated unless the expressive-motor components are activated. Again, in theory, it is thus possible to explore and challenge dysfunctional beliefs about interpersonal relationships at a conceptual level without ever modifying some of the more fundamental dysfunctional beliefs about interpersonal relationships encoded in expressive motor form.

As Safran and Greenberg (1986; 1987) hypothesize, an important precondition for modifying schematic structures with an emotional or expressive motor component involves gaining access to some of the expressive-motor components associated with that schematic structure. The greater the number of components evoked, the greater the access to the schematic structure and the more amenable it will be to change (Foa and Kozak, in press).

Consider the following example. A young man with agoraphobic symptoms comes to see the therapist and, in the course of the interview, reveals a history characterized by both emotional and physical abandonment by his parents and subsequent experiences of having been hurt as a result of trusting people. At first he seems eager for help and eager to participate in active behavioral intervention, but as the interview proceeds, it becomes apparent that he is actually cynical and skeptical about therapy. He maintains that he already understands his problem, has tried implementing a behavioral program himself, and has difficulty seeing how anything the therapist could do would really help.

The therapist, in tuning into her own feelings, discovers an experience of being "talked at," almost as if the patient were speaking to a tape recorder rather than engaging in a dialogue. The patient is speaking about various events that, on the surface, seem to be quite intimate, but the therapist's experience persists. When she discusses her feelings with the patient and invites him to explore his reactions, the patient says that, indeed, he feels as if he is talking to a machine, that he has told the story "a thousand times before," and that the therapist is just one more person trying to help.

On the face of things, the patient is discussing intimate details about interpersonal events and issues that are relevant to a core interpersonal schema. And yet, he manages to talk *about* relevant historical events without tapping into the associated emotions. One might hypothesize that the patient appraises the situation as too dangerous to engage in a real interpersonal encounter with the therapist, because of the risk of abandonment. As a way of protecting himself, he depersonalizes the therapist and speaks about intimate experiences without attending to the relevant expressive motor cues. We hypothesize that before any fundamental changes could take place in this patient's interpersonal schema, he would first have to gain access to his associated feelings while he is describing relevant interpersonal events to the therapist and also be able to express his real feelings about the therapist.

Memory Retrieval and
the Process of Change

We have already hypothesized that interpersonal schemas develop as a result of the persistent influence of maladaptive interpersonal experiences, not from one or two specific traumatic events. Interpersonal schemas can thus be thought of as prototypical representations of many interactions related to the maintenance of interpersonal relatedness, and not the representation of one specific interaction. In fact, as Stern (1985) suggests, because a schematic structure is an abstraction, it is possible that no single, specific interpersonal event will correspond precisely to an individual's interpersonal schema.

If the schematic structure is an "averaging" of a variety of interpersonal events similar in nature, what factors would then lead to the retrieval of a particular episodic memory? As research on memory retrieval indicates (Alba and Hasher 1983; Hasher and Zacks 1979), stimulus distinctiveness plays a key role in whether a particular memory will be retrievable. If a particular interpersonal event is sufficiently different from other interpersonal events that have been averaged into a specific interpersonal schema, then it will be grouped in memory along with interpersonal events of a different type, and will not be part of that particular interpersonal schema. On the other hand, if a particular interpersonal event is highly characteristic of a particular class of events, the memory for that event may be retained because of its salience for the individual as a prototypical exemplar of the relevant interpersonal experience.

We hypothesize, therefore, that memories that emerge spontaneously when an interpersonal issue is being explored in an emotionally immediate way, are often prototypical exemplars of the interpersonal experience that contributed to the development of the interpersonal schema being activated. It may also be that some memories accessible in therapy do not correspond to the events that *actually* took place, but may instead be prototypical constructions that capture the essential features of a class of relevant events.

We, thus, view memories retrieved in therapy as significant, not as unassailably accurate information about the patient's history, but as prototypical exemplars of interpersonal experience that is significant to the patient. What is important to the therapist is not the details of the memory, but rather the meaning of the memory for the patient.

CHAPTER 6

Experiential Disconfirmation
and Decentering:
I. Out-of-Session Focus

Experiential Disconfirmation with an Out-of-Session Focus

This change mechanism is most commonly associated with more behaviorally oriented approaches. As Bandura (1969; 1977) has argued, enactive therapeutic strategies are one of the more powerful ways of facilitating change, even when change is conceptualized from a cognitive perspective. To mobilize patients into re-entering problematic situations with a new framework that facilitates a change in perceptions or construal (Beck, Rush et al. 1979; Goldfried 1980), cognitive therapy takes advantage of procedures such as scheduling activities, graded task assignments, and other homework exercises.

Unlike the earlier behavioral tradition, the cognitive perspective asserts that it is useful to understand the process of change in cognitive terms even when the level of intervention is behavioral. Engaging in new behaviors such as staying in an anxiety-producing situation may or may not change the patient's subjective experience. Ultimately, the mediating factor will be the way in which the patient construes the new experience. Because other sources offer extensive descriptions of enactive techniques (Beck, Rush et al. 1979; Beck and Emery 1985; McMullin 1986), we will confine our discussion to their use from a cognitive-interpersonal perspective.

Although empirical research indicates that in vivo exposure is effective in treating a variety of fear-avoidance problems, patients obviously cannot benefit from the behavioral program unless they are willing to engage in it. Because many patients are not willing to experiment with new behaviors when they first start therapy, it is necessary to clarify potential mediating variables. Many people are reluctant to experiment with new behaviors because they have never developed the kind of secure attachment relationship that is first necessary if one is to engage in exploratory behavior to overcome childhood fears (Safran and Greenberg 1989).

M. D. S. Ainsworth (1982) and others (for example, Main 1983; Pastor 1981) have consistently observed that infants vary considerably in the extent to which they use the attachment figure as a secure base from which to explore and master unfamiliar and potentially anxiety-provoking situations. An extremely useful dimension for classifying these observations involves the *security* of the child's attachment. The secure child is one who is able to explore novel situations relatively freely, using the mother or attachment figure as a base. Securely attached children will thus roam around and explore their environment, returning from time to time to the attachment figure, or simply visually checking to ensure the attachment figure's availability and responsiveness.

The *insecurely* attached child, however, engages in minimal exploratory behavior, even in the attachment figure's presence. The insecure child is not able to use the attachment figure as a base for exploration, becomes extremely distressed in the mother's absence, and may not greet the mother upon her return.

The balance between withdrawal and exploration thus appears to be mediated by the child's belief that the attachment figure will be available and responsive when necessary. As Bowlby (1973) suggests, people with multiple-anxiety problems may never have developed the secure attachment relationships necessary to engage in the kinds of exploratory behaviors essential to developing familiarity with, and mastery of, the environment. In these situations it may be vital for the therapist to develop a trusting relationship with the patient gradually, over an extended period. Once such a relationship has developed, the therapist can then function as a secure base from which the patient can engage in exploratory behavior, as a parent does for a child.

A second consideration is ensuring that the relevant interpersonal schema is activated when the individual is engaging in the behavioral exercise (Foa and Kozak 1986; Safran and Greenberg 1989). Again, it is possible for an individual to engage in a behavioral exercise that should, in theory, provide information that would challenge dysfunctional interpersonal schemas, yet not change. Just as one must gain access to a computer program before one can modify it, before an interpersonal schema can be modified in response to new information, one must first have access to it. One obstacle may be that the relevant schema is associated with emotions that lead to the experience of anxiety. Take, for example, those whose feelings of vulnerability and longing for nurturance and support were met with rejection repeatedly as a child. Because of the anxiety that becomes associated with such feelings, they may have difficulty fully accessing them in new relationships. This will prevent them from discovering whether these feelings are in reality as threatening to interpersonal relatedness as anticipated. Anxiety thus interferes not only with the experimentation with new behaviors, but also with the processing of inner experience.

Because anxiety plays such a central role in mobilizing security operations that distort the nature of both inner and outer experience, it is essential for the patient to develop some degree of tolerance for anxiety in therapy. A useful stance involves helping the patient reframe the meaning of anxiety by explaining that one of the best ways to learn and grow in therapy is to seek out and pursue experiences of anxiety.

A nice metaphor for describing this process was once provided by a patient who flew gliders as a hobby. He explained that gliders are typically buffeted about by convection currents called thermals, which are created when an air pocket is heated. When the wing tip of a glider touches one of these thermals, the glider is automatically pushed away. Experienced glider pilots know this, however, and also know that by harnessing these thermals, they can use them to propel the glider as they wish. Experienced pilots thus set about *looking* for thermals, and learn to counteract the wing's automatic tendency to move away from the thermals by intentionally turning the wing into them.

In the same way, it is useful to tell patients that every time they experience anxiety or negative feelings, there is a learning opportunity as long as they are able to stay with the experience, whether it is an internal or an interpersonal encounter. By reframing the meaning of anxiety for patients in this way and by reminding them of this reframe when they begin to engage in security operations, the therapist can help the patient tolerate anxiety and facilitate the learning process.

A final consideration relates to learning to assess which kinds of new behaviors in the real world are likely to evoke the environmental responses most likely to facilitate real and enduring change. This assessment, in turn, depends on the therapist's accurate assessment of the patient's cognitive-interpersonal cycle and core dysfunctional interpersonal schema.

Decentering with an Out-of-Session Focus

Decentering is a change process of ubiquitous significance in psychotherapy, and one that has been described in different terms by therapists from different orientations. What exactly is it?

Decentering is a process through which one is able to step outside of one's immediate experience, thereby changing the very nature of that experience. This process allows for the introduction of a gap between the event and one's reaction to that event. By developing the capacity to observe oneself and one's own reactions, one begins to distinguish between reality and reality as one construes it.

Stepping outside of one's current experience fosters a recognition that the reality of the moment is not absolute, immutable, or unalterable, but rather something that is being constructed. In addition to the process of reflexive self-observation, there is a second component that is involved in the process. This is one of seeing oneself as an agent in the construction process (Rice 1984). There is thus also a process of accepting responsibility by seeing one's own role in the construction process.

These two interdependent processes of stepping outside one's immediate experience and observing oneself in the process of constructing that experience are common to a variety of forms of psychotherapy. Moreover, it is a central change process in many mystical traditions. In psychoanalysis, this process has been referred to as developing an "observing ego." In his analysis of change in the mystical traditions, A. J. Deikman (1982) refers to this process as "developing the observing self."

At the heart of Buddhist epistemology, for example, lies the concept of Shunyata, which means "empty of inherent existence." The idea here is that all phenomena lack absolute existence independent of one's construction of them. In this tradition, meditation is used specifically for the purpose of helping the student to obtain an experiential realization of the role that his or her own mind plays in constructing reality. In the same way, a growing number of cognitive therapists (for example, Guidano 1987; Guidano and Liotti 1983; Liotti 1987; Mahoney 1988), are arguing that cognitive therapy should be

117

based upon a constructivist perspective that recognizes that the individual plays a continuous and active role in constructing his or her reality.

For change to take place, however, patients must have more than an intellectual grasp of this notion. They must have the experience of actually seeing themselves construct reality. With this experience, the very nature of the experience changes for them.

It is worth dwelling on this distinction between a conceptual and an experiential realization of this construction process. Patients will often say that because they are already aware of their negative, self-critical thinking, they question the value of monitoring their thinking. Moreover, in our experience, therapists in supervision will often question the value of encouraging their patients to continue to monitor their thinking when they have already become aware of it. But knowing that one engages in negative self-critical thinking is very different from having the *tangible experience* of observing oneself in the process of interpreting a situation negatively. It is the stance of the dispassionate observer of one's own construction process that is the essential ingredient. It is thus vital for therapists to appreciate this distinction if they are to help patients see it and appreciate it. Moreover, once the patient has had this kind of experiential realization, the battle is not over. For change to continue, the patient must maintain a continuing awareness of his or her constructive processes.

Awareness versus Challenging

We will now extend our argument for awareness one step further, and hypothesize that the efficacy of any challenging technique in cognitive therapy can be explained by its role in promoting awareness of the way in which one constructs reality.

It is tempting to assimilate this discussion into the old controversy in behavioral and cognitive therapies about the relative merits of insight versus skills acquisition in the change process. This distinction, however, does not do justice to the relevant theoretical issue. The awareness we hypothesize lying at the center of the change process can be just as accurately thought of as a skill acquisition as it can be thought of as an insight. It is, however, more of a *perceptual* skill acquisition. Many discussions about insight are complicated by a lack of clarity about the meaning of the term. It is vital to distinguish between tangible experiential awareness of the kind described here and conceptual insight.

This distinction can also be useful in clarifying the meaning of existing cognitive-behavioral research on the topic. A number of studies have attempted to evaluate the relative importance of exploring versus challenging cognitive processes. J. D. Teasdale and M. J. V. Fennell (1982), for example, found that periods of time devoted to a "challenging" version of cognitive therapy consistently produced more change in targeted belief than did similar periods of time devoted to "exploring or getting more information relevant to the belief."

At face value, it appears that the results are consistent with the hypothesis that challenging cognitive processes plays a much more important role in the change process than exploring. As with any psychotherapy study, however, it is vital to ascertain how the particular therapeutic intervention was operationalized. In listening to recordings of sessions from a number of different cognitive therapists, we have observed that the exploration of automatic thoughts by the therapist is often not conducted in a way that promotes the kind of tangible awareness of one's own constructive processes that we have described. Often, the exploration process involves a dry report of a particular thought that the patient may have had, rather than an emotionally alive account of the details of the subjective construal, here and now.

Because the patient's observation of his or her subjective construal process, as it takes place and in an emotionally alive way, is essential for decentering, any study in which the "exploration" condition does not intentionally facilitate this process cannot stand as a true test of the hypothesis.

The Role of Historical Reconstruction

An important point of divergence between cognitive therapy and psychoanalysis has traditionally been the role that exploration of the patient's past plays in the therapeutic process. While psychodynamic approaches have always emphasized the importance of focusing on the patient's history both as an essential part of the assessment process and as an intrinsic part of the change process, cognitive therapists have traditionally avoided an extensive focus on the patient's past.

119

This is beginning to change, however. Guidano and Liotti (1983), Guidano (1987), and Liotti (in press), for example, focus extensively on assessing the patient's past as a way of clarifying the patient's tacit beliefs and they engage in a systematic historical reconstruction with the patient as a way of facilitating the decentering process. Similarly, Young (in press) suggests that exploring the patient's past can be particularly useful for gaining access to and modifying schematic structures.

The belief that change occurs as a result of understanding the historical origins of one's problems, was part of Freud's earliest perspective on psychoanalysis. As F. Sulloway (1979) has argued, this view of the change process was part of Freud's legacy as an intellectual writing during the age of enlightenment in a culture where it was believed that understanding and rationality were curative.

Even in the early history of psychoanalysis, however, this assumption was challenged by analysts who believed that change would only come from new awareness taking place at an experiential level. Thus, for example, J. Strachey (1934) emphasized that any interpretation, to be therapeutic, had to involve an emotionally immediate interpretation of an event taking place currently in the therapeutic relationship. Contemporary psychoanalytic theorists such as Gill (1982), H. Kohut (1984), and Strupp and Binder (1984), have increasingly come to deemphasize the importance of engaging in historical reconstructions and instead emphasize the importance of providing the patient with a new constructive interpersonal experience by not participating with the patient in his or her characteristic maladaptive interpersonal transaction. Indeed, both Gill (1982) and Strupp and Binder (1984), advocate a sparing use of genetic transference interpretations in which a link is made between the patient's current interpersonal behavior and the relationship with parents. It is thus interesting that at a time when leading psychodynamic theorists are moving away from an excessive emphasis on historical memories and experiences toward a greater emphasis on the exploration of the therapeutic relationship in the here and now, cognitive therapists are beginning to speak about the importance of focusing on memories for relevant historical experiences.

While we believe that historical experiences play an important role in the development of interpersonal schemas and that in certain contexts the exploration of relevant historical experiences can be therapeutic, we also believe it is important to develop a differentiated understanding of when and how the exploration of historical memories can contribute to the change process and when it will be counter-therapeutic.

One of the more important potential pitfalls of using systematic historical reconstruction as a standard practice is that it may contribute to a kind of intellectualized understanding of the problem that may, in the final analysis, be incompatible with real change. Moreover, as we will explore in chapter 7, a focus on the past can deflect attention from what is really happening in the therapeutic relationship. This, in turn, can lead to the perpetuation of a dysfunctional cognitive-interpersonal cycle.

Although the exploration of historical memories in the wrong context can be counter-therapeutic, in the right context it can facilitate change. First, the exploration of the historical events leading to the development of the patient's interpersonal schema may, in the right context, help patients develop a greater perspective on the way they themselves have constructed many of their important tacit beliefs. This in turn can help them understand that these attitudes and beliefs are not immutable but potentially modifiable. Second, the exploration of relevant historical antecedents may help patients understand their dysfunctional attitudes and beliefs as a function of certain historical circumstances and as a necessary and reasonable adaption to those circumstances. Understanding these beliefs and attitudes as an appropriate adaptation to the relevant historical circumstances may help patients feel less guilty and responsible and may thus make it easier for them to accept and acknowledge some of their important dysfunctional attitudes and beliefs. This process of acceptance of responsibility and owning is a necessary precursor to any change (Greenberg and Safran 1987). Third, there is a natural tendency to want to make sense of one's own experience. By coming to understand the historical context leading to the development of certain beliefs and attitudes, patients may begin to develop a sense of mastery.

What is the right context for exploring historical memories? Often, in the course of exploring a patient's thoughts, beliefs, and attitudes in an emotionally immediate way, there is a spontaneous recall of historical events that led to their development. In this context, the activation of associated memories and accompanying feelings provides evidence that a relevant interpersonal schema has also been activated, one that consists of episodic memories, images, and associated emotions. In this process there is typically a sense of experiential discovery rather than an intellectualized attempt at analysis.

In contrast, when the relevant memory is discussed in a matter-of-fact way as a standard part of a historical reconstruction, without the quality of emotion and newness associated with a memory's evocation, it is less likely to facilitate the change process. The therapist, thus, must always assess whether the exploration of historical memories is the patient's attempt to avoid the here and now or whether it is a genuine activation of memories, images, and associated feelings that will help the patient further clarify the meaning of current interpersonal transactions.

Examples of Decentering
with an Out-of-Session Focus

In activating the decentering process, the context determines the most useful intervention. To examine the decentering process in two contexts, we will follow Rice and Greenberg (1984) and use the term "patient marker" to refer to a patient verbalization that reflects an underlying construal process indicating receptivity to specific kinds of intervention. We have observed two markers with different implications for cognitive intervention: the *fully immersed marker*, and the *divided awareness marker* (Safran 1985). In the fully immersed marker, patients verbalize a dysfunctional or problematic perception and do not appear to question its validity. They are, hence, fully immersed in that perspective. For example, the patient may say: "I will never succeed in meeting someone compatible." Or "What a mess! This feels just like I was five years old again." Assuming there is an adequate therapeutic alliance, a fully immersed marker can be an appropriate context for a challenging intervention, such as examining the evidence or considering alternative perspectives.

In the divided awareness marker, patients provide evidence of a maladaptive or dysfunctional perception, yet simultaneously question or invalidate their own perception. For example, the patient may say, "I feel that people are judging me negatively, but I know that that's not really true." For reasons we will soon explain, divided awareness markers do not provide a good context for challenging interventions.

The following transcript illustrates the decentering process in the context of a fully immersed marker. In this example, there is a sufficiently strong therapeutic alliance to allow the patient to construe the therapist's actions as fundamentally validating and thus to feel fully amenable to engage in the therapeutic task of using the intervention to help herself distinguish between reality and reality as she construes it.

The patient has been referred for treatment from out of town and finds herself with no friends, in a city she is completely unfamiliar with. Initially, she was treated on an in-patient basis, but just before this session, she moved out of the hospital and is now staying at the home of a fellow patient's mother. The entry point for the therapeutic intervention is the patient's feeling that she is imposing upon her host and that she is an inconvenience. Because the transcript is extracted from the twelfth session of therapy, the therapist already has a working hypothesis of the patient's core cognitive processes.

THERAPIST: Okay, so where are things for you—bright and early this Friday morning?

PATIENT: The mornings are always worse for me. I always feel worse in the morning, particularly when I got up this morning—see when I start feeling better it takes a little longer. I don't know why. Maybe it's because I don't feel very good physically. I feel just like I'd like to curl up some place and sleep for about a week.

THERAPIST: So you're feeling really weary?

PATIENT: I'm really tired—physically and emotionally. Just really kind of run out. I'm staying at my friend Susan's mother's place, and I'm feeling really badly. I really don't know Susan's mom that well and I don't want to be an imposition for her—so I kinda try and stay out of the way as much as possible—she's really a nice lady and I—I'm imposing. It's an inconvenience for them. It was very nice of them to let me stay there. She said she didn't really like to be alone either, but she's got to resent it at some level.

Here, the patient presents a fully immersed marker. She articulates her perception that she is imposing, that it is an inconvenience, and that Susan's mother must resent it at some level. This articulation reveals an unquestioned acceptance of her perception as reality. The patient sees her experience as inherent in the situation rather than as partially dependent on her own construction of the situation. In the next segment, the therapist responds to the fully immersed marker with a challenging intervention that involves examining the evidence.

THERAPIST: So you're saying it's an inconvenience for Susan's mother?

PATIENT: Yes.

THERAPIST: Uh-huh. And that she must resent it at some level?

PATIENT: Uh-huh.

THERAPIST: How do you know this?

PATIENT: I don't know (pause)—I guess I just see it as an inconvenience.

THERAPIST: Uh-huh. Okay, so you're making some assumptions.

PATIENT: Uh-huh.

THERAPIST: What are some of the other assumptions you're making about how she feels about it?

PATIENT: Well, when I went there she didn't know me at all. I guess—I found that kind of surprising, you know? Especially in as big a city as this is. She just said, "Susan, bring her over here" and she handed me the keys to the apartment and said "Come and go as you please" and it made me feel (pause, voice becomes emotional) kind of guilty, I guess, ah, I'm not sure where that comes from. I felt—uhm—like I was taking advantage of her. That maybe I should find some place that I could stay and, you know, how I didn't want to be an inconvenience. And I still feel that way.

THERAPIST: Okay. Good. We have a situation we can explore here. (Laughter from the patient.)

The therapist's question, "How do you know this?" begins to activate a decentering process in which the patient starts exploring her own role in constructing the experience. The patient begins to explore some of the assumptions she makes that contribute to her feelings of discomfort and also to explore the true nature of her feelings ("It made me feel kind of guilty, I guess"). Here, there is a change in the quality of the patient's voice tone as the patient appears to re-experience some of the emotions that she had actually experienced in that situation.

PATIENT: She says it's not an inconvenience, but——

THERAPIST: Uh-huh. Okay, so I wonder if you can just really elaborate a little bit on your concerns about your being there right now.

PATIENT: I don't know. I guess I feel like I should have borrowed the money or whatever I needed to do to stay someplace else, because it's hard having somebody living with you—and—I don't want her to feel that she has to go out of her way at all and (pause) I just feel like I'm in the way (voice becomes more emotional). If I stayed with somebody else other than—I think that it goes back to—uhm—being independent.

THERAPIST: Okay. So, "I should have stayed somewhere else," "I should have borrowed the money," "I'm imposing on her." Any other "shoulds"?

PATIENT: I guess I feel like that in most relationships. I don't—I can't "take" comfortably. Like, when we moved to our new house and I had (pause) I had been sick for quite a while. I was scheduled to go into the hospital on February 1st and we moved on January 28th. And (pause) I had a lot of offers to help move and, uh—I could handle it. And I seem to think I have to do it myself. It's not acceptable if I don't.

THERAPIST: Okay. So, "I have to do it by myself" sounds like this is hooking up with a common theme for you. So in this situation, there's some sense that you "should" be more independent?

PATIENT: Uh-huh. And find some place to stay.

THERAPIST: So, what does this mean about you that you didn't—so that, that you were staying there?

PATIENT: That I'm taking advantage or that it's my own responsibility.

THERAPIST: Uh-huh. So, "I'm being irresponsible—taking advantage."

The patient begins this segment by further exploring associated thoughts and feelings. Gaining access to the relevant emotional state appears to facilitate the process of tapping into relevant construal processes. She becomes aware of her feeling of being in the way and her injunctions to herself ("I should have stayed somewhere else, I should have borrowed money"). She, herself, then becomes aware of how this hooks up with a core theme that has emerged previously in therapy, her belief that she should be independent, that she should take care of herself. In terms of the theory outlined earlier, this would be understood as a tacit rule for maintaining relatedness, which is part of an interpersonal schema.

In this process, the patient shuttles back and forth between the level of automatic thoughts and higher level constructs or dysfunctional attitudes. Thus, it is not a linear sequential process of moving from automatic thoughts to dysfunctional attitudes, as some of the written material on cognitive therapy suggests.

PATIENT: It just seems strange that things that I have always taken for granted, that I had to be independent and in control and responsible, have affected just about everything—ah—I feel like I must really have messed up.

THERAPIST: So now you're—as often happens when we start to explore what this really means to you, you start spinning off into a negative, self-critical type of spiral, is that right?

PATIENT: I don't recognize it right away. Sometimes, I'll recognize it, but not—it's automatic.

THERAPIST: Okay. So it's important for us to note that this is predictable for you, that when you start to make a new discovery about yourself you're going to start getting down on yourself. Right?

PATIENT: I guess I'm still not far enough. I'm not aware enough of what I'm feeling sometimes. I don't realize that it happens so fast.

THERAPIST: But as you look at it now, you do see that?

PATIENT: Yeah.

THERAPIST: Okay, so just let's leave that aside for a second now that we're aware that it goes on and focus in on your reactions to living with Susan's mother, all right?

Here the patient clearly recognizes how this situation is tied to her general belief that she must be independent and in control. With this realization comes a new cycle of self-critical activity as she realizes how pervasive a theme this is in her life. This cycle of self-critical activity accompanying a new awareness of a dysfunctional style is a common occurrence in therapy. When it occurs it is essential for the therapist to determine whether this new cycle of self-criticism is sufficiently intense to override the initial focus. If so, it is important to shift focus to the current self-criticism because it will be more experientially alive for the patient than the original focus and would consequently impede its progress.

It is the therapist's assessment, however, that in this case the original focus is more salient, and he bypasses the new cycle of self-criticism by helping the patient decenter from it. This is done by labeling it and alluding to previous occasions when this has happened. He then proceeds with the investigation of the initial theme, which seems to be more central.

PATIENT: I guess I don't feel anything positive about it. I don't feel it as anything other than an inconvenience, being there—and her Mom—I'm doing the same thing that I always tend to do. It doesn't matter what anybody else says, but I seem to have my mind made up on how they feel about it, and it doesn't make any difference what they say.

THERAPIST: Well, let's look at what you're saying. There are a bunch of assumptions you make about what's going on, so let's look at evidence you have which might be relevant to it. Okay? What evidence do you have right now that it's an inconvenience for her?

PATIENT: I guess I think it's an inconvenience that she feels that she has to come home at night and fix a meal, or that she feels like she's saying all this stuff over breakfast and you know, those kinds of things and I think that it's got to be inconvenient when she's used to being alone, and I guess I feel that it's an inconvenience for her and the added—any time you have another person living in the house there's always more washing and that kind of stuff. Just sheets and towels—and I feel that's an inconvenience.

THERAPIST: So you know that it's going to mean a change in her routine and more work for her and you're assuming that she's going to feel badly about it—that it's going to be negative for her?

PATIENT: And even though she's said that she much prefers having someone there because she doesn't eat and she's lost a considerable amount of weight because she eats alone and there's nobody here and why should she bother so she just didn't, and—so she can say that she likes it better having someone there—but I still feel I'm in the way.

THERAPIST: So she's telling you that it's actually to her advantage, that it actually is a positive thing for her, rather than a negative thing. What do you think about the reasons that she told you? Are they believable?

PATIENT: I guess they're believable, but on the other hand, I guess that I think she's just being nice and trying to make things comfortable—which is something that I would probably do, even if it's something that is inconvenient for me, I would try to make someone comfortable—I don't accept when people say, you know, if I—if I question or have evidence on the other side. I guess it just depends.

THERAPIST: Uh-huh. If you question, or have evidence on the other side?

PATIENT: I just discount them.

THERAPIST: So you see yourself discounting some evidence right now?

PATIENT: Yes.

THERAPIST: Okay. So you're aware of yourself discounting. What specifically is the evidence you're discounting?

PATIENT: When she said, "It's nice having someone there," that it's nice not being alone in the apartment, and having someone to sit down and eat with and to help with supper and clean up and that kind of thing and—I guess I still feel that I'm inconveniencing her.

THERAPIST: Well, for now, what's important is just that you're able to see yourself discounting.

PATIENT: I didn't recognize it before, but that's what I'm doing—I do that in everything (pause), so even if what I wanted is positive reinforcement, I don't accept it even if I get it.

Here, the patient oscillates between two contrasting constructions of reality. She contrasts seeing herself as being an inconvenience with her host's statement that it's to her advantage to have her staying with her. Through this process of oscillation between her construction of the situation and the evidence, she spontaneously becomes aware that she is discounting the evidence ("I just discount them"). This juxtaposition of her construal with the evidence (or in other situations, of two alternative constructions of reality) appears to be instrumental in helping the patient develop a metaperspective on her own dysfunctional processing style. In the rest of the segment she consolidates her perspective of "discounting" ("I didn't recognize it before, but that's what I'm doing—I do that in everything, so even if what I wanted is positive reinforcement, I don't accept it even if I get it").

THERAPIST: What's going on for you right now? What are you experiencing?

PATIENT: Uh—I've started thinking—back when I wanted to go back home—it was made very clear to me that they would tolerate me, but they didn't really want me to do that. And I think this had an effect on, on the way I feel about anyone going out of their way for me. That I don't want that. I feel like it's always an imposition.

THERAPIST: That your parents, you wanted to return home to your parents' place, then?

PATIENT: I never asked to go home.

THERAPIST: Uh-huh.

PATIENT: I think it would have made things much better if I just stayed home a few months.

THERAPIST: This was after your separation?

PATIENT: Uh-huh. It was made very clear to me that I was alone— that I was an independent adult and they were my children. I was responsible for them and, uhm, to take it as it comes—that I would survive.

THERAPIST: Uh-huh.

PATIENT: So I stayed independent and I became almost, uh, fiercely possessive of that independence. There were times we didn't have anything to eat, but I wouldn't have asked for any help.

THERAPIST: So, that experience, it was a very powerful, painful experience for you?

PATIENT: I felt very cut off (pause). It forced me into a lot of growing, and the things that happened because of it—there are a lot of positive things that happened because of it. Because I was forced to be very independent. And I did survive.

THERAPIST: So, it forced you really to take care of yourself, to be independent and you learned that you can do that, that you can survive anything.

PATIENT: I think I also learned that I can *never* depend on anybody else (said with emphasis).

THERAPIST: And you also learned that you could never depend on anybody else, all at the same time. So there was some positive learning that came out of it and some learning that looks like it's affecting you in a negative way.

The patient's recognition of her processing style appears to trigger a chain of associated memories that have a definite emotional tone. She recalls a significant incident in her past that is related to the entire theme of independence/dependence, a painful memory of wanting to stay with her parents after the break-up of a disastrous marriage. Her parents refused and she was forced to stand on her own two feet. This served to reinforce or consolidate previous beliefs about not being able to trust and depend on other people, and strengthened her resolve always to be completely independent.

It was thus a significant learning experience that contributed to the development of her generalized expectations of self-other interactions. As indicated earlier, this type of spontaneous retrieval of an associated memory suggests that it may be prototypical. Exploring propositions related to the theme of independence/dependence, gaining access to specific automatic thoughts and a specific emotional state, becoming clearly aware of her pattern of discounting reassuring feedback in the moment, all combine to activate an important, schematically linked memory.

We hypothesize that although the material in the session that was schematically related to the independent/dependent theme served to prepare the context for the retrieval of this spontaneous memory, the patient's awareness that she was discounting reassuring information in the moment had an activating, emotional impact upon her that helped trigger this painful memory. It is as if suddenly becoming aware of her own discounting activity provides the patient with dramatic evidence that she actively constructs reality in a dysfunctional way and triggers a memory search in an attempt to make sense of her own behavior. In this context, the spontaneous retrieval of an emotionally toned memory thus indicates that the relevant interpersonal schema has been activated.

At this point, with very little assistance from the therapist, the patient goes on to evaluate the significance of this past event, clarifying for herself the way in which this experience contributed to her belief that she can never depend upon anyone else and that she must always be completely independent. As the therapist summarizes, the attitude she has developed has both advantages and disadvantages.

> PATIENT: At the time that I was going through the divorce it was obvious that I couldn't depend on my husband and it was obvious that I couldn't depend on my parents, either, for any kind of emotional or physical or monetary support in any way. And I felt very cut off (voice becomes emotional here). I guess I was twenty when my son was born and I got the divorce.
>
> THERAPIST: Uh-huh.
>
> PATIENT: There were some real good things that came out of it. I did stand on my own two feet and I did take care of the kids and I did go back to work, probably much earlier than I should have. My son was only four weeks old and I got a special doctor's release, I had to feed the kids and we did survive. I can remember weeks that, uh, the kids had something to eat, but I

lived on whatever—tomatoes. I remember, it's surprising that I still like tomatoes. They're kind of bad as a single diet.

THERAPIST: Uh-huh.

PATIENT: But, you know, we all survived it, and it didn't seem to do them any harm.

THERAPIST: As you talk right now, I experience you as, as sort of getting in touch with——

PATIENT: It makes me feel sad (voice breaks). It still hurts, because it was a really bad experience in some ways.

THERAPIST: Uh-huh.

PATIENT: On the other hand, it can make you feel good that you did survive it, that you did go it by yourself, and you didn't have to ask for help.

THERAPIST: So, it's a mixed thing, right? There's a real sadness and a pain; on the other hand, there's a self-satisfaction, a sense of strength. "I did it. I can take care of myself."

In this segment, the patient explores the complex, multifaceted nature of her feelings about both the particular event under discussion and the general theme of independence/dependence. There is both a sadness as she recalls the pain of being rejected and the hurt of being alone, but there is also a fierce sense of pride and self-satisfaction in her ability to look after herself. This realization of her multifaceted feelings surrounding the independence/dependence issue helps her clarify what the true meaning of being independent is for her, and thus facilitates the decentering process. This, in turn, increases the degree of choice she has in determining whether or not she wishes to continue this way. Her emotional voice tone continues to suggest that there is a real process of self-exploration taking place, rather than an intellectualized avoidance of painful feelings.

PATIENT: The one fact is that I always had to take care of myself. This is based on everything that I've had to do. No other way is acceptable and I think that's when I learned that lesson. So, all that stuff that I never dealt with back then, that I just went on with, I guess I'm going to have to sort through it—all of it. Because there were positives and negatives in all of it (pause). I hope my children learn a different lesson. I don't want them to think they can't depend on us. I want them to know that we're there if they need us; that we're there——

THERAPIST: Right.

PATIENT: My parents are very, uh, have just really been super and they—you know, felt for the kids and everything, since I've been sick and have just done whatever—I guess if I really think about it, I wonder what was going on for them at that time that they felt that way. My brother kind of seemed like he always wanted to depend on them.

THERAPIST: They probably had their reasons——

PATIENT: Uh-huh.

THERAPIST: Nevertheless, it was a very painful experience for you.

PATIENT: It really was. And I guess my mom made it very clear that you can't come home. Don't even think about it.

THERAPIST: Uh-huh.

PATIENT: So, and I think now if it were one of the girls and they were in that kind of a situation, I wouldn't want them to come home and stay forever, but I think that I would want them to come home to get their feet on the ground and be able to handle it on their own, so that it didn't come all of a sudden. And that's kind of the way it happened to me, that I seemed to lose everything at once. It has affected the way I feel about life.

THERAPIST: So, you would want your children to reach out to people sometimes and take help from people.

PATIENT: It makes me feel like, I feel like I have to reciprocate, not just in the normal sense that you reciprocate, that I always have to do more for them. It's really frustrating to think about all that (crying a little), but I never looked at why I was sick.

THERAPIST: So, this is clarifying for you—looking back and making some connections and seeing where some of these things actually came from.

PATIENT: Well, it's going to be very difficult to change the way—the automatic feeling, but I think that I'm making some headway in that I can see some of the stuff that I'm doing—and it's especially affecting my relationship with John [her current husband], because I know that he could tell me anything—I don't trust him. It makes me feel bad that I don't trust him.

THERAPIST: So that, if he says that he cares about you, or if he says that, uhm, something is okay with him, you'll discount that in the same way you'll discount what Susan's mother says.

PATIENT: Yeah.

Here, the patient realizes the absoluteness of her belief that she must always be completely independent and again tries to make sense of the tacit rule that has been guiding her actions, in terms of previous learning experiences. As reflected in the statement: "I hope my children learn a different lesson," she is becoming more and more aware of the detrimental effect this dysfunctional attitude has had on her life. Also, it suggests that she is beginning to see a degree of arbitrariness in this attitude.

Let us now consider the transcript as a whole. The process taking place involves the modification and reorganization of fundamental cognitive structures and belief systems by inferring core themes ("I must always be completely independent") at the deep structural level from the surface structure (that is, specific automatic thoughts and dysfunctional processing activities such as discounting reassuring information). By gaining access to a constellation of schematically associated automatic thoughts and then exploring the nature of the interpersonal schema that shapes this self-evaluative activity, the therapist and patient promote a process of overall construct loosening.

One of the important features of this session is that the patient is able to have a concrete, meaningful experience of how deep structural rules (dysfunctional attitudes) and the surface level activities (automatic thoughts, discounting activity) are linked. Oscillating between the exploration of high-level constructs and the reality testing of cognitive activities guided by these constructs, keeps the patient's recognition of the impact of these constructs grounded in immediate experiences, thereby contributing to the loosening of her constructs.

Once both the negative self-evaluative activity and the guiding dysfunctional attitudes have been made explicit, and the patient becomes aware of the complex interconnection between deep structure and surface structure in the moment, cognitive interventions, such as reality testing or inspecting evidence, can then contribute to the modification of the underlying interpersonal schema.

Our experience has been that interventions such as inspecting evidence or examining alternative perspectives are most effective in precisely this context. Thus, challenging randomly selected automatic thoughts is not a particularly potent therapeutic intervention. However, under certain conditions, encouraging the patient to "check out" the veridicality of a particular self-critical thought, perception, or assumption, in context of an appreciation of the way in which the thought being tested fits into the overall cognitive organization, can facilitate a change in core cognitive structures.

A crucial feature of the patient's change process is that she was fully immersed in her dysfunctional perspective prior to the intervention and that she experienced her perceptions ("It's an inconvenience for her") in an emotionally immediate way. This complete immersion in her perspective allows her to experience an alternative perspective as *new* information, thus facilitating the decentering process.

When patients do not fully allow themselves to experience their dysfunctional processing activity, disconfirming evidence does not have the same kind of impact. Instead, disconfirming evidence simply becomes assimilated to the old schema or the old way of viewing things. When, however, patients allow themselves to experience their dysfunctional cognitive activity fully, the discrepancy between reality and reality as construed becomes more apparent and there is a greater possibility of schematic accommodation.

We will now illustrate the process of change with a divided awareness marker. This patient has been troubled by chronic procrastination. He has just described an event preceding the session where he has avoided arranging for his transcripts to be forwarded from high school to university, but has no idea why he has procrastinated.

Because the dysfunctional appraisal was not manifest on the surface, as it was in the previous case, the therapist has begun by encouraging the patient to reconstruct the situation as vividly as possible, using imagery, and becoming aware of relevant feelings and dysfunctional cognitive processes.

THERAPIST: Can you put yourself back in the situation and describe it as if it were happening right now?

PATIENT: Well, I can sort of get hold of it, but I can't articulate it. It's, I see a picture of some of the people that I have to contact and try to get something moving on this, and I see them hating me. They see me as a nuisance.

THERAPIST: Uh-huh.

PATIENT: And they've got all the power and I don't have any.

THERAPIST: Can you actually visualize those people?

PATIENT: I can see, I can see, a face of one woman that I have to deal with, yeah. And I can see the look on her face. She's thinking I'm a nuisance.

THERAPIST: Uh-huh. Okay. So, you can see her and her reaction. She's thinking you're a nuisance.

PATIENT: Hmm, yeah.

THERAPIST: Yes.

PATIENT: That I'm sort of, just a troublemaker, a sort of punk trying to stir up trouble, and there's this—"Sorry, you've got your answer and that's all there is to it"—that's her reaction.

THERAPIST: Uh-huh.

PATIENT: And that she's sort of actually conniving in case I should manage to get someone higher up than her. She's gonna connive. I mean, it's a ridiculous fear, I suppose.

The patient provides a divided awareness marker. He imagines that the clerk in the transcript office might actually connive against him. At the same time, he begins to invalidate his subjective perception: "I mean, it's a ridiculous fear, I suppose."

THERAPIST: But very real for you?

PATIENT: Yeah, very real, yeah.

THERAPIST: Okay, so here's this woman and—you're very good with imagery, I think. You're able to get an image of her, of this woman. She's conniving.

PATIENT: Uh-huh, right (laughs).

THERAPIST: You laugh right now, but it's real, right?

PATIENT: Yeah, real for me, yeah.

THERAPIST: She sees you as being kind of a punk.

PATIENT: (Laughing) Yeah. Yeah.

THERAPIST: And again, you laugh a little bit. It seems—what—a little——

PATIENT: Yeah, it's funny when I hear things that I say, said, back to me.

THERAPIST: Uh-huh.

PATIENT: Why do I laugh there, umh. Because it really, when I hear it from you, it isn't accurate. She's not like that. She wouldn't think of me as a punk at all, but then, yet, from another point of view, when I say it, it's really what I mean—kind of.

THERAPIST: Uh-huh.

The therapist intervenes by encouraging the patient to suspend self-critical judgment and to accept the subjective validity of his appraisal. In response, he continues to reveal his hidden, preattentive subjective appraisal ("She sees me as being kind of a punk"). At the same time, he continues to invalidate it, partly because of his discomfort, as indicated by his laughter. At the end of the segment, the patient sums up his subjective experience nicely when he says that he realizes that the perception is not objectively valid, but that it is *subjectively* real for him.

PATIENT: Peculiar.

THERAPIST: Yes. It's very real for you at the time, right?

PATIENT: Yeah.

THERAPIST: And then somehow or other, when you hear me say it, you kind of step outside, very quickly.

PATIENT: Yeah, yeah, and just, "Oh, that's ridiculous, you know."

THERAPIST: Uh-huh.

PATIENT: "Of course, she doesn't see me as a punk"—you know.

THERAPIST: Uh-huh. So, before you step outside—I'm going to ask you to try to stay with your subjective experience for a while, okay?

PATIENT: Got ya.

The patient continues to establish a metaperspective on the way he is now invalidating his own subjective perception. This process is a kind of subtask.

THERAPIST: Okay. So, here's this woman, you look at her and you have thoughts like, "She's going to think that I'm a punk and I'm trying to create trouble." Can you elaborate on the imagery at all?

PATIENT: Well, I can't really elaborate on the image, but on the action, like, I'm lying here in bed and the thought occurs to me, "This is what I've got to do. I've got to phone that woman." Ah, it's funny, after describing all this, suddenly it doesn't seem as surprising to me, that what happens is that I stay in bed for another hour.

THERAPIST: So, in your mind you see this woman, and if you try to do something, you might get connected to her. There's a sense of futility about it in a way, right?

The patient begins to gain a tangible understanding of the impact that his subjective construal has on his experience. His procrastination is becoming less mysterious to him the less he invalidates his construal, and he begins to see what he is doing to himself.

PATIENT: Uh-huh. Uh-huh.

THERAPIST: Can you actually imagine a scenario, or a confrontation between the two of you, if you did get connected to her?

PATIENT: Yeah. Ah, well, she'd answer the phone saying "guidance department." And I'd say, "I'd like to speak to a guidance counselor. I'm an old alumnus," etc. She'd ask my name, I'd tell her and then say: "I was wondering if we could do anything about it." I guess now as I fantasize it, I don't see how she could say anything but "Okay, I'll see what I can do." But she might not be very active in arranging it. Like, I mean, it's entirely within her power to let the memo sit on her desk for a day.

THERAPIST: Uh-huh.

PATIENT: Umh, that's the most reasonable fantasy I can come up with.

THERAPIST: How about an unreasonable fantasy?

PATIENT: Okay, just for the heck of it?

THERAPIST: Yeah.

PATIENT: Ah, then her voice would get sharp, and she'd say, "Now listen, we cleared all that up two weeks ago. You can go ahead and apply with your grade 12, and that's all you have to do. That's all you're gonna need, and you just—you don't have the other marks, so why should you be bothering staff here with nonsense like this." Ah, and then she'd threaten—something—

THERAPIST: Like what?

PATIENT: Ah, I don't know. It's sort of ridiculous. Like, she— nobody threatens in this society.

THERAPIST: Uh-huh. So now again, you sort of stepped outside.

PATIENT: (Laughing) Yes.

THERAPIST: Yeah, okay. Can you stay inside your subjective experience for a minute?

PATIENT: Okay, I'll try. Ah, "If you keep calling, keep this charade up, maybe we'll"—oh, that's ridiculous, too. I was going to say, "send the college your," ah, like there are poorer marks that I have, that I re-did. Like, I re-did them in summer school. Upgraded them, like she would be threatening to send the prior marks.

THERAPIST: Uh-huh.

PATIENT: But, I mean, that's so silly.

THERAPIST: So, now you step outside again and you say, "that's really silly."

PATIENT: Hmm.

THERAPIST: But you are able to create that scenario quite easily, huh?

PATIENT: (Laughing) Yeah, I see, yeah. There's something really weird going on here. Like this is fucking strange; it's like I can very easily, in fact, I *am* fantasizing about those possibilities, this

woman sending my entire reports from grade 11 and 12—all the
bunged-up marks——

THERAPIST: Yeah.

PATIENT: To a college. And she isn't even going to know which col-
leges I'm going to be applying to.

THERAPIST: Uh-huh.

PATIENT: But somehow I've got it in my mind that she could do
this to me.

THERAPIST: Uh-huh.

PATIENT: And that is a very strong fantasy, like, it's very real, very
visceral. And somehow I'm not letting myself see those fantasies
exactly for what they are or something.

The patient continues to tap into his hidden appraisal of the situation and to construct a scenario in fantasy that captures some of his
real perceptions. More than once, he invalidates his own perception,
but the therapist encourages him to suspend his rational perspective
and his self-criticism and to continue to articulate his real perception.
He continues to gain more tangible understanding of his hidden
appraisal of the situation and its impact on his experience and continues to consolidate his metaperspective on the process of invalidating his subjective appraisal.

PATIENT: 'Cause I'm always dodging out and saying "That's ridiculous" and "I never thought that."

THERAPIST: Uh-huh.

PATIENT: But I did! I did think it!

THERAPIST: So continue. Go with that a little now, generate some
more scenarios like that.

PATIENT: Okay, I'll try. It's embarrassing for me.

THERAPIST: Uh-huh.

PATIENT: Like, I really feel like I'm stupid, when I'm doing it, but
I'll try.

THERAPIST: Okay. As much as you can, just suspend self-judgment.

PATIENT: Yeah. Back on the phone with her?

THERAPIST: Sure.

PATIENT: (Laughing) Okay, ah (more laughter)—there's a quick fantasy there, and she says—she's given me all this about how she's
gonna maybe even get me and then she says, "As a matter of
fact, I'm going to phone the principal right now, and it's all set.
We're gonna come over and we're gonna spank you."

THERAPIST: Uh-huh.

PATIENT: Yeah (laughs), it's like that—it's like—she's gonna phone the principal right now, and like I've got to hang up and run and hide or something.

THERAPIST: Right.

PATIENT: 'Cause he's—I'm gonna be in big shit.

THERAPIST: Uh-huh. So, I'm gonna be spanked. I'm gonna be punished.

PATIENT: Yeah, yeah.

THERAPIST: It's like, I'm a bad little boy, I'm in the wrong.

PATIENT: And I'm gonna get squashed like a bug. Yeah.

THERAPIST: Okay, that——

PATIENT: And I have no defense, no defense at all.

The patient's statements here reveal his interpersonal schema—the heart of his idiosyncratic perception of self and others—more fully. He sees himself as a powerless child who is in danger of being punished by powerful adults; as a powerless, defenseless child who can be squashed like a bug by malicious adults. Note the powerful metaphorical language here, indicating the emotional immediacy of the experience.

Comparison of the Two Change Processes

Let's compare the two processes of change we have illustrated. In the first case, the therapist begins the intervention at the fully immersed marker by encouraging the patient to clarify the evidence the perception is based on. For this kind of change to take place, it is necessary for certain conditions to exist in the therapeutic alliance. The patient must be able to experience the therapist's active challenging of the patient's appraisal as part of a collaborative process rather than as personal invalidation. This kind of intervention makes strong demands on the alliance, because it is very easy for the patient to experience it as criticism. Alternatively, patients who are particularly submissive or compliant may deny or invalidate subjective perceptions, and hide them from the therapist and possibly from themselves.

Assuming that both the right marker and the appropriate alliance conditions are there, however, the patient will use the intervention to begin actively to question the degree of fit between perception and reality, and begin to treat the perception as a hypothesis to be evaluated, thus becoming open to an alternative construction of reality. By oscillating between the evidence and perception, the patient begins to establish a metaperspective on the dysfunctional cognitive-perceptual process, and gains a tangible understanding of the impact the subjective appraisal has on experience. The patient thus begins to distinguish between reality and reality as construed. (Note, however, that the efficacy of the process depends on the alternative perspective coming as genuinely new information.) Finally, the patient begins to examine and re-evaluate tacit beliefs associated with her interpersonal schema ("I must always be independent or in control").

In the second case, the therapist begins the intervention at the divided awareness marker by encouraging the patient to suspend his self-critical judgment or rational perspective. This process can be regarded as a necessary kind of subtask that allows the patient to experience relevant emotions and hidden appraisals fully. This subtask also has particular alliance requirements. Specifically, the patient has to feel sufficiently confident of the therapist's goodwill and acceptance to risk accessing a hidden appraisal in which he sees himself as childish.

Note how difficult it might be to meet this kind of alliance requirement when, as in this case, the patient sees himself as a powerless child who was doing something wrong and others as capriciously malicious, punishing adults. Here the therapist tries to help the patient attain a metaperspective on the ways in which he invalidates his own appraisal, which then also helps him suspend his rational perspective.

The next subtask involves gaining access to relevant emotions and the patient's hidden appraisal. Here, because the danger is one of *prematurely* invalidating the subjective appraisal as it begins to emerge, it is essential for the therapist to continue to encourage the patient not to do so. In the next subtask, the patient gains a tangible understanding of the impact his subjective appraisal has on his experience and begins to establish a metaperspective on what he, in essence, is doing to himself.

To summarize the similarities and differences between the two change events:

Both events involve a process of decentering through which patients come to see themselves actively constructing reality and become open to alternative constructions. In the first event, however, the process becomes activated by a challenging intervention which encourages the patient to treat her perceptions as hypotheses and actively attempt to

140

clarify the degree of correspondence between her perception and reality. In the second event, the process of gaining access to a perceptual appraisal, previously hidden, allows the patient to understand the impact of his own construal process on his experience and also to appreciate the self-evident absurdity of this perception. This change event is similar to what Rice (1984) has described as a "problematic reaction," in which patients are puzzled by their own reactions to a situation because they have not completely gained access to the underlying construal processes that are problematic.

CHAPTER 7

Experiential Disconfirmation and Decentering:
II. In-Session Focus

Experiential Disconfirmation with an In-Session Focus

The first change mechanism we shall examine in context of an in-session focus consists of the disconfirmation of the patient's interpersonal schema through the therapeutic interaction. By unhooking from the patient's cognitive-interpersonal cycle, the therapist can provide opportunities for new learning.

This perspective converges in many ways with the Mount Zion group's (Weiss, Sampson, and the Mount Zion Psychotherapy Research Group 1987) view on the role that the disconfirmation of pathogenic beliefs plays in psychodynamic therapy. J. Weiss and colleagues (1987) hypothesize that neurotic problems arise from pathogenic beliefs about interpersonal relationships that people develop as a result of traumatic experiences with significant others. An example of a pathogenic belief would be that one will be abandoned by the therapist for asserting or standing up for oneself. The Mount Zion group theorizes that patients unconsciously submit their therapists to what it calls "transference tests." In a transference test, one tests, either consciously or unconsciously, whether the therapist will confirm a pathogenic belief. For example, a patient who believes that independence will be punished will speak about quitting therapy, hoping the therapist will not react in a concerned or controlling way. If the therapist passes the transference test by not confirming the pathogenic belief, therapeutic progress takes place.

The proposition that patients submit their therapists to transference tests, consciously or unconsciously, is not a necessary component of our position, but we accord a central role to disconfirming dysfunctional beliefs through the therapeutic relationship.

If one is to refrain from participating in the patient's cognitive-interpersonal cycle and challenge his or her dysfunctional beliefs about relationships, it is essential to distinguish between being hooked and unhooked, which, in turn, requires the therapist to assess the therapeutic process at both interpersonal and cognitive levels.

At an interpersonal level, one must determine what responses are complementary to the patient's interpersonal pull, and what responses are noncomplementary by identifying one's feelings, action tendencies, and the interpersonal markers that evoke them. Thus, for example, if one is aware of a continuing pull from the patient to provide support and reassurance, one can lessen this kind of response. Or, if one finds oneself responding to the patient competitively, one can intentionally refrain from doing so.

The assessment at the interpersonal level, however, provides only a rough guideline to the kind of stance in the relationship that will be therapeutic. A more finely tuned guideline requires an assessment of the patient's interpersonal schema. To the extent that one can understand the patient's internal working model, one will be more likely to understand the kind of interpersonal stance that will disconfirm rather than confirm the patient's dysfunctional interpersonal schema.

For example, when patients believe that others will abandon or reject them when they act independently, one can infer that a stance that conveys anger or rejection when they act independently will confirm their interpersonal schemas. If the therapist learns that a patient believes that others will abandon them if they are emotionally vulnerable, it can be hypothesized that an interpersonal stance that suggests discomfort with the patient's emotional vulnerability will confirm their dysfunctional interpersonal schema. Thus, the more able the therapist is to understand the patient's interpersonal schema, the better able they will be to make fine-tuned predictions about what type of therapeutic stance will disconfirm it.

Unhooking from
the Cognitive-Interpersonal Cycle

As indicated in chapter 5, to unhook oneself from the patient's dysfunctional cognitive-interpersonal cycle, one must function effectively as a participant-observer. In other words, one must simultaneously participate in the interaction with the patient and observe the interaction in which one participates. This kind of parallel processing, in which the therapist functions as both the subject and the object at the same time, is similar to the psychological process involved in the change that patients go through when decentering from their automatic thoughts. Therapists, too, must develop the skill of splitting their attention.

In developing this skill, the first step involves turning one's attention inward to detect the subtle feelings and thoughts that one experiences during the interaction. Since cognitive therapists typically are not trained to turn their attention inward in this way, this is an important shift. In fact, it is vital, because only when therapists are able to become aware of their own feelings and action tendencies can they begin to develop hypotheses about the kinds of responses a patient evokes in other people.

Therapists who attempt to generate hypotheses about the patient's interactional style that are not truly grounded in their feelings will often be in error. As noted earlier, one of the greatest obstacles for therapists in becoming aware of their own feelings during the therapeutic transaction are their rigid beliefs about what feelings are and are not acceptable for them to have. Those who believe, for example, that it is not appropriate to have angry feelings toward a patient, will have difficulty truly acknowledging and becoming aware of angry feelings that may be influencing the therapeutic interaction. Just as unacknowledged feelings color the patient's interactions without his or her full awareness, the therapist's unacknowledged feelings color the therapeutic interaction without the therapist's awareness. One may experience oneself as saying something to help the patient, when in fact the statement is fueled by angry feelings that are not fully acknowledged. The therapist who insists, for example, that a patient take responsibility for coming late to a session may do so in a subtly (or not so subtly) punitive way. Similarly, the therapist who is sexually attracted to a patient, or who enjoys the patient's sexual attraction, but has difficulty acknowledging this, may unwittingly behave in a way that encourages flirtation.

A clue that one is not fully acknowledging one's own feelings in the interaction is when one jumps quickly to hypotheses about what is going on for the patient in the interaction without first going through the vital stage of acknowledging one's own feelings and action tendencies. Becoming aware of one's own feelings and action tendencies is particularly difficult when one is firmly hooked by the patient's interpersonal pull, because to be hooked, by definition, implies that one is not fully aware of one's own feelings and action tendencies and thus participates unwittingly in the interaction.

A useful process, particularly when one is having difficulty unhooking oneself from the interaction, involves watching or listening to a recording of a relevant session, either with or without a colleague or supervisor. Because the demands of responding to the immediate interaction have been removed, one can pay more attention to monitoring inner feelings and action tendencies. This practice can also be particularly useful in the early phases of training when therapists are first learning to work as participant-observers.

Observing a recording of the session with a supervisor or a colleague can also be valuable, since another person can function as a facilitator to help the therapist clarify feelings and experiences that are not entirely clear (Kiesler 1982c).

The process of clarifying and articulating tacit feelings that one may have can be slow and painstaking, and one should be prepared to devote as much time to it as to the process of helping the patient to clarify tacit feelings through empathic reflection. If one begins with preconceptions about one's true feelings, they may well impede the process of discovering one's true feelings.

A true discovery process goes on here. The therapist attends to bodily felt sensations, gradually contacts a felt sense, and subsequently abstracts a conceptual meaning from this bodily sense. Simple one-word descriptors such as "angry," "sad," or "frustrated" will not adequately capture the complex flavor of emotions that the therapist is actually experiencing.

Once one has begun discovering one's true feelings in the therapeutic interaction it is then possible to return to therapy and allocate part of one's attention to monitoring the inner state, and noting whether the feelings that emerged when listening to session recordings actually emerge in therapy.

Of course, therapists who do not wish to or cannot use session recordings, can immediately begin to allocate attention to monitoring their inner states during interaction. Once again, to do this requires starting without preconceptions about one's own inner state, and adopting a nonjudgmental stance toward one's inner feelings. Moreover, it is important not to feel pressured. When therapists come to a supervision session confused or stuck, it can be helpful to advise them to spend a minimum of one or two sessions with the patient focusing solely on sitting back calmly to observe their own inner experience and their interaction with the patient. It is often the feeling of urgency to accomplish something, to solve the problem, that prevents therapists from developing the relaxed state that is a necessary condition for monitoring inner experience and beginning to unhook from the interaction.

To observe one's inner experience without being hooked by it, one must work on developing an attitude of nonattachment. It can be helpful to think of one's inner feelings and thoughts as if they were clouds passing in and out of awareness. The task is to note them without grasping at them; to observe them dispassionately, without trying to change them in any way.

Once one is able fully to acknowledge one's inner experience and begin to observe it without attachment, the process of unhooking begins. Consider the following example. A therapist, working with a patient who is constantly challenging him, attempts to give the patient feedback on his challenging behavior. The patient, however, will not acknowledge that he is challenging the therapist in any way. The therapist has difficulty acknowledging any feelings of anger toward the patient because he is judgmental of himself for being angry. He thus continues to attempt to give the patient feedback about his challenging behavior because he will feel vindicated only when the patient acknowledges his role in the interaction. This keeps the therapist hooked into a vicious cycle of accusation, denial, and counter-accusation.

If, however, the therapist could acknowledge his own anger in a nonjudgmental fashion, he would have less of a need for the patient to become aware of his own role in the interaction because the therapist's self-esteem would no longer be dependent on the patient's accepting part of the responsibility for what is going on. The pressure to convince the patient of his perspective would thus be reduced, and he would unhook from the interaction and by freeing himself up, be open to new possibilities.

Once one has begun observing one's own feelings or thoughts in a dispassionate, nonattached manner, one can begin to monitor and identify the patient's nonverbal behaviors and communications one's own feelings appear to be linked to. By observing the therapeutic interaction over time it is possible to determine whether the relevant feelings one has identified in oneself and the associated interpersonal markers occur together with some degree of regularity. If the therapist observes a consistent relationship between the distinctive feelings experienced with the patient and a particular interpersonal marker, he or she can then use this marker as a cue to explore the patient's experience.

One therapist, for example, observed that she was spending a considerable amount of time giving her patient a rationale for therapy together with reassurance that things would improve. She had a feeling that something was not working properly, but was confused about what exactly this was. After spending a few sessions monitoring her own inner experience, she discovered that she had a feeling of anxiety and a desire to look after the patient. She then began using these feelings as a cue for monitoring interpersonal markers or patient-evoking communications.

After some time, she was able to identify a particular fragile tone of voice and nonverbal posture that her patient displayed at such times. After identifying these interpersonal markers, she was able to refrain from reassuring the patient and to explore what was going on cognitively and emotionally for him at those times.

Once one has begun to unhook oneself through participant-observation, one can begin to metacommunicate with the patient or talk about their interaction. Metacommunicating serves two functions. First, it continues the process of unhooking the therapist from the interaction, thereby providing the patient with an experiential disconfirmation of his or her dysfunctional interpersonal schema. Second, it helps the patient begin to see his or her own contribution to the interactions. It thus activates a process of decentering. Although in reality, these two processes are so intertwined as to be inseparable, we will discuss them separately.

Decentering with an In-Session Focus

As noted previously, cognitive therapists traditionally have rejected two important features of psychodynamic therapy: the interpretation of the transference, and the extensive use of historical information.

Thus far, it should be clear that the use of the therapeutic relationship to explore and disrupt the patient's cognitive-interpersonal cycle is a central feature of our approach, but the use of the therapeutic relationship as described in this book corresponds more closely to contemporary psychodynamic theorists such as Strupp and Binder (1984) and Gill (1982) than to the practice of transference interpretation in classical psychodynamic theory. In classical psychoanalytic theory, fantasies that the patient transfers onto the therapist provide an opportunity to help the patient recover memories about important childhood experiences and gain insight into the way in which these experiences shape his or her current interpersonal functioning.

As Strupp and Binder (1984) point out, this understanding of the mechanism through which transference interpretation works is based on the assumption that rational knowledge and understanding will set patients free from their repetitive maladaptive interpersonal transactions. This conceptualization is based on two assumptions, first, that rational thinking plays an important role in the change process and, second, that it is possible to unearth, accurately, previously hidden memories. The first assumption is challenged by the growing evidence of the importance of affective processes in change (Greenberg and Safran 1987), while the second is challenged by critics such as D. P. Spence (1982) and E. Peterfreund (1978) who view psychoanalysis as a hermeneutic science. As we have suggested, memory is a constructive process and consequently one can never be confident of a memory's historical accuracy.

As indicated in the previous section, the process of metacommunication operates, in part, by derailing the dysfunctional cognitive-interpersonal cycle, thus providing the patient with an experiential disconfirmation of his or her dysfunctional interpersonal schema. The second mechanism consists of allowing the patient to observe his or her own contribution to the interaction, thus facilitating a decentering process not unlike that described in chapter 6.

Through empathically exploring the patients' expectations, beliefs, and appraisals of the therapeutic interaction as it unfolds, the therapist helps patients see how their own cognitive processes shape their experience. They thus begin to distinguish between reality and reality as they construe it. They begin to regard their perceptions as hypotheses that can be tested. By giving patients feedback on their emotional reactions and by pinpointing behaviors that evoke these reactions, patients can gradually move from the position of powerless victims, caught up in circumstances beyond their comprehension, to a position of agency in which they see themselves as active contributors to interactions.

Once the therapist and a patient have used the therapeutic interaction to begin to identify beliefs and expectations that contribute to the patient's dysfunctional cognitive-interpersonal cycle, the therapist can use *active* cognitive interventions that *explicitly* identify dysfunctional expectations and help the patient clarify whether they have been confirmed or disconfirmed in the therapeutic relationship. Behaving in such a way that is inconsistent with the patient's dysfunctional interpersonal expectations may sometimes modify those expectations and sometimes not. A patient may fail to process interactional information that is disconfirming. It seems reasonable to assume that information processing in the context of the therapist-patient interaction follows the same rules of confirmatory biasing that have been documented in other domains (Nisbett and Ross 1980).

For this reason, it can be helpful for the therapist to metacommunicate with the patient explicitly about what his or her expectations are, and whether the interaction has confirmed or disconfirmed these expectations. This kind of metacommunication can take place both during or following an interaction (Safran 1990b).

A further advantage of this kind of metacommunication is that it can help the therapist to evaluate his or her hypotheses about some of the patient's dysfunctional interpersonal expectations, to refine these hypotheses in response to patient feedback, and to evaluate the patient's expectations continually to see whether they are being confirmed or disconfirmed. The therapist can encourage the patient to find active ways of testing dysfunctional expectations that have been identified *in-session* (by trying on new ways of being with the therapist) and in interactions with other people *between sessions*.

For example: An assessment of one patient's interpersonal schema revealed a belief that any expression of the patient's independence or emotional interest in other people would be construed as disloyalty by the therapist and would lead to retaliation and abandonment. After the therapist, in collaboration with the patient, explicitly clarified the specifics of this working model, the therapist suggested that the patient generate a strategy for evaluating the accuracy of his expectation, and the patient, in turn, suggested that he might try being more friendly with the clinic secretary. The focus then switched to clarifying how he would know whether or not his hypothesis had been confirmed or disconfirmed. Would he be able to tell by evaluating the therapist's manner in the following session? Was there a possibility that he might misread the therapist's manner? In this way, the patient was encouraged to test out actively his dysfunctional belief and to be wary of his tendency to interpret events as confirming his usual expectations. In subsequent sessions, the patient was encouraged to look for similar patterns in his relationship with other people and to generate other active strategies for disconfirming this interpersonal schema between sessions.

Our perspective thus emphasizes the importance of working with patients to articulate their dysfunctional beliefs about interpersonal relationships explicitly, and to devise active ways of testing them in the therapeutic relationship. Weiss and colleagues (1987) theorize that patients unconsciously evaluate their pathogenic beliefs by submitting their therapists to transference tests. The current approach integrates this perspective with the position of collaborative empiricism proposed by Beck and coworkers (1979) by encouraging patients to treat their perceptions as hypotheses and to *actively seek* ways of using the therapeutic relationship to evaluate hypotheses. The assumption is that promoting this type of active and intentional hypothesis testing will facilitate the change process by encouraging a conscious hypothesis-testing set rather than leaving this process to chance (Safran 1990b).

In addition, this approach reflects the cognitive-behavioral emphasis on generalizing changes to situations in the patient's everyday life. Thus, rather than assuming that learning taking place through the therapeutic relationship will automatically generalize, patients are explicitly instructed to use out-of-therapy interactions to test expectations and beliefs that have been explored and evaluated through the therapeutic relationship. In this way, the patient is encouraged to become an active collaborator in the therapeutic process and to continue the work between sessions (Safran 1990b).

In theory, the more rigid and restrictive the patient's interpersonal schema, the greater the amount of corrective interpersonal experience required. Given that a patient has abstracted a generic representation of self-other interactions from a lifetime of experiences, it is unlikely that one or two disconfirming instances will change it. Moreover, unless the patient begins to behave differently, thus activating new patterns of interactions in the real world, it is unlikely that new experiences with the therapist alone will change his or her *generic* representation of interactions.

Weiss and colleagues (1987) theorize that one naturally tends to test others in an attempt to disconfirm one's dysfunctional expectations. Even if this is true, it seems reasonable to hypothesize that in many instances, the fear of confirming one's dysfunctional expectations would prevent one from actively testing these expectations.

Paying explicit attention to the issue of generalization and encouraging patients to use, consciously, both the therapeutic relationship and interactions *in vivo* to test out their beliefs can thus play an important role in providing the kind and range of interpersonal experience required to gradually change their interpersonal schema.

Metacommunication

Metacommunicating about the therapeutic relationship plays a central role in facilitating the processes of experiential disconfirmation and decentering. We will discuss four kinds of metacommunication:

1. The therapist conveys his or her own feelings to help patients become aware of their impact on others and thus their role in the interaction;
2. The therapist conveys his or her feelings to patients to probe for the patients' internal experience;
3. The therapist identifies and points out the patients' interpersonal markers to help patients become aware of their role in the interaction;
4. The therapist uses the identified interpersonal marker as a juncture for cognitive/affective exploration.

Although we will discuss them separately, typically in practice two or more kinds of metacommunication are combined. The first two forms of metacommunication to be discussed involve the disclosure of the therapist's own feelings to the patient. Since the discussion with the patient of the feelings that are evoked in the therapist when interacting with him or her plays such an important role in treatment, it is vital to have some guidelines regarding when and how to disclose such feelings.

When should one talk about one's feelings with the patient and when should one withhold information? The rule of thumb here is that before discussing one's feelings with the patient, one should have enough distance from them to be a true participant-observer in the interaction. Thus, even though one may feel confused and locked into a dysfunctional interactional cycle with the patient, one should still be able to have some experience of observing oneself in this confused and locked-in state.

If, however, one's feelings (either negative or positive) are so intense that one cannot be a true participant-observer, it is best to withhold the feedback until one can clarify one's own experience and gain some degree of nonattachment (Kiesler 1988). The guiding principle is that when therapists give feedback to patients about their own feelings, they must be feeling sufficiently balanced so that their motivations are clear and fundamentally positive.

In situations where the patient elicits very intense feelings in the therapist, it may be useful for the therapist to spend some time exploring these reactions (either alone or with a colleague) before exploring them with the patient. Sometimes, for example, the patient's interpersonal style hooks into a particular sensitivity one has because of previous experiences with significant others. When this happens, the therapist's own emotional issues may cloud his or her ability to maintain balance in the therapeutic interaction. Therapists should, thus, be alert to extremely intense emotional reactions and should consider the possibility of clarifying the meaning of these experiences for themselves before exploring things further with the patient.

In the first kind of therapeutic self-disclosure, where the objective is to help patients become more aware of the impact they have on others to help them clarify what they are contributing to the interaction, a therapist who becomes aware of a tendency to behave nurturantly toward a patient might say: "I feel like protecting you right now." A therapist who becomes aware of feeling insulted by a patient might say: "I'm feeling put down right now."

The manner in which this feedback is delivered is vitally important. It should be tentative and exploratory so that the patient understands that the therapist is honestly trying to clarify his or her own feelings and to share them in a way that invites further exploration, rather than trying to blame the patient. As Kiesler (1982b; 1988) maintains, it is often useful to combine this kind of feedback with specific feedback about those patient actions and communications that are linked to the therapist's feelings.

In the second kind of self-disclosure, the therapist shares his or her own feelings so as to probe for the patient's internal experience. For example, the therapist says: "I'm feeling very cautious with you right now . . . as if it would be easy for me to say or do the wrong thing. Does that connect with anything you experience?" Or: "I feel like I'm playing a game of chess. Does that make any sense to you?" A therapist becomes aware of feeling irritable and says: "I feel like I've been attacking you in little ways. Does this fit with your experience at all?" A therapist becomes aware of feeling helpless and says: "I feel really powerless right now—like nothing I could do would be helpful. Does this connect with your experience at all?" Or: "I feel pushed away, or kept at a distance. Does this make any sense to you in any way?"

Again, it is vital that the feedback invite exploration rather than place blame. It can also be useful to comment on the interaction. For example: "I feel we're involved in a struggle right now. Does this connect with your experience at all?"

In the third kind of metacommunication, the therapist comments on the patient's actions or communications to help clarify the patient's contribution to the interaction. As indicated above, this is often linked to the self-disclosure of feelings that are evoked by the behavior. For example: "I feel patronized right now and I think it's connected with the tone of your voice and the smile on your face."

It is also possible for one to give the patient direct feedback without linking it to one's own feelings, but in doing so one must fully acknowledge the subjectiveness of the perception and accept responsibility for the observation, rather than treat it as objective reality. For example: "I experience you as cautious right now," or, "I experience you as skeptical right now." By emphasizing the subjective nature of the perception, the therapist clearly acknowledges the possibility that he or she could be wrong and invites the patient to use the therapist's perception as a stimulus for exploration. Failure to acknowledge the subjective nature of the perceptions tends to undermine the patient's confidence in his or her own perceptions. This kind of metacommunication is, of course, consistent with the view that the therapist is not the expert on the patient's reality, and that one of the therapist's objectives is to help the patient become more trusting of his or her own experience.

The fourth kind of metacommunication provides feedback on the therapist's perception of the patient to facilitate exploration of the patient's subjective experience. There are two major subtypes here. In the first, the therapist provides general feedback and then invites the patient to explore his or her internal experience. For example: "I experience you as being very cautious with me right now. Does that connect with your experience at all?" Or, "I experience you as kind of irritable right now—what's your experience?"

In the second subtype, the therapist provides more specific feedback and then probes for the patient's internal experience. For example: "I'm aware of your clenching your fists as you talk. Are you aware of that? What are you experiencing?" Or, "I'm aware of your lowering your voice, and rushing through it as you talk about this. What's happening inside?"

By drawing the patient's attention to a nonverbal behavior they may not be aware of, the therapist may facilitate awareness of an associated internal experience. For example, the patient who is clenching a fist while speaking may become aware of an associated feeling of anger. The patient who is lowering the voice may become aware of a feeling of shame and a belief that he or she is being evaluated negatively by the therapist.

Once the therapist has begun the process of metacommunicating with the patient, it is important to continue to maintain the discipline of a participant-observer, otherwise the metacommunication itself can maintain the interactional status quo rather than lead to the desired outcome of unhooking. For example, a therapist had a patient who constantly digressed. The therapist decided to intervene by bringing this to his attention. In response, the patient briefly acknowledged the therapist's point, and continued to digress. Once again, the therapist interrupted and brought the patient's digression to his attention. Only by first becoming aware that he was engaged in a struggle was the therapist then able to unhook himself from the interaction by telling the patient that he had the feeling of being involved in a struggle and by asking whether the patient had similar feelings.

In this situation, the therapist's initial attempt to metacommunicate with the patient led to and fueled a struggle between the therapist and patient for control of the interaction. Only by unhooking himself, once again, and metacommunicating on the current interaction was the therapist able to facilitate the therapeutic process.

The Focus on the Present

Throughout the metacommunication process the emphasis is on the here and now of the therapeutic relationship. The reasons are twofold. First, allowing patients to test out their dysfunctional beliefs about relationships in the interaction with the therapist as it occurs facilitates the process of experiential disconfirmation. Second, helping patients discover how they contribute to the interaction as it is taking place facilitates the decentering process. Both facilitate a learning process grounded in concrete experience, rather than an abstract intellectual exercise.

To facilitate enduring change, the relevant interpersonal schemas must be fully activated. The patient must explore cognitions about the therapeutic interaction in an emotionally immediate fashion. Patients are often reluctant to focus on the here and now of the therapeutic relationship because of their anxiety that such a focus will lead to an exploration of feelings and thoughts that will alienate the therapist, thereby confirming their worst fears about interpersonal relationships. They will often speak about their concerns generally rather than deal specifically with their concerns about the therapeutic relationship. It is also common for patients to speak about related situations outside of therapy or to narrate historical experiences with parents and other figures that, although thematically similar to the immediate interpersonal transaction, may serve to deflect rather than directly confront anxiety-provoking issues that are occurring in the therapeutic relationship. For example, the patient who is feeling dominated by the therapist may speak about a dominating father rather than about the relationship with the therapist. This behavior, referred to as "allusion to transference" by psychoanalytic theorists (Gill 1982), can be understood as an avoidance of the anxiety associated with directly confronting the therapist with a topic potentially threatening to the therapeutic relationship.

In this kind of situation, the therapist who encourages patients to explore the historical memory rather than what is currently occurring in the therapeutic relationship, colludes with them in avoiding the here and now. As a result, the potentially constructive interpersonal experience that can come from patients facing their immediate anxieties does not occur.

It is just as common for therapists to avoid the here and now of the therapeutic relationship by talking about historical events or by attempting to draw links between what is currently transpiring in therapy and other situations in the patient's life. Many therapists are understandably anxious about the possibility of fully exploring their own contribution to the current interpersonal transaction and will often avoid doing so by distancing themselves from the interactions through framing the patients' problems in terms of their relationship with their parents. For example, the therapist with a patient who tends to experience others as being critical may focus on the origin of the construal style in the patient's experiences with a critical parent, rather than explore the possibility that he or she may be currently participating in the patient's dysfunctional cognitive-interpersonal cycle by being critical.

By focusing excessively on the developmental origin of the patient's dysfunctional interpersonal schema, the therapist may be failing to fully explore his or her own role in perpetuating the patient's dysfunctional cognitive-interpersonal cycle and the possibility that he or she is being critical of the patient. Thus, the therapist may be unwittingly perpetuating the patient's dysfunctional cognitive-interpersonal cycle by transmitting the message that the problem is in the patient's head rather than in the current interaction. This would confirm the patient's dysfunctional belief that others are, indeed, critical. *For this reason it is essential that the therapist always be aware of the current interpersonal meaning and function of his or her actions while exploring the patient's historical past, or when linking the therapeutic interaction to other relationships in the patient's life, or when making links to the past to facilitate decentering in the therapeutic relationship.*

Making Links to the Past to Facilitate Decentering in the Therapeutic Relationship

With this caveat, we will now examine a particular context in which drawing a link between the therapeutic interaction and previous relationships *can* be a useful intervention and the process through which this takes place. This kind of intervention, which in psychodynamic therapy is usually practiced as a genetic transference interpretation, has traditionally been rejected by cognitive therapists.

The mechanism through which a genetic transference interpretation operates, however, is similar to the way other cognitive interventions operate. If effective, it activates a decentering process through which patients develop an awareness of the way they construct current experience by superimposing a grid from the past. In this sense, a transference interpretation is no different from other interventions, like inspecting evidence, more commonly used by cognitive therapists.

To be effective, a genetic-transference interpretation must take place in an emotionally immediate way. Thus, just as becoming aware of one's automatic thoughts in an emotionally immediate way is more likely to lead to change than does developing an intellectualized appreciation of one's automatic thoughts, an effective, or what Strachey (1934) referred to as a "mutative," interpretation must be emotionally immediate. If a genetic transference interpretation does not have this emotionally immediate quality, it may promote an intellectualized way of avoiding the here and now. We have already examined the dangers of drawing a link between the current interaction and the past. There is a specific context, however, in which making a link of this kind can be particularly useful. In situations where the patient's distortion of the therapist's characteristics and actions is so extreme that the quality of the therapeutic alliance is severely impaired, drawing a link between the patient's current experience and a particularly significant memory about a relationship with a significant other can be a way of breaking into an otherwise closed perceptual system.

For example, if patients see the therapist as extremely critical, any attempt by the therapist to challenge this perception may simply be interpreted as another criticism. If, however, patients have already described specific, detailed memories to the therapist of interactions with a critical parent, asking patients whether their current experience in any way resembles the experience with that parent can provide an "ah ha" experience if they suddenly recognize the similarity between the two situations. The effectiveness of this kind of intervention will be even greater if patients have already described the earlier experience in detail and have experienced the relevant emotions while describing them. The process of having gained access to relevant memories and associated feelings earlier in therapy will provide a solid emotional memory that patients can identify as similar to the current emotional experience. Moreover, the fresher in memory, and thus more accessible the thematically similar emotional experience, the more effective the intervention will be. For this reason, if the therapist is particularly concerned about the patient's distortion of the therapeutic relationship and intends to use this kind of intervention, it can be useful to prepare the ground by actively exploring for relevant memories of interpersonal experiences.

Rather than suggesting to patients that their present interpersonal experience in the therapeutic relationship is related to a historical relationship, it is better to intervene by simply asking whether the current emotional experience is similar in any way to an earlier one. This kind of questioning is less threatening because rather than implying that their current perception is distorted, it establishes a climate for patients' active search for similar feelings. It is thus more consistent with the principle of treating patients as the final arbiter of their reality.

The Process of Healing an Alliance Rupture

As suggested in chapter 5, the healing of an alliance rupture is a particularly potent in-session change event. This emphasis on the importance of detecting and repairing alliance ruptures is consistent with the emphasis on working through empathic failures in self psychology (Kohut 1984) and with the intersubjective approach (Stolorow, Brandhoft, and Atwood 1983). Because alliance ruptures often occur when the therapeutic intervention activates an important interpersonal schema, the constructive resolution of a rupture provides an ideal opportunity to explore that interpersonal schema and also modify it.

The process through which this takes place typically involves a combination of experiential disconfirmation and decentering. Exploring and resolving an alliance rupture allows the patient to test out and challenge important dysfunctional hypotheses about self-other relationships. It also provides an opportunity for the patient to explore the way in which his or her own construal processes contribute to the rupture.

The research on affective miscoordination and repair, discussed in chapter 4, can be useful in further clarifying the processes involved in causing and healing alliance ruptures. People who have not had the developmental experience of having interactive errors with their parents consistently repaired, do not develop interpersonal schemas representing themselves as interpersonally acceptable and effective and others as trustworthy and reliable. If they experience their affective state as misattuned to, they are unlikely to persist in attempting to articulate their experience either to themselves or the therapist. In such a situation, they will experience a secondary affective response to the original misattunement (for example, anger or sadness). Even this, however, may not be fully experienced or expressed because of the potential threat to interpersonal relatedness.

For example, a patient whose parents consistently misattuned to the emotion of sadness, or who experienced anxiety in this context, may have difficulty fully experiencing that feeling. In addition, because the patient expects sadness to be unacceptable, incipient feelings of sadness may be followed by a secondary emotion of anger. The patient may, however, have difficulty directly expressing this anger, because he or she believes it will threaten the relationship. It will be essential for the therapist to accept and empathize with the secondary emotion of anger, before the primary emotion of sadness can begin to emerge more fully and be attuned to. By responding to both the secondary and primary emotions empathically rather than with anxiety or defensiveness, the therapist can help the patient learn that interpersonal ruptures are potentially resolvable and that the patient does not have to disown his or her inner experience to maintain relatedness. This process, referred to by Kohut (1984) as a ''transmuting internalization,'' involves a modification of the patient's interpersonal schema in a way that represents the self as acceptable and the other as available.

The first step in resolving an alliance rupture is to detect it. This is often difficult because many patients are reluctant to disclose negative feelings for fear of alienating the therapist. Moreover, many patients have difficulty fully articulating negative feelings to themselves. It is thus extremely important for the therapist to be alert to the rupture markers described in chapter 5.

The principles involved in resolving an alliance rupture are the same as those involved in any form of metacommunication. The therapist goes through the process of becoming aware of his or her own feelings, unhooking from the transaction, providing feedback to the patient, and exploring and empathizing with the patient's experience. Of critical importance is the principle of accepting responsibility for, and acknowledging, one's own contribution to the interaction (Gill 1982). When there is an alliance rupture, the patient and the therapist often become locked into interactional positions in which they are both trying to validate themselves and it is very easy for the therapist to make comments that subtly blame or pathologize the patient.

Consider the following example. The therapist and patient are involved in a struggle over what the topic will be. In an attempt to metacommunicate with the patient about what is going on, the therapist says: ''I feel as if you're trying to control the interaction.'' The patient, who is involved in the struggle to maintain self-esteem, experiences this comment as ''blaming'' and feels an even greater need to control the interaction.

It is thus important for one to begin by including oneself in the description of interaction and to acknowledge one's own role in the interaction. When this takes place, it once again frees the patient to view the process of exploration as a collaborative activity, because he or she is not feeling blamed. A better response in the foregoing example would be for the therapist to make a statement such as: ''I feel as if I'm involved in a struggle with you and I'm not sure what's going on. How does this relate to the feelings you are experiencing?'' With this response, the patient no longer feels quite so blamed or invalidated and is thus freed up to try to discover—in collaboration with the therapist—exactly what is going on in the situation.

In some situations, if one acknowledges one's role in the interaction and then comments on the patient's role, the patient may still continue to feel criticized or blamed and thus have difficulty letting go of a self-protective stance. In these situations, it can be important for the therapist to stop short of commenting on the patient's contribution to the interaction. Simply accepting responsibility for part of the interaction may help free the patient to explore his or her role in the interaction.

Another reason for one to begin by acknowledging one's role in the interaction is that often patients feel particularly threatened because they are not quite sure where reality lies. Their own responses to the situation may seem unreasonable to them, and they may thus have difficulty truly acknowledging their own feelings either to themselves or the therapist. This can make it particularly difficult for patients to begin to understand their roles in the interaction.

If, however, the therapist is able to clarify his or her own role in the interaction, the patient may begin to understand the context of his or her own reactions and thus begin to be more accepting of them. For example, one therapist experienced the patient as being angry at him and in response made comments that were unintentionally critical of the patient. When he asked the patient whether she was angry, the patient denied such feelings. When, however, the therapist became aware that he had been critical of the patient and acknowledged this to her, the patient's own responses became more understandable to her, and she found it easier to acknowledge her feelings of anger at the therapist. The therapist's acceptance of responsibility for his contribution to the interaction in this situation thus made it easier for the patient to begin the process of self-exploration that eventually led to the resolution of the alliance rupture.

In addition to acknowledging their contributions to the interaction, it can be useful for therapists to convey to their patients their empathic understanding of their experiences. In the foregoing situation, for example, it might have been useful for the therapist to say that if he were the patient, he imagined he would be feeling angry. If the therapist is able to empathize with the patient's experience accurately during an alliance rupture and convey understanding of this experience to the patient, the patient may feel understood and find it easier to begin to explore what is going on in the interaction. An accurate empathic response in this situation may also help the patient acknowledge feelings that he or she is not fully aware of.

Finally, if it is to be facilitative, any metacommunication must be grounded in an accurate empathic understanding of the patient's interpersonal schema. Attempts to resolve alliance ruptures through metacommunication are often blocked even though the intervention seems technically correct. When, however, the therapist is finally able to get a real feeling for the the patient's internal working model, an important shift takes place in the interaction, and the therapist is able to metacommunicate in such a way that the patient experiences it as facilitative rather than critical.

Clinical Illustrations

The following transcript illustrates the use of metacommunicating about the therapeutic relationship to facilitate the processes of decentering and experiential disconfirmation. It also demonstrates the resolution of an alliance rupture. This session, the fourth of twenty, is from the therapy of a fifty-year-old man who presented with chronic dysthymia. The previous session had centered on the patient's concerns about being observed through a one-way mirror. He had reported that he had seen one of the observers (Eric) in the hallway after the second session and that Eric had not said hello (the observers had been introduced to the patient at the beginning of therapy). The patient thus felt rebuffed and angry.

In the session, the patient had begun to explore his feelings of anger and concern about being observed through the one-way mirror—but without any resolution. The therapist's perception had been that the patient had explored the whole situation timidly, as if unwilling to take the interpersonal risks necessary to bring things to a resolution that satisfied him. The patient begins the current session by describing a chronic situation with his boss.

PATIENT: I haven't got too much done this week. Hmmmm. Had a little talk with the boss yesterday about things. Don't feel—terribly satisfied with myself. I suppose I got some things said that I've been wanting to say for a long time, but I never get much back from her—you know (laughs)—so it left me feeling basically unsatisfied.

THERAPIST: So you said some things that were on your mind?

PATIENT: Yeah, but—well, I did get something out of her (laughs). I did get a little bit out of her, so, I don't know. But, I still feel basically unsatisfied with uhh (sighs)—Like I told her that I would—like, you know—felt that she was setting all the objectives and priorities and that things weren't really up for discussion and that uhh—and she said that, well, she hadn't meant it to come across that way, but—you know—she was on a campaign to set deadlines, which you know is fine. I mean, it's good to know when she expects something. But I just—oh, I don't know. My feeling is that—you know it's more than that. There's—I asked her—I *did* ask her straight out—I said, "You know, I really feel that—" I said, "If you are unhappy with my performance I would really like to know." And uhh, and she paused a long, long, long time. (Laughing) And she said that, "Well, yes," she had been unhappy last May, June, but it wasn't the case this year. And she said that she felt—you know—we weren't on the same track last year, but that we seem to be on the same track this year. (Laughing) I said, "Well, maybe that's because you're setting all the objectives and priorities." And she said, "Well, I hadn't thought of it that way." So it turned into a discussion of was I managing my time correctly. And whether I was delegating properly—and this kind of thing. I'm feeling kind of confused about it all. I mean I was—I told her, I said, "If I—" I indicated that I was very—I said, "If I can't do the job to your satisfaction, then perhaps I should just get out of the way." I was seriously—I guess I still am seriously thinking about quitting. Certainly not functioning very well, you know. Once I get to work—you know—I can more or less focus and concentrate and get things done, but this past week I just haven't been able to concentrate. I don't know—I go to work and I sit there and I can't remember things, and I sit and shuffle papers and—I can't build up any energy or commitment to get going on things so— I don't know—I guess—just throw in the towel and——

THERAPIST: Uh-huh. So, it sounds like you really opened things up with her—brought things out into the open in a way that you haven't really quite done before—something that you've been avoiding, because of your fear of the consequences?

PATIENT: Yeah, yeah, that's reasonable to say.

THERAPIST: And so you brought out a number of things that you've been reluctant to, and you were left feeling kind of, sort of confused and unsatisfied.

PATIENT: Uh-huh. Uh-huh. Well, I mean as—yeah, confused and unsatisfied.

The patient's characteristic interpersonal style is wordy, unclear, and equivocal. Although one might tentatively hypothesize that this style might contribute to his leaving interactions confused and unsatisfied, it is difficult to sort out what precisely took place in the interaction with the boss—to determine just what his contributions were, and what her contributions were. Nevertheless, it is worth recognizing the patient's equivocal style of communication as a potentially important interpersonal marker embedded in an as-yet-to-be-revealed cognitive-interpersonal cycle.

There is a striking similarity between his encounter with the boss and the encounter that had taken place in therapy the preceding week. Gill (1982) would probably classify the patient's description of the former as an allusion to the transference. Whether or not the patient is indirectly referring to the therapeutic relationship, however, if the pattern is similar, it may be profitable to use the relationship as a laboratory for exploring the patient's cognitive-interpersonal cycle in greater detail. The therapist begins to do so a few minutes later in the session.

THERAPIST: So you were still dissatisfied, but you're saying there is something about the fact that perhaps you confronted her and were clear?

PATIENT: Yeah, yeah. But, you know, it's not—yeah, right, I think so. I mean it's not the first time I've confronted her—you know—I *have* confronted her before in the past, but I just—I don't know. It's like I have to expend so much of my energy to confront her and try to convince her that I'm doing something, or—you know—I just don't know that it's working, really—you know.

THERAPIST: So, it seems like you may have come out of your meeting wondering whether it's worth all the trouble and the bother that it is.

PATIENT: Yeah.

THERAPIST: You know, as you're talking right now, I can't help thinking back to our last session.

PATIENT: Yeah. Right. That's still kind of on my mind too.

THERAPIST: That seemed to me to be the kind of situation in which you were unhappy and frustrated and you were kind of confronting me, and I'm wondering how that resolved for you.

PATIENT: Well, I guess I sort of was putting that issue on the back burner. I mean it was on my mind. It was there for me this morning. You know, "Well, am I going to follow through or not, or what are we going to do to follow through on that?" You know—"Am I going to bring it up again—will I make an issue out of it?"

THERAPIST: So, you really haven't sorted out whether or not you want to bring it up again?

PATIENT: Yeah. Right.

THERAPIST: Okay. I'm not wanting to derail you. In other words, if you would rather focus on the situation with your boss, that's fine with me.

PATIENT: Hmm. Well, I'm just thinking that—you know—there seem to be some similarities there that—you know—I confronted you last week, and now I'm not sure whether I want to follow through or not. And I confronted her yesterday, and I'm saying, "Well, you know I achieved some things, but, I'm not sure whether it's worth the hassle of following through."

THERAPIST: So, it seems like there's a common thread there?

PATIENT: Uh-huh.

THERAPIST: It's like you take the first step, and then you're not sure whether it's worth following through. What are some of your concerns about following through? When you say you're not sure whether it's worth it—I wonder if you could just elaborate.

As this segment begins, the therapist attempts to speak positively about the patient's having confronted his supervisor directly and thus attempting a new constructive behavior. This intervention is consistent with the cognitive strategy of drawing attention to positive events that may be missed as a result of selective abstraction. In this context, however, it is unempathic, because the patient is more connected with his feelings of frustration and confusion. It may also unwittingly contribute to a recapitulation of the pattern with his supervisor, that is, feeling that he is not being heard. In this situation, it is possible that the therapist's empathic failure and eagerness to find a solution is partly a response to his frustration with the patient's communication style.

The therapist, however, is subsequently able to pick up on the patient's real concern about feeling unheard and wondering whether it's worth it. The therapist then begins to explore whether the experience is similar to last session's. It is quite possible that a more immediate focus on the current interpersonal transaction (that is, the therapist's empathic failure) would have been more productive, or just as productive.

The patient agrees that there is a similarity between the situations, and implicitly gives his consent to explore the parallel between the two situations. This is important because without this, he might construe further exploration of last week's session as another instance of other people imposing their agenda on him, thus perpetuating a dysfunctional cognitive-interpersonal cycle. The therapist begins to explore the dysfunctional expectations that block the patient from seeing interpersonal encounters of this kind through to resolution. In a transcript segment which, for the sake of brevity, is not included here, the patient identified a feeling that it seems pointless—like a losing battle with his boss. In the next segment, the therapist begins by empathizing with this feeling.

THERAPIST: It feels like a losing battle, then, is that what you're saying?

PATIENT: Yeah, uh-huh.

THERAPIST: Is that how it was feeling with me, last week?

PATIENT: Well, yeah, I guess I did come away from the session feeling—you know—I guess one of the reasons I put it on the back burner was because I thought, "Where are we going to go with this?" And "I don't see any movement—you know—forthcoming." Maybe I'm not pushing hard enough, but—you know—I don't uh, when we started out you indicated that—that Eric wasn't there at the time, but that he might show up some time during the session. Well, we never followed that through. You know, did he, or didn't he? And if he did, what were we going to do about it? Or is he there now? Or are we going to do anything about it? I don't feel as emotional about it today as I did last week. But uh, I—you know—I guess I got the feeling that there really wasn't much movement there or not much possibility of movement.

THERAPIST: Uh-huh. So you were left with the feeling that things weren't going to go anywhere, that this was a losing battle. You're saying there are also some things that we didn't follow up on. Right?

PATIENT: Uh-huh.

THERAPIST: What stopped us from following up on them?

PATIENT: (Long pause.) Well, I don't know. I guess one thing that didn't happen is I didn't—I didn't push to—we discussed various things that might happen and uh (pause) I never made a choice I guess. I didn't say, "Well, okay, I would like this to happen." (Long pause.) I guess I'm afraid that if—um—if we did ask Eric in and, and, uh, talked about it, I really wouldn't feel any better about it anyway. It really wouldn't prove anything. He'd come in—and have a little chat, and go back out.

THERAPIST: So—you had an idea—something to try.

PATIENT: Uh-huh.

THERAPIST: And it sounds like you chose not to follow through because you believed it wouldn't help anyway.

PATIENT: Uh-huh, yeah, yeah. God, it sounds terrible!

THERAPIST: You don't like the sound of that?

PATIENT: No, no.

THERAPIST: What don't you like about it?

PATIENT: Well, it sounds so defeatist. But—that's the way I am.

THERAPIST: Okay, so that when I sort of mirror that back to you, you're saying you don't like the way that sounds. If that's—if that's true, you don't like what that says about you?

PATIENT: Uh-huh. Right.

THERAPIST: What are you feeling right now?

PATIENT: (Long pause.) Well, I'm feeling anxious now.

THERAPIST: Do you have a sense of what that anxiety's about?

PATIENT: Yeah, I think it's about—I'm faced with a decision here, and um, um (pause) and I'm making a big deal out of it. "Should I, or shouldn't I?" I guess I do that a lot, spend a lot of energy on feeling anxious about decisions.

Here the patient sees more clearly how he *chose* not to push for resolution in last week's session because he expected it wouldn't help. This acceptance of responsibility is an important shift from his earlier stance ("*We* never followed that through") and appears to bring the situation back to life for him in the here and now. He is once again confronted with the decision he has been avoiding by not accepting responsibility for his role in the interaction and his feelings of resentful resignation give way to anxiety.

THERAPIST: Uh-huh. So, right now you're feeling anxious about a specific decision—"Should I, or shouldn't I?" And you're saying that it's not an unusual experience?

PATIENT: Yeah.

THERAPIST: Okay. Now, just to step back for a second, to kind of get a perspective on what's going on right now——

PATIENT: Uh-huh.

THERAPIST: If what's going on is similar to what happens in other situations, my hope would be that we could use this as an opportunity for us to work together to understand just a little bit better what happens in these situations. You know—just sort of explore and examine how it is that you get yourself stuck in a way, and see whether there are some options that may not be immediately apparent right now.

PATIENT: Uh-huh.

THERAPIST: Does that make sense?

PATIENT: Sure.

Because of the potentially anxiety-provoking nature of the theme they are exploring, the therapist attempts to strengthen the alliance by clarifying the rationale for the task they are engaging in, and seeking the patient's agreement to continue.

THERAPIST: So, what's happening for you right now?

PATIENT: (Long pause, sighing) Well, I'm still feeling anxious about the decision to get—umm—you know—how it would—how things would play out, if for example, I made a decision to—ask Eric in to talk about it.

THERAPIST: Uh-huh. So, as a way of thinking about the decision you're projecting into the future, you're kind of imagining a scenario?

PATIENT: Yeah, sort of. It's not very detailed though. (Laughing) Just sort of, it's kind of fuzzy.

THERAPIST: Uh-huh.

PATIENT: Sort of imagining Eric sitting over there, me trying to articulate my concern, and—it's not very clear. I'm shutting down.

THERAPIST: You're shutting down right now. In other words, you start to play it out, and then you shut it down. What prompts you to shut it down? Are you aware?

PATIENT: Well, I think the—I think the anxiety about what might happen, prompts me to shut it down. That I might not—you know—whether or not I express myself well. And uhh, uncertain about what might go on between us, or what your response might be. And that—I think a basic assumption that opening things up is just going to make things worse. That's what shuts things down, I guess. It's the safest way. I think.

Here the patient is able to identify a basic working assumption—that bringing up his concerns will make things worse—and gains a tangible sense of how this influences his behavior. He develops an awareness of the way he avoids thinking about the problem situation because of the anxiety associated with it. In the next segment the therapist further explores the fears leading to the patient's avoidance.

THERAPIST: How might things become worse? How might things get worse if you were to pursue them further with me right now?

PATIENT: I guess maybe part of the risk is that whatever—no matter—that there is nothing really that we can do of any substantial nature, and that I will be left with my negative—and whatever we can do in this context is not really going to—uh, resolve my negative feelings about it, and I will be left with negative feelings and then I will also be left with a situation—well, you know— we'll see each other and establish eye contact and we'll say, "hello" and I'll feel it's all just a game, and so the risk is piling some sort of game playing on top of the negative feelings. And maybe it's better to just (laughing)—oh, God! Incredible!

THERAPIST: Uh-huh. So, what are you experiencing?

PATIENT: Oh, it's—I don't know, geez—It's just, it seems ludicrous. The whole thing seems ludicrous. It's just——

THERAPIST: I'm unclear when you say, "It seems ludicrous."

PATIENT: It's a very complicated process, isn't it?

THERAPIST: Right. It seems what you're doing is that you sort of work out all the possibilities and then ultimately decide that it's not worth doing anything, because of the fact that it's not going to help matters, and might probably just make matters worse.

PATIENT: That's probably one of the reasons I've come to the conclusion that it's not going to help. I make it so complicated. I expect too much from situations.

THERAPIST: Well in this situation you say you expect too much. So what, what would satisfy you? What is it that you expect?

The patient further reveals his experience of utter futility. He believes that there is no way that the therapist can satisfy him, perhaps because his expectations are excessive. Rather than risk confirming this expectation and having to live with the further negative feelings that would be engendered by the frustration of his needs should they be made explicit, he avoids the situation. An important piece of the picture that appears to be emerging is that the patient believes that his own needs are invalid or excessive. The therapist thus begins to explore the patient's needs.

PATIENT: I'm not sure.

THERAPIST: What would satisfy you with me right now, around this issue? Do you have any sense of what you want, and whether you are getting what you want or not?

PATIENT: (Long pause, sighing) I guess I do feel dissatisfied. I'm not sure. I don't know. Maybe, maybe I'm looking to you to spoon feed me or something. You know, sort of tell me what is reasonable to do in this situation, or you know——

THERAPIST: So you're feeling dissatisfied, right now. You're wanting something other than what I'm giving?

PATIENT: Uh-huh. (Long pause.) Well, I was all worked up last week about—you know—what I was perceiving as a lack of respect. I'm not worked up about it this week, so it's a little—but I guess thinking back to last week, I guess I was looking for some direction as to what my options were. I guess to put it bluntly—you know—was one of the options to say I don't want Eric behind there anymore? That kind of thing.

THERAPIST: Okay, so that was last week, and what about now?

PATIENT: Well, I'm working up to that again now, because now that we've refocused on it—you know—it's becoming an issue again.

THERAPIST: So you were wanting me to indicate further what your options were? What are you working up to? What about in terms of what I'm providing? Are you satisfied? Are you getting what you want from me right now?

PATIENT: Well, I, no, no. I mean, I don't feel you're being very responsive. I don't know whether—Okay, let me put the question to you. Is one of the options for me to say, "I don't want Eric behind there"?

THERAPIST: Yes.

PATIENT: Okay. Is one of the options for me to say, "I don't want anybody behind there"?

THERAPIST: Yes.

In response to the therapist's probing, the patient begins to explore what he wants in the situation. At first, he avoids speaking directly about his needs and what he wants now by speaking about last week. Rather than support an indirect bid for reassurance, however, the therapist encourages him to state directly his desires in the *present* ("So that was last week, what about now?" And, "Are you getting what you want from me right now?"). This is important because the patient's fear of stating his wishes directly is a major theme, which appears to contribute to his continuing inability to have his needs met. Finally, the patient asks the therapist what would happen if he were to decide he doesn't want to be observed ("Is one of the options for me to say I don't want Eric behind there?" "Is one of the options for me to say I don't want anybody behind there?").

This is still one step short of directly stating what he wants, but it nevertheless constitutes a considerable risk that will test his belief that his demands are excessive and that articulating them will be futile or dangerous. The therapist's response is direct and unequivocal: Yes. A more ambiguous response might be experienced as similar to the confusing response the patient felt he got from his supervisor and confirm his belief that it is futile to attempt to state his needs directly.

PATIENT: Okay (long pause), I guess that leaves me a little confused again. Maybe I was making assumptions, but I sort of—you know—came into the clinic—and there are certain norms—well, of course I chose whether to allow our sessions to be observed— but then those norms would appear to be up for grabs. Do I accept what appear to be the norms and don't bother to question? Actually, one of the thoughts that occurred to me last week was, well, okay, I suppose one of the reasons the observers are behind the mirrors is because that is supposedly unobtrusive observation. Except that there is a lot of noise going on back there which—you know—now that it's become an issue, I am very conscious of. So, in that sense it's not really unobtrusive. What would be wrong with having them in the room? I mean I can appreciate the value of the observation which is why I initially didn't feel that I objected to it. But now it's become an issue, and I wonder what would be wrong with having them in the room, so that there could be more of an ongoing relationship, and one could—you know—sort of establish and satisfy oneself whether—you know—respect that one knows that they are there.

THERAPIST: I'm open to exploring that with you.

At first the patient appears to be a little confused by the therapist's response. Perhaps he does not experience the therapist's response as sufficiently supportive. Perhaps he finds it hard to shift from finding the therapist at fault for his dilemma toward recognizing his own responsibility. Because the latter implies he had not previously acknowledged his contribution to the situation, he may be experiencing it as an assault on his self-esteem.

This experience, however, does not appear to last for long, as he shifts into a more active and constructive state and spontaneously suggests the possibility of having the observers sit in the room rather than behind the mirror. The energy and enthusiastic style with which he makes this suggestion contrasts with his previous caution and tentativeness, and suggests that the interaction with the therapist has begun to disconfirm his dysfunctional interpersonal schema.

THERAPIST: Okay, we are going to have to stop in a second. You know, we are right in the middle of things obviously and this is to be continued. But, I just want to try and extract some themes of what's been going on, okay?

PATIENT: Okay.

THERAPIST: There were a lot of different things going on. Let me ask you. Can you extract any themes out of what's been going on that might be useful to you?

PATIENT: Well, yeah. One is to ask for clarification. Try to avoid making assumptions and just ask for clarification.

THERAPIST: Okay, so that's what stands out for you, right?

PATIENT: Umm, well, the other thing is the trouble that I have making decisions. But, I suppose one could link the two. Indecision is probably linked to the assumptions and might be made easier by requests for clarification.

THERAPIST: What assumptions?

PATIENT: Whatever, you know. Whatever they might be in a situation. Well in this case I think I was making an assumption that while there had to be observers and they had to be behind the mirror, I thought there might be some openness on who was there, but—And I suppose too, the difficulty that I have, is that it's easier to go with my assumption, instead of asking for clarification. I think that—like my feelings coming away from yesterday's confrontation, you know, the basic dissatisfaction that I was asking for clarification about certain things, and I wasn't getting it.

THERAPIST: So that what happens is, it seems like you make an initial foray sometimes, right?

PATIENT: Yeah.

THERAPIST: And then you're not quite satisfied with the result of that, so that you are reluctant to try again.

PATIENT: Yeah, yeah. I suppose that is another theme. Persistence.

THERAPIST: Okay. Sort of a general underlying assumption that it's not going to help anyway, so what's the point. The final thing I just want to highlight—it was really striking me as we were talking, was the sort of general question of, are you getting what you want, right? And if not, what can you do about things to get what you want?

PATIENT: Uh-huh. Yeah.

THERAPIST: So this last interaction between us, for example, you know when I was asking, "Are you getting what you want?" You sort of became clear, "Well, no, I'm not getting what I want." And then you actually did something. You phrased things in a point-blank way. So I think unless a person is really clear on whether they are getting what they want or not, then it's difficult for them to do what they need to do in order to get what they want.

PATIENT: Well that's sort of an overriding theme for me.

THERAPIST: To be continued?

PATIENT: To be continued, yes.

THERAPIST: Okay.

The patient appears to be encouraged by the therapist's response to the test, as indicated by the detail with which he proposes an alternative plan of having the observers in the same room. The session concludes by clarifying the themes that have emerged in the session. Subsequent sessions confirmed that this had been a particularly important session for the patient. The basic question of whether he is getting what he wants, and if not, what can he do to change the situation, became an important theme for him, one he spontaneously returned to again and again. To summarize some of the important features of this patient's cognitive-interpersonal style as it has displayed itself in the present transcript, the following picture emerges:

The patient has a fundamental belief that his needs and wishes are invalid and unreasonable, and that any attempt to get them met will be futile. Because of these beliefs he has tremendous difficulty stating his desires directly. This difficulty is revealed in his reluctance both to bring up the topic and then to pursue it once he has raised it. It is also revealed in the very style of his communication, which is highly equivocal, qualified, and unclear. All these factors presumably make it difficult for people to satisfy his needs, thus confirming his dysfunctional beliefs and leaving him frustrated and resentful.

The following transcript provides another illustration of the processes of experiential disconfirmation and decentering and various kinds of metacommunication. The therapeutic alliance is tenuous throughout most of the transcript and it thus provides a good example of working through alliance ruptures, and an equally good example of the relationship among the patient's interpersonal schema, the kind of therapeutic dilemma discussed by Ryle (1979) and Horowitz and Marmar (1985), and the importance of refining one's understanding of the patient's interpersonal schema in the process of developing a therapeutic alliance.

The patient in this transcript is a thirty-eight-year-old man whose presenting problems are difficulties in interpersonal relationships in general (he maintains that people seem to mistrust him and are wary of him), and with his girlfriend in particular. He complains that they constantly fight, that he does not feel that she is as available to him as he would like, and that he consequently feels rejected by her.

The patient has a strong, forceful presence. He is amiable and friendly, but his style is aggressive and his friendliness somewhat forced. He also has an analytical, problem-solving kind of orientation toward human relationships with little role for emotional experience. This transcript is taken from the sixth session of a twenty-session protocol.

PATIENT: I've been thinking about how much progress we've been able to make since we started and I don't know how you feel, but I would like to see if we could do something to get more progress, and uh, I don't know what we will have to do to do that. Maybe revisit our objectives or—you know—see where we're going? Maybe figure out what it is that is happening that's preventing us from—like me feeling that we're not making progress. How do you feel? Do you think we're making progress (pause) of any kind?

THERAPIST: I'm aware that you're somewhat frustrated with what's going on, and I have a sense that we're not always on the same wavelength.

PATIENT: Are you—how do you feel about the actual amount of quote, unquote, progress? I know it's a tough word to define but how do you feel about it? Are you frustrated for example—about what's going on?

THERAPIST: There are certainly times when I feel frustrated, yeah.

PATIENT: What do you—what do you recommend us doing, um, differently than what we've been doing till now?

THERAPIST: I'm not sure right now.

In introducing the topic of his dissatisfaction with the way things are proceeding in therapy, the patient is direct and forceful about his dissatisfaction, but at the same time attempts to temper or modulate his dissatisfaction by enlisting the therapist in a mutual problem-solving process. By gauging the therapist's feelings about their progress, he attempts to reduce the possibility of saying something potentially disruptive to the relationship by, in a sense, "surveying the lay of the land." He then asks the therapist to assume responsibility for proposing another approach, rather than taking the risk of being more explicit about the nature of his own dissatisfaction.

THERAPIST: What is the nature of your frustration and dissatisfaction?
PATIENT: I'm not sure we're getting to the core of my situation or my, at least my beliefs, um, whether they're right or wrong or uh, maybe what's causing me to think in certain ways or certainly what's causing me to behave—you know—'cause it's the behavior that I'm interested in changing, uh, we're obviously making headway. Don't get me wrong. It's just that if you're feeling frustrated and I'm feeling frustrated is there anything that we can do to change the process so that both of us don't feel frustrated?

The therapist attempts to return the focus to the patient by exploring the nature of his frustration and dissatisfaction more fully. In response the patient slightly elaborates on his feelings and then retreats to the safety of a "pseudo-alliance," by speaking about *their* mutual problem and concern ("If you're feeling frustrated and I'm feeling frustrated, is there anything we can do to change the process so that both of us don't feel frustrated?"), thereby handing the responsibility back to the therapist.

THERAPIST: I'm not sure what to do right now, but my experience is that I feel pressured by you, and at the same time, I feel you're kind of pulling back. It's like you kind of say things to me and then take them back.
PATIENT: Take them back?
THERAPIST: Uh-huh.
PATIENT: You mean make them softer?
THERAPIST: That's right, you'll soften them. It makes me feel like it's difficult for me to have contact with you, because you'll be

very nice—but at the same time—it feels like an iron fist in a velvet glove.

PATIENT: Well, I guess I'm kind of frustrated and I don't know what to do about it. I don't know how to proceed. I still want to, if possible, work within your program. You said you don't know what to do. That's fine. That's fair. I didn't want to give you the impression that I was—you know—pushing you around. I just, I would like to find out what options we have in terms of either me understanding the process better and understanding where we are in it or rearranging things so that we both feel like we're making some progress.

The therapist responds by metacommunicating about his sense of feeling pressured in a "nice" or relationship-protecting way. It is unclear whether this metacommunication has helped deepen the patient's self-exploration or not. On one hand, his statement that he doesn't want to give the impression that he is pushing the therapist around, may provide further insight into the construal process associated with the "iron fist in the velvet glove." On the other hand, the patient may still be attempting to convey his dissatisfaction, while pulling back or reassuring the therapist. If the latter, he may have construed the therapist's last remark as critical and continue to have negative feelings mixed with a fear of the consequences. The therapist (as the next segment begins) thus probes for the patient's current experience.

THERAPIST: What's happening for you now?

PATIENT: Well, I was just thinking about how I felt about you saying that uh, I treated you like uh, velvet glove. Iron fist, velvet glove, and uh, it's obviously disappointing to find out that that's the way I'm coming across.

THERAPIST: It didn't feel good when I said that?

PATIENT: I wasn't delighted (soft laugh), no. I didn't, I'm not, I mean I believe what you're saying. You're being honest with me, so I don't feel depressed in any way. I guess I'd like to be able to figure out how to come across in a way that doesn't make you feel—like you know—you're being hammered.

THERAPIST: What I'm having difficulty with is not so much the feeling of pressure. Of course nobody likes to feel pressured, but I can live with that. That's where you are. What's difficult for me is that it feels like you pressure me and then "make nice."

PATIENT: Okay.

THERAPIST: So that I find it difficult to feel really in contact with you.

PATIENT: Okay.

THERAPIST: It's like I start doubting my sanity.

PATIENT: Oh (laughs). Well, I want to make it clear that I wasn't attacking you personally, I was looking at the process. I think I was pulling the argument back a bit. I started getting the feeling internally that maybe I was crossing the boundary. We were getting into—I was getting you—you know, I was leading into the area of personality with you—you know—so I wanted to go back so that it would be clear that I wasn't going beyond that boundary.

The patient's response suggests that he has construed the therapist's comment as critical ("It's obviously disappointing to find out that that's the way I'm coming across"). He responds to his feelings of disappointment, however, by continuing with the same interpersonal strategy of trying to soften the impact of his negative feelings so as not to jeopardize the relationship ("I guess I'd like to be able to figure out how to come across in a way that doesn't make you feel like—you know—you're being hammered"). The therapist tries to make it clear that he is not critical of him for having negative feelings. Rather, it is the attempt to soften them that is problematic. Note that the therapist takes responsibility for his own feelings ("I find it difficult to feel really in contact with you," "It's like I start to doubt my sanity"). This appears to help deepen the patient's self-exploration ("I started getting the feeling internally that maybe I was crossing the boundary. We were getting into—I was getting you—you know—I was leading into the area of personality with you").

THERAPIST: You're concerned that I might start taking this personally.

PATIENT: Something like that.

THERAPIST: Are you willing to explore this further?

PATIENT: Yes.

THERAPIST: What if I did start taking it personally?

PATIENT: I'm concerned about the relationship.

THERAPIST: Uh-huh. What might happen? You say, "I'm concerned about the relationship."

PATIENT: Well, if you got the feeling that I was attacking you personally, that would not be the impression I was trying to give.

Okay, regardless of how you took it, if you took it positively or negatively. Obviously if you took it negatively, it would be worse. If you took it positively, that's fine. Uh, you know, it wouldn't cause us problems but in either case it would be the wrong impression of me. You know, I wasn't trying to attack you. You're trying to help me. I'm just frustrated by—you know, our lack of apparent progress.

THERAPIST: See, now in this moment I see you doing exactly the same thing. I still feel like you're saying, "Don't take this personally." I'm asking you, what's your concern if I did take it personally? If you're open to exploring this right now.

The therapist continues to explore the patient's interpersonal schema by asking him to elaborate on his fears. Sensing the difficulty he has in exploring this theme, he attempts to strengthen the alliance by asking for the patient's permission to explore further, thereby explicitly obtaining an agreement to proceed with the task ("Are you willing to explore this further?"). The patient, however, continues to assure the therapist that he does not mean it personally and the therapist first metacommunicates that he is experiencing this statement as a reassurance as well, and then attempts to explore further, once again asking the patient's permission to do so.

PATIENT: Yeah. Well, um, I can—If I take things personally—and then I guess there are two aspects, positively and negatively, but personally, okay? If I took it negatively personally which is the worse, I might get the feeling, and this is why—you know—I'm concerned that you might get this feeling, um, that the person doesn't feel that I've got their best interest at heart or uh, that I'm treating it impersonally and—you know—there is a process here and we have to follow it and you are just a cog in the wheel—you know—so that if that happened to me I would want to re-establish a personal connection—you know. Why do you feel this way? What is it about—you know—what I'm doing here? Those are the kinds of questions that would come to mind, if I got hit with the feeling that I was being personally attacked. I didn't want those negative—you know—those kinds of reactions to hurt you.

THERAPIST: That I might just, uh, I'm having a bit of difficulty following you. If I took it personally, then what might happen? I might——

PATIENT: You might feel like you have to try to re-establish—you know—some understanding on a personal level, or that you might consider that I don't have your interest at heart or that I don't like you and I'm not going to cooperate.

The patient's rather convoluted response here suggests it feels very threatening for him and is likely an important interpersonal marker. The therapist does not, however, probe for the construal processes associated with it because the patient appears to have such difficulty in gaining access to his immediate experience. Instead, the therapist simply asks for clarification. In response, the patient is able to explore further, acknowledging fear that the therapist might believe that he doesn't have his best interests at heart, doesn't like him, or won't cooperate. This constitutes some articulation of his interpersonal schema but it still leaves out the core of the schema because it is not self-referrent. The therapist continues the exploration in the next segment.

THERAPIST: I might feel that you don't like me or won't cooperate?
PATIENT: That's right.
THERAPIST: Okay. What if I felt like that? That you don't like me? I don't think this is easy stuff to explore.
PATIENT: (Pause) It would divert us from what it is that—certainly I'm trying to do.
THERAPIST: Can you elaborate?
PATIENT: It would set up a chain reaction of questions and answers and digressions where we would end up trying to re-establish a connection.
THERAPIST: You say we might have to—it seems like there's a step missing here—Okay, you're saying that we might have to spend time re-establishing a connection. What might happen before then?
PATIENT: I'm not sure I see a step missing. If I gave the impression that there is something wrong at a personal level, you might want to re-establish a connection because you might feel that before we can make any progress there would have to be some sort of mutual understanding about things. And then we could spend an hour discussing it and at the end I wouldn't feel any better about our ability to make progress in these kinds of, these sessions.
THERAPIST: Somehow or other, your answer for me is, sort of, it's

missing, um, it's missing the heart in a way. It's like missing the guts.

PATIENT: Uh. Okay. I think I know what you mean. Yeah, it's uh, uh—you know—while you and I are not bosom buddy friends— you know—who come over to your place in the evening for drinks, uh, and I rely on your support as a friend, I wouldn't certainly want to set up an antagonistic element in our discussions. You know what I mean? Maybe that's the part that's missing. Neither of us would want any antagonism.

THERAPIST: You're speaking for me?

PATIENT: I'm speaking for you, yeah, I'm thinking we share the same point of view. I don't think you'd be very happy if I came in here—you know—and said, "Your program stinks, you stink, I can't stand this any longer" (laughs).

The patient continues to have difficulty exploring his concerns in personalized, self-referrent terms. He speaks about not wanting to be diverted from the task, implying that the concern is one of efficiency. The therapist metacommunicates that the patient's response is missing a lively emotional quality. Once again, he takes responsibility for the perception ("Your answer *for me* . . .").

This metacommunication appears to facilitate deeper self-exploration. The patient acknowledges concerns about antagonism. He still, however, has difficulty speaking about either his fears of the therapist's antagonism or owning his own antagonistic feelings. Instead, he speaks about "an antagonistic element" as if it were an impersonal aspect of the situation rather than an emotion that he or the therapist might feel.

The statement "neither of us would want antagonism" creates a kind of false alliance ("we want the same thing"). There's an assumption that any anger on either side would be too threatening for the relationship to tolerate. In response to the therapist's comment ("You're speaking for me?"), the patient is able to acknowledge a little more fully his fear that the therapist would be upset if he expressed negative sentiments. The patient's laughter, when he expresses negative sentiments even in hypothetical form, indicates his anxiety about these feelings.

THERAPIST: See—I experience you even in this moment as trying to protect our relationship. It's a funny kind of thing, it's a kind of paradox because I experience you as trying so hard to protect the relationship, um, and it feels almost suffocating, in a way, it feels like there's no room for us to have a real relationship because you're trying so hard to protect it.

PATIENT: Well, under normal circumstances—you know—in conversations with people, um, I guess you don't get into this kind of conversation. It's like bringing you down into a vortex like an onion—you know—there's the surface of the conversation and there are deeper layers. Because you bring me down to looking at it at a very detailed level, it's like using a microscope. You're looking at something very small, maybe at the nub. But because you're using a microscope you see it in a large picture and so it, it makes all the words that we use about this small thing, big, and what I'm getting from you is a sense of this suffocating you, that is, it's now *so* big it fills the entire room up.

THERAPIST: Now, could I ask you, when I said that, "This is suffocating," do you have any recollection of what you felt?

PATIENT: Yeah. Um—that I was overbearing you and overwhelming you, uh, I was maybe too controlling, um, you know, so I was disappointed. And I could, I could see how you sat on your side of the room there looking at it and I thought, well, what is it about it that's doing that and——

THERAPIST: Okay, so again, see, a number of times I think what's happened is that I will say things and when I ask you how you feel you say disappointed. My experience is that when I say something that disappoints you, at that point, um, I feel sort of a barrier go up between the two of us.

PATIENT: Because of my persistent trying to explain things?

THERAPIST: Right. (Pause.) At this moment what are you experiencing?

At first, the therapist metacommunicates about the way the patient's consistent attempt to hold the relationship together—his difficulty in thinking about himself and the therapist as separate individuals who can have angry feelings toward each other—affects him. One might hypothesize that his girlfriend, Lisa, experiences similar feelings of suffocation and that this contributes to her constant withdrawal from him. At this point, however, it would only be conjecture. Moreover, for the therapist to draw a parallel now might involve some denial of his contribution to the interaction and may leave the patient feeling blamed or pathologized. The patient's rather detailed, convoluted explanation appears to have elements of self-justification and suggests that he may, again, be feeling criticized. Because, as we said earlier, this kind of response can be an important interpersonal marker for the patient, the therapist decides to explore his internal experience in this context. The patient's response ("I was disappointed"), confirms that there has been an alliance rupture. At this point, the therapist again gives feedback on the impact that this interpersonal marker has had on him in the hope of facilitating the decentering process by helping the patient experience his contribution to the distancing process. The therapist probes to explore how the patient is receiving this feedback. Is it facilitating the decentering process or does the patient still experience it as critical?

PATIENT: Well, I'm sort of getting an insight that what I should do is (pause)—is change the style here. I'm trying to get analytical with you and it's not analysis that you're looking for. I'm looking for analysis but you're not looking for analysis. So (pause), I'm going to hold off on the analysis.

THERAPIST: I'm concerned that when I say something to you like "When you analyze, I feel like a wall goes up," that you will take that as a criticism. It's like I'm telling you to be some way other than the way you are.

PATIENT: Yeah.

THERAPIST: Is there any of that?

PATIENT: Yeah. Well I think it does happen, you know, I do get a sense of disappointment—you know—I do get down, but the approach I'm using isn't working.

THERAPIST: It's a tricky thing because um, it's like we're caught in a kind of a, it's like a——

PATIENT: A dance.

THERAPIST: A dance in a way, yeah, in a sense it's almost like your relationship with Lisa. You know, it's like she's saying to you, "You're not good enough the way you are." So you'll respond by trying to do things to make the relationship work because you don't want to lose that relationship. At some level it's not feeling very good, though. It's my concern that some of that is happening in our relationship.

On one hand, the patient's response suggests that the feedback has facilitated decentering ("I'm sort of getting an insight that what I should do is change the style here"). On the other hand, there's a quality to the response that concerns the therapist. When he says,

"I'm looking for analysis but *you're not looking for analysis,*" it conveys a hint of the patient's doing something for the therapist rather than for himself. This perception of course is partly influenced by the therapist's assessment of what has taken place in therapy so far, as well as his relationship with other people, particularly his girlfriend. Another potentially important piece of information here for the therapist is his own feelings. Is he feeling frustrated? Is it possible that the tone of his questions and comments is colored by such feelings? If so, this may contribute to a feeling on the patient's part of not being accepted for who he is.

The therapist attempts to convey an empathic understanding of what the experience may be like for the patient ("It's like I'm telling you to be some way other than the way you are"). This time the patient acknowledges his disappointment, while at the same time indicating that he's open to the feedback. The quality of the interaction suggests that the alliance is improving at this point. The therapist begins a sentence ("It's a tricky thing because it's like we're caught in a kind of a . . .") and the patient, who is now on the same wavelength, finishes it ("dance"). There is thus an empathic resonance. The therapist goes on to draw a parallel between what may be happening here and in his relationship with his girlfriend. This time, drawing the parallel in no way denies the therapist's contribution to the interaction or blames the patient. Instead, it is an empathic recognition of the patient's dilemma. In Horowitz and Marmar's (1985) terminology, the patient has a particular role-relationship model that makes it difficult to form an adequate therapeutic alliance *in the present context.*

On one hand, he is eager to change. On the other hand, his intense need to protect the relationship leads him to change for the other person rather than for himself. This leaves him feeling resentful that he is not acceptable the way he is. The dilemma for the therapist is that by metacommunicating with the patient about his distancing style and by pushing him to explore his feelings, he may be confirming the patient's dysfunctional interpersonal schema rather than providing him with experiential disconfirmation.

THERAPIST: What are you experiencing now?
PATIENT: Well—I'm feeling more optimistic in the sense that I don't think we're that far apart. Uh, in getting you to feel more connected with me, uh, it's sort of like me trying to find out where the fog is and moving it out of the way so that you could feel

connected. It's like, I feel like I'm sort of issuing the fog. I think it's clear, you don't see it, uh, but it's not the intent on my part, I don't think, to fog you.

THERAPIST: You see—I imagine—just trying to get inside your head and get a sense of what it would be like to be you. I have a sense of you trying so hard to make things work, um, and they're not quite working——

PATIENT: Right.

THERAPIST: And I imagine that would be very, very frustrating. That you try so hard. (Pause.) What do you experience when I say that?

PATIENT: Well, it's obviously—you know—very frustrating 'cause I know what I want to accomplish. I know what's inside that I'm trying to get out, uh, it just doesn't work.

THERAPIST: It's like—I get an image right now of you, kinda trapped inside some kind of a container in a way and not being able to get out.

PATIENT: Yeah. It's like I'm trapped in a room with all these doors. And I try this door and it doesn't go anywhere. So I try that door—and it doesn't go anywhere. There's a door there that works—I'm sure. I just haven't figured it out.

THERAPIST: It sounds incredibly frustrating.

PATIENT: Yeah, right. (Long pause.) But you don't get a sense that my heart isn't in the right place, do you?

THERAPIST: Not at all. No. That's the sad thing in a way, right? That there really is a yearning. You're yearning so much for contact. Wanting so much to make things work and somehow no matter what you do, it never quite works for you.

PATIENT: Right.

THERAPIST: Does that fit with your experience?

PATIENT: Yeah. Very much, both here and in a lot of conversations with Lisa.

THERAPIST: I have a sense of you being so effortful—trying so hard to make things work. Does that correspond to your experience in any way?

PATIENT: Yeah. And Lisa always gets down on me for bludgeoning her with details and explanations.

The alliance continues to improve as the therapist is able to empathize with the patient's incredible frustration—the sense of being trapped and not being able to escape. The patient's response to the therapist's empathic comment about being trapped in a container is illuminating. He provides the metaphor of being trapped in a room with multiple doors and of an endless search for the right door.

This metaphor is very consistent with the patient's general style of trying so hard to make things work that he ironically destroys what he wants most. The intensity of his yearning for interpersonal relatedness and the belief that he is not worthy enough to have it if he just *is*, underlie his tremendous effortfulness in relationships. The paradox, however, is that what he yearns for can only come from a type of letting go—from simply *being* rather than *trying to be*. This transcript represents only the beginning of this man's change process. By metacommunicating with him about his interpersonal style and by refraining from participating in his cognitive-interpersonal cycle while working toward an accurate empathic understanding of his dysfunctional interpersonal schema, the processes of decentering and experiential disconfirmation have been initiated.

The following transcript illustrates the use of an interpersonal marker as a juncture for cognitive/affective exploration. It is extracted from a later session with the same patient. By this session there has been some improvement in the therapeutic alliance and an increase in the patient's capacity for self-exploration. The patient has just responded to some feedback the therapist has given him, with the same kind of convoluted analytical style illustrated in the last transcript. Recognizing this style as an important interpersonal marker for this patient, the therapist begins to probe for his experience.

THERAPIST: Any sense of what you're feeling as you're saying this to me?

PATIENT: I'm sort of in an analytical mode, I guess.

THERAPIST: What might happen if you were to leave this analytical mode right now?

PATIENT: Well—when you made that comment, I guess I felt a little disappointed. But I wasn't feeling buffeted or anything like that. I mean, you're giving me your impression and I'm responding, I'm not, you know—It's sort of a give and take discussion right now. I'm open to hearing you and I'm not responding negatively, other than a mood of disappointment perhaps but not, you know, "I don't want to hear what you have to say, 'cause you're not saying great things to me," or something like that.

THERAPIST: What if you were? You assure me, "I'm not feeling buffeted, I'm not feeling too strongly about this." What if you were?

PATIENT: Well, I probably would be a lot stronger in my reply, you know, a lot more extreme. Like I might become very silent or I might be very nervous or, um (laughs), whatever. I might start thinking, "What am I doing here?" I don't feel—I feel comfortable, you know. Generally speaking I feel a high level of comfort.

In response to the therapist's probe, the patient begins to reveal some negative feelings. At the same time, however, he hastens to assure him that his feelings are not that intense, and that he feels comfortable.

THERAPIST: Do you have any objection to feeling strong feelings— here with me? Ahh, you know, strong negative feelings.

PATIENT: Probably. Umm, it's not something that I strive for and, um, um (pause),—I guess to, um, hmmm—it's kind of scary to think about it, but ahh, like if umm—you know if you, if you were to become very personal in attacking me or something like that, I would, I would really be in a bit of a flap (voice very low). Or if I felt that this was a personal attack or something of that nature (voice almost inaudible), I would get, well, upset.

Noting the patient's persistent and unconvincing denial of any strong negative feelings, the therapist probes for dysfunctional attitudes prohibiting such feelings ("Do you have any objection to feeling strong feelings here with me?") The resulting shift in the patient's voice tone suggests that the probe has facilitated an experientially real contact with both the fear prohibiting the expression of negative feelings ("It's kind of scary to think about") and the underlying feelings ("I could get, well, upset").

THERAPIST: Uh-huh. What's happening for you right now?

PATIENT: Oh, I'm just, uh, thinking about me reacting stronger, and it really displeases me to think about that, you know like, I'm not looking forward to doing that (laughs).

THERAPIST: What is it about that prospect that seems so unpleasant?

PATIENT: Oh it, it means sort of, out of control, and, um, and I've been feeling in a pretty good mood and I'm not looking forward to switching it around.

THERAPIST: There's something about being out of control?

PATIENT: Yeah.

THERAPIST: Can you imagine if you were to—to lose control when you're here, what would that be like?

PATIENT: Well, I can tell you how it feels when I'm—when I'm in that situation with Lisa and, um, so I'm gonna assume it's very similar here. I would, feel (pause) like well (voice lowered) worthless, or, um, or not appreciated or, um, you know, and it makes me feel, um, really disappointed in me, um, frustrated, or really angry, you know. Sometimes a great sense of futility. So my reaction to that is—is just "I want to get out of here." I wanta just clear the whole thing away. I'm just, you know, embroiled in this mess and I can't, I can't handle it.

THERAPIST: So, you just um——

PATIENT: So, I walk away sometimes—very often with Lisa.

THERAPIST: Uh-huh. So that if you start feeling strong emotions, if you start losing control, you just want to escape from that.

PATIENT: One thing I do is I escape. Another thing I do, other times, is I'll rant and rave, you know. I'll just pour out a whole bunch of—things—and how I feel, what it's doing to me, what I think is happening, what I think of the other person, you know. All kinds of things like that. Just a big hemorrhage of words, and——

THERAPIST: And then you feel worthless—at times like that?

PATIENT: Yeah.

THERAPIST: Okay, so now just to bring this back to the situation right here. Just imagine if you were to lose control with me, what would that be like?

PATIENT: Well (sigh), it would be pretty awful. Yeah, I'd be disappointed in myself. I'd be, uh, you know, into having these initial feelings of anger and maybe confusion and—you know like—inability to grasp what's going on and that kind of stuff. And just no sense of support and, um, I'd probably—I'd probably leave. I'd probably say, "I really don't see the value of doing this right now." I might just disengage and say, you know, "Call you later" or something like that—if I was able to calm myself down, I might just say, "Okay, let's stop and have a five-minute coffee break" or something like that. If I was so upset that I couldn't even do that, I would just say, "I've got to go," you know——

THERAPIST: Okay, so it sounds like for you, it would feel pretty catastrophic, right?

PATIENT: Oh yeah, yeah.

THERAPIST: It feels so, so catastrophic that you couldn't stay in contact with me——

PATIENT: Right.

THERAPIST: If you were not feeling in control of yourself.

PATIENT: Absolutely (pause).

THERAPIST: So it's not so surprising that you might respond in a more analytical way.

PATIENT: That's right.

In this segment the patient further explores his fears of expressing negative feelings. Various nonverbal markers (laughing, lowered voice) continue to indicate the anxiety-laden nature of the topic and the fact that this is an experientially real rather than an intellectualized exploration. The patient spontaneously makes a link to his experience with his girlfriend Lisa. His vivid words ("I'll rant and rave"; "Just a big hemorrhage of words") reveal his distaste for himself when he feels out of control. When the therapist returns the focus to the here and now of the therapeutic relationship, the patient is able to articulate to a greater extent than before the nature of his discomfort with losing control and expressing negative feelings with the therapist.

Although the precise nature of the patient's interpersonal schema will require further clarification, this exploratory process has been an important start. It has also helped the patient begin to explore negative feelings that he has been avoiding for fear of the consequences. This in turn will further facilitate the process of experiential disconfirmation.

CHAPTER 8

Accessing Action-Disposition Information

The Role of Empathy

The process of acknowledging emotion or action-disposition information is mediated by the interpersonal context in which it takes place. Thus, if patients feel accepted by the therapist, they can begin acknowledging action dispositions and exploring inner experiences that may not have been fully processed previously. Moreover, whenever a patient contacts feelings that previously have not been fully processed, the therapist's perceived reaction will be critical in determining whether the experience will be therapeutic. For example, if a patient begins to direct angry feelings at the therapist, a hostile or defensive reaction may confirm a dysfunctional belief that it is dangerous to experience anger. In response to a patient who begins to contact previously unacknowledged feelings of sadness, the therapist's attempt to dispel the sadness by rationally re-evaluating the situation, may only confirm the patient's belief that sadness is unacceptable. In contrast, an accepting and empathic response may challenge dysfunctional beliefs about his or her emotions and help the patient be more open to internal experience. The therapist's receptiveness will facilitate the processing of internally generated information, which then will lead to a change in the patient's sense of self.

As we have discussed earlier, because some inner experiences pose a threat to interpersonal relatedness, patients may disown or distort parts of those experiences, which then become, in Sullivan's (1953) terms, the ''not me.''

As Stern's (1985) work on affect attunement suggests, the ''not me''

188

becomes established not only by disowning the inner experience pre-cipitated by anxiety but also from failing to articulate aspects of one's inner experience fully because of the lack of empathy from significant others in one's childhood for those experiences. For this reason, inner experiences that have led to the disintegration of interpersonal rela-tionships, or have not been accurately empathized with by significant figures in one's developmental past, may never become fully articu-lated. The therapist's ability to empathize accurately with internal experiences of patients may thus play an extremely important role in helping them develop a better understanding of their internal expe-riences and who they really are, rather than who they should be. By accurately empathizing and accepting patients' inner experiences, the therapist can provide one of the most powerful challenges to the patients' dysfunctional beliefs about who they must be to maintain relatedness to other people. True empathy does more than provide the necessary precondition for effective cognitive intervention; in and of itself, it can be one of the most powerful means of challenging the patients' dysfunctional interpersonal schemas.

Exploring Attitudes
Prohibiting Emotional Experience

When one decides to explore and challenge explicitly a patient's atti-tudes governing emotional expression, it is best done in a gentle and accepting fashion, with the emphasis on *discovering*, in an emotionally immediate way, the patient's blocks to experiencing and expressing the emotion, rather than on pushing the patient to express the emo-tion. The expression of the emotion is not an end in itself (Greenberg and Safran 1987). It is more important for patients to have a direct experience of how they interrupt the emotion, and then to begin choosing to contact and express these feelings only as they feel suf-ficiently trusting to take the interpersonal risk (Safran and Greenberg in press). Although patients may, under the therapist's influence, force themselves to express particular emotions, this may not be ther-apeutic if they do it to please the therapist rather than because they are ready to take the risk. This is coercion and will serve only to rein-force the dysfunctional beliefs that a patient must be a certain way to maintain relatedness.

The following transcript illustrates the process of exploring dys-functional attitudes and automatic thoughts that prohibit the experience of particular emotions. This patient has a rigid belief that she must always be strong and that feelings of vulnerability are unacceptable. As a result, she has difficulty contacting feelings of sadness. As the transcript begins, she is discussing her relationship with a man she is romantically interested in.

PATIENT: I met this guy in the summer. He'll phone me every now and again. He's come down a couple of times to see me and I know he's interested, but there's still something going on in his life with—you know—a girlfriend, too. So he's kind of battling with that, I guess. Or—you know—deciding whether or not he wants to change girlfriends or whatever.

THERAPIST: Sounds like a very hurtful situation.

PATIENT: Uh-huh. It is. It bothers me a lot. Last week, last Friday, it really hurt. I had gone out shopping. That's what I do just to keep myself busy. Just go shopping. And I came in and I was making dinner and all of a sudden the tears just started coming down my face. Here I am, you know, alone. I usually don't like to stay in weekends, or stay in through the week, but—I don't do it that often, but still it bothers me.

THERAPIST: That sounds painful.

PATIENT: Uh-huh.

THERAPIST: To be left alone——

PATIENT: Ummm.

THERAPIST: Are you in contact with some of those feelings right now?

PATIENT: A little bit. I mean, I don't like to dwell on those feelings. That's why I stop myself—because it's such a rotten feeling. And it's so hard to get out of. You know, I start feeling a little bit down. It takes all my strength to get me back up again, and I can't afford to do it.

THERAPIST: So you say you stop yourself?

PATIENT: Uh-huh.

THERAPIST: Are you stopping yourself right now?

PATIENT: Yeah.

THERAPIST: How are you doing that? How are you interrupting this feeling?

When the patient describes her feelings of sadness in retrospect, the therapist immediately attempts to bring the situation into the present by asking whether she currently has access to the relevant feelings.

This question may lead to an in-depth and alive exploration of the construal process associated with them. When the patient reveals that she has difficulty allowing herself to experience these feelings, the therapist then begins to explore the process through which she blocks her feelings. The emphasis is on *discovering* how she is actually blocking her feelings now, rather than on conjecturing about reasons for avoiding feelings.

PATIENT: I just cut the thoughts off. Just stop thinking about it.

THERAPIST: Uh-huh. How do you do that? How do you cut them off?

PATIENT: I don't know. I just don't think about it. I guess I say to myself mentally, "Don't think about it. Stop." And I do.

THERAPIST: So that's what you're doing right now. You just kind of shut them off. "Don't think about it. Stop"?

PATIENT: Uh-huh. Right. I guess I kind of throw in other thoughts like, "Well, you have to go to work today and you have to perform and you have to put a smile on your face." And, you know, there's something in there saying, you know, "Be strong."

THERAPIST: "Be strong. Pull yourself together."

PATIENT: Uh-huh. "Be a fighter." You know.

THERAPIST: "Be a fighter"?

PATIENT: Yeah. My father's famous words, "Be a fighter. Don't throw in the towel."

THERAPIST: Is that right?

PATIENT: Uh-huh.

THERAPIST: So you're always kind of pulling yourself together. "Don't throw in the towel, be a fighter."

PATIENT: Yeah. Probably sometimes I hear my father saying like, "Oh, you've got nothing to worry about" or "Don't let it get you down," or——

THERAPIST: Uh-huh.

PATIENT: Things like that. Or my aunt saying like, "Now, what have you got to be crying about?" You know, things like that. It kind of starts me thinking: "Well, maybe I'm just feeling sorry for myself." You know, "You haven't got time to feel sorry for yourself."

THERAPIST: So you start to feel that pain.

PATIENT: Uh-huh.

THERAPIST: And then it's like another voice chimes in, saying, "You're really feeling sorry for yourself."

191

PATIENT: Uh-huh.

THERAPIST: "Be a fighter."

PATIENT: Uh-huh.

THERAPIST: "Pull yourself together."

PATIENT: I don't know if that's healthy or unhealthy or what but that's what I do anyways.

THERAPIST: Uh-huh. And what about right now? Where are you?

In response to the therapist's probes, the patient does a good job of articulating the automatic thoughts blocking the feelings ("Be strong. Pull yourself together. Be a fighter"). The patient spontaneously recognizes how these attitudes reflect beliefs of important figures in her life, such as her father and aunt. Toward the end of the segment, the patient appears to be distancing herself from her experience by reflecting on it, wondering whether it is "healthy or unhealthy or what." The therapist intervenes by refocusing on her current experience by asking where she is "right now."

PATIENT: I guess I'm in the middle.

THERAPIST: In the middle?

PATIENT: Yeah.

THERAPIST: Describe that to me. Being in the middle right now.

PATIENT: I feel—like a sadness. And yet I don't want to show it. You know, it's just like a—just enough to let me feel something but not enough to keep me down.

THERAPIST: Uh-huh. Okay, so you say that you feel the sadness, and you don't want to show it?

PATIENT: Uh-huh.

THERAPIST: Okay. What's your objection to showing it?

PATIENT: Well, like my sister said, "It doesn't look nice." Appearances, you know.

THERAPIST: Wouldn't look good?

PATIENT: Doesn't look good. Makes other people feel uncomfortable. Doesn't make me feel good. Just like a real negative situation. One to be avoided.

THERAPIST: If you showed your true feelings to me right now, it wouldn't look good to me?

PATIENT: No. Then I wouldn't feel comfortable either. So, the reason is that I'm just not comfortable with it.

THERAPIST: Okay. Are you willing to explore this a little further?

PATIENT: Yeah, all right (said tentatively).

THERAPIST: You sound hesitant.

PATIENT: Yeah, but I'll try.

THERAPIST: Before you leap into something—what's your hesitancy?

PATIENT: How I'm going to feel. How it's going to affect me. I guess I'm protecting me.

THERAPIST: Okay. That sounds sensible—to protect yourself. Like, your concern is that if you explore it further, that what might happen? You say, "How I'll feel"——

PATIENT: I might bring up feelings that I don't want to face. I don't want to feel, I don't want to face them. I don't know. And I don't know if I'm—you know—sometimes I just wonder, am I ready for it? Or, I have to be in the frame of mind for it.

THERAPIST: So this is important, I think, to pause here and not rush into something. To really respect where you are. You're saying "I'm not sure if I'm ready to look into this further."

PATIENT: Uh-huh.

THERAPIST: "I might get into some feelings that I'm not ready to deal with right now. And I feel like protecting myself."

The patient reveals further concerns about contacting her sadness ("It doesn't look nice"). The therapist attempts to keep the exploration grounded in the current interpersonal situation. ("If you showed your true feelings to *me right now* . . . it wouldn't look good to me.") The emphasis is consistently on encouraging the patient to make an active decision about whether she wishes to explore further, rather than on pushing her into it. When the therapist notices some hesitancy in her voice, he explores it rather than ignoring it. Rather than rushing her, the therapist also respects the patient's expressed desire to protect herself. The assumption here is that only thus can the patient truly begin both to experience herself as in control and to decide to share her feelings or not, depending on her appraisal of the situation.

Duplicitous Communication and Responsibility

As discussed in chapter 4, cognitive therapists have traditionally rejected the psychodynamic concept of disowned experience, a concept that has been particularly problematic because it is associated with one of the thorniest issues in psychotherapy: the issue of responsibility.

H. Kaiser (1965), in an important article, clarifies some of the central problems surrounding the issue of responsibility in a way that is particularly relevant here. As he notes, therapists often use the term "responsibility" moralistically without understanding its conceptual link to a theory of change. It is not uncommon for therapists to blame patients for not accepting responsibility when they are not benefiting from the therapy. As Kaiser points out, however, blaming patients for not accepting responsibility does little more than give therapists an opportunity to vent their own frustration and irritation with noncooperative patients.

A deeper conceptual understanding of responsibility in the context of therapy can, however, enable the therapist to be helpful to the patient who is not accepting responsibility. In Kaiser's terms, failure to accept responsibility means failure to stand behind one's own actions. One who speaks with an angry tone of voice yet does not acknowledge the experience of being angry, or who presents in a way that calls for protective behavior from others yet does not acknowledge the desire to be taken care of, is engaging in what Kaiser (1965) refers to as duplicitous communication. The communication is duplicitous because there is inconsistency between the meaning of the communication as acknowledged by the patient and the impact the communication has on others. Clearly something is awry. The patient is perpetuating maladaptive, repetitive interpersonal cycles with others by engaging, without awareness, in behavior and communications that pull for complementary and confirming responses.

A converging perspective is provided by R. Schafer (1983), who treats emotion as a kind of action and conceptualizes the failure to acknowledge intentions and wishes that are being expressed nonverbally as an act of disclaiming one's actions. As discussed in chapter 4, the psychological process through which this disclaiming takes place can be clarified by contemporary theory and research on emotion in psychotherapy. As Greenberg and Safran (1987), and Safran and Greenberg (1988), have summarized, contemporary perspectives on affect view emotion as a form of information about the self in interaction with the environment. All emotion has an important expressive motor component which can be understood as preparedness to act in a certain way (Arnold 1970; Izard 1977; Plutchik 1980; Tomkins 1963). Emotion can thus be thought of as an action disposition (Lang 1983).

One whose interpersonal schema restricts the range of acceptable feelings and actions may thus have difficulty synthesizing expressive motor information consistent with emotions that are inconsistent with the "good me," in Sullivan's framework, and may thus engage in a kind of incongruent communication. Others may then respond to a message or intention that one communicates nonverbally, but of which one is not fully aware.

The process of taking responsibility involves discovering the interpersonal impact of one's nonverbal communications and coming to experience oneself as their author. When one begins to "own" one's actions and communications, the maladaptive, self-destructive interpersonal cycles in which one is helplessly caught up, are gradually illuminated. One gains some control and can now choose to act, rather than experience life as a victim. The process of acknowledging disclaimed action dispositions can thus play a central role in both challenging one's constricted sense of self and modifying the duplicitous communication that evokes unexpected negative responses from others.

As patients develop more flexible interpersonal schemas and begin to process affective information more fully, their verbal and nonverbal behaviors become more congruent, and duplicitous communication decreases. They become more aware of, and are able to assume more responsibility for, their dysfunctional interpersonal patterns. For example, a patient with a rigid self-definition as someone who is always agreeable will begin to shift that sense of self as he or she attends to, and begins to process, feelings of anger more fully. A patient whose self-definition is one of always being strong or in control will begin to broaden that self-concept to include vulnerability as he or she gains access to feelings of sadness.

This increased awareness of one's own contributions to interactions fosters a sense of agency rather than one of helplessness. Moreover, as one becomes more aware of one's feelings and less concerned about the risk of the associated actions, one is better able to get one's needs met directly rather than indirectly.

The following transcript illustrates the process of accepting responsibility through contacting previously unacknowledged feelings about the interaction with the therapist. The patient's style is to comply superficially with the requests of others and then act in a way that blocks true fulfillment of the task. This creates problems in her relationship with others and interferes with progress in therapy as well.

Because she feels she has no choice but to comply with the therapist's requests, she often completes therapeutic tasks with a grudging quality that undermines the usefulness of the tasks. The process of accepting responsibility in this case thus involves coming to acknowledge and articulate any negative feelings she has about the therapist's requests. Only after she truly acknowledges and accepts where she is *now* in her relationship with the therapist will she be able to move forward.

In this session, the patient had been complaining about a recent interaction with her aunt in which she felt criticized. To help reveal relevant cognitive processes, the therapist has adapted the two-chairs method from gestalt therapy (the patient is instructed to play alternatively the role of her aunt in one chair and of herself in the other). As the transcript begins, the therapist asks her to switch to the second chair.

THERAPIST: Can you switch to the other chair please?

PATIENT: May I sit in the same chair (spoken with a grin and a humorous tone)?

THERAPIST: When you ask that, are you serious or——

PATIENT: Yeah, back and forth, back and forth, yeah. I can tell you, you can ask me questions.

THERAPIST: Uh-huh. So you don't like the idea of moving back and forth between the two chairs?

PATIENT: No, not really. No.

THERAPIST: What is it about that that you object to?

PATIENT: Just back and forth. I think it changes things for me.

THERAPIST: Uh-huh.

PATIENT: I guess it interrupts what I'm thinking of. And as far as envisioning somebody else sitting there—I mean—maybe my imagination doesn't work that way.

THERAPIST: Uh-huh. So something about this is difficult?

PATIENT: Not difficult, but I don't know. It just doesn't feel right somehow.

THERAPIST: Uh-huh, yeah. Can you say, it's important, can you tell me more about what it is you don't like about it?

The patient simultaneously voices her objection to the exercise and cancels the seriousness of the message by smiling and speaking in a humorous tone. One might hypothesize that the function of her nonverbal behavior here is to minimize the risk of offending the therapist. This kind of nonverbal behavior is probably self-defeating because it increases the possibility that people will not take her seriously and then push her to do things against her will. The therapist, however, begins to probe in an attempt to clarify the patient's objection to the exercise.

PATIENT: Just moving back and forth and, like I say, it stops my train of thought. And having to envision somebody else sitting there, I just don't, 'cause I see it as being a chair.

THERAPIST: Uh-huh.

PATIENT: No matter how much I try I see it as being just a chair, and it's not the other person.

THERAPIST: Okay. So, I see this as being a tool which can be useful to help see things in a way—to help see things in a new way.

PATIENT: Uh-huh.

THERAPIST: As I understand it, there is something about it which changes things for you, or isn't quite right. Are you willing to try it, even though it doesn't seem quite right?

PATIENT: Yeah, sure, I'll go through with it. *I mean I'm easy* (laughs). Yeah.

THERAPIST: Uh-huh. Yeah. What's the——

PATIENT: 'Cause I always give up, I always give in and say, "Yeah, okay, I'll do it." It doesn't seem to matter what I say—somebody always seems to be able to tell me, "This is better for you. This is the way it's done," and I say "Okay" rather than argue and maybe lose out on something. "All right, I'll do it that way, I'll try it." Cause it's new to me and everything else, so——

THERAPIST: So this is—it's not uncommon for this to happen—that you will want to do things one way, somebody else wants to do it the other way——

PATIENT: Yeah.

The patient indicates some difficulty with the exercise, and some reluctance to go through with it. At this point the therapist could retreat. The nature of the patient's resistance to the task, however, has not been fully articulated. Perhaps she feels self-conscious doing the exercise. Perhaps she feels resentful toward the therapist for pushing her to do something she feels uncomfortable about. The therapist thus encourages her to experiment with the task in the hope that this will bring the real issue into focus. The patient agrees to give it a try, but at this point the therapist senses an odd quality of capitulation in her voice. Now the exploration of the transaction between the therapist and patient assumes priority over any attempt to have the patient engage in the task as initially defined.

THERAPIST: And then you end up giving up?

PATIENT: Yeah, I say, "Forget about it, we'll do it your way." And then if it works for me, then great, you know? 'Cause I don't want to seem—like be really argumentative, or shut my eyes to something that might work, you know? Just 'cause I don't know about it, I mean obviously I don't know everything so I'll try it, and then if I try it and afterward if it really doesn't work for me, then I'll say to the person, "Well, I'm not doing it, that's it! I've tried it your way now and it doesn't work for me, so thank you very much!" But, I do, I seem to give in quite a bit. And I'll say, "Okay, fine." You know, as soon as there's a little bit of discussion about things I'll say, "All right, fine."

THERAPIST: Uh-huh.

PATIENT: Rather than go into a big spiel and everything else, just "Okay, I'll do it to make you happy, I'll do it."

THERAPIST: What's the risk of going into a big spiel?

PATIENT: Maybe winding up in an argument and having—you know—bad feelings.

THERAPIST: Uh-huh.

PATIENT: It might stick in your head for a long time. People store things away and they use it against you later on. You know— "You're uncooperative"—"You're negative"—and blah, blah, and all that crap.

In response to the therapist's probing, the patient begins exploring a characteristic style of capitulating to people to avoid being seen as argumentative. As the therapist probes further to explore the dysfunctional expectations or fears that lead to her acquiescence, the patient articulates a general fear of people believing she is uncooperative.

In the next segment, the therapist begins by attempting to explore the patient's feelings and beliefs in an emotionally immediate way by grounding the exploration in the here and now of the therapeutic relationship.

THERAPIST: So that I might be sitting here believing that you are uncooperative and negative?

PATIENT: Ummmm, I wouldn't say *you* necessarily—not you in this situation, but—you know—other situations, yeah.

THERAPIST: People in general.

PATIENT: Yeah, yeah.

THERAPIST: What about in this situation?

PATIENT: I don't think you would. I mean, you're a therapist. I don't think you're here to pass judgment.

THERAPIST: So what's the risk of getting into a big spiel then?

PATIENT: I don't know. I guess I'm just like an old dog—you can't teach me a new trick. I don't know.

THERAPIST: You're saying it's habit in a way?

PATIENT: Yeah, I guess it is. It's a habit, uh-huh.

THERAPIST: What's that like for you, that experience you know, when you have kind of given in: "All right, we'll do it *your* way"?

PATIENT: It's like taking a piece out of me—like I have no value, no worth, and it doesn't matter what I say. It's never the right thing. It's like I'm stupid.

THERAPIST: That doesn't sound very nice.

PATIENT: No, it's not. It's not. So when things don't work out, then I can have my victory and say to the other person, "Well, I told you so in the first place, it wasn't a good idea," or something, and I feel like, "Well, now I've won a point this way by going along with it and letting someone else know that it really hasn't worked out."

THERAPIST: So it's like the only way to kind of win a victory and make a point, to maintain some integrity, is to go along with it and kind of prove that the other person was wrong in a way.

PATIENT: Uh-huh. And if it turns out that they were right, well then, great. Then I've benefited from it and the other person has. But if it doesn't turn out that way, then it's like I'm saving face, like, why make a big argument out of it—you know—it didn't have to start off with bad feelings and it showed them, probably in a nice way, afterwards, too, that they're not always right—you know—maybe they should listen to somebody else, too, for a change.

Here the patient begins by denying that her expectations about being judged or condemned for asserting herself are relevant to the current situation, even though the incident began with her capitulating to the therapist. This denial may be thought of as an avoidance of the here and now of the therapeutic relationship because it currently provokes too much anxiety in her. Paradoxically, a certain sense of security is required before one can admit vulnerability. The patient's denial may also reflect a split between what she knows intellectually and what she knows emotionally.

Particularly important is that the therapist has avoided a stalemate of accusation and denial, a struggle that could perpetuate precisely the kind of interpersonal cycle the therapist is exploring, that is, the patient feeling she has to comply to avoid a confrontation. This illustrates the necessity of keeping constantly vigilant so as to avoid becoming re-hooked into the old cycle at a new level. Instead, the therapist pursues a different tack, and explores the feelings resulting from the patient's complying. This exploration evokes some vivid and poignant feelings and thoughts ("It's like taking a piece out of me—like I have no value, no worth, and it doesn't matter what I say").

With the emergence of these feelings, the patient apparently accepts responsibility for her indirect attempt at self-assertion ("So when things don't work out, then I can have my victory and say to the other person, 'Well, I told you so in the first place, it wasn't a good idea' "). This is a critical transition in the therapeutic process: the patient begins to own a previously disclaimed action. The therapist attempts to facilitate the acknowledgment of an action disposition, which the patient may potentially construe as unacceptable, by conveying his understanding that it is currently the only way she has of maintaining her integrity.

THERAPIST: So if it doesn't work out——

PATIENT: Well, if it doesn't work out—I didn't start an argument, and I won't get the label of being uncooperative but the other person will see that what I have to say is of value also.

THERAPIST: I see. So then you can say, "I told you so" in a way.

PATIENT: Yeah, like in my head. I wouldn't say it to them verbally but—you know—it would be in my head, "I told you so. If you would have listened in the first place, or if you hadn't of been so determined, just set on getting things your own way—you know—maybe things would have been different."

THERAPIST: Yeah, you wouldn't say out loud what you're thinking.

PATIENT: No.

THERAPIST: But in your head?

PATIENT: Uh-huh.

THERAPIST: You'll show the person that you are cooperative, and then you will have the satisfaction at the end of being able to think, "Well, I told you so," in a sense, "I was right"?

PATIENT: Uh-huh.

THERAPIST: It would be important, I think, after feeling that—like—another piece of you is being taken away, when you agree to do something.

PATIENT: Uh-huh. A lot of people pooh-pooh my thoughts and yeah, a lot of people I run into, like supervisors and what not—you know—you give a suggestion and it's like, "Oh, we can't do that! That will never work!" And two, three months down the line somebody else will suggest it, somebody else that they like better, that they've known a little longer or something, and it will be like—I've had it happen to me. Somebody else brought up an idea in a meeting, and the supervisor would say, "Oh, that's a wonderful idea!" And I'd like to see the other person say, "Well, that was Christine's original idea, that she brought up—you know—a few months back." And I'd like to see their faces go, afterwards, like, "Oh, I screwed up this time." And I could sit back and say, "Now I know what I thought wasn't crazy."

The patient further acknowledges the satisfaction and sense of validation she will experience if things don't work out. Again, the therapist empathizes with her experience of losing a part of herself so as to validate an attempt on her part to maintain her integrity, and so she can begin acknowledging any indirect attempt on her part to sabotage things as a way of doing this.

THERAPIST: Okay, so if we can come back to our situation for a minute?

PATIENT: Uh-huh.

THERAPIST: Now I'm asking you to do something.

PATIENT: Uh-huh.

THERAPIST: You're feeling that you don't want to do it for various reasons, right? And now I'm saying, "Well, will you do it anyway?" And you're saying, "Well, okay, I'll do it."

PATIENT: 'Cause I don't want you to think I'm uncooperative.

THERAPIST: And can you get a sense of what's going on inside for you while this is happening?

PATIENT: Well, part of me is hoping that things will work, and part of me is hoping that they won't.

The therapist now attempts to return the focus to the current interpersonal situation. Although exploring the patient's interpersonal style in general terms may be of some value, directly acknowledging her

previously disclaimed action with the therapist is particularly important, because this process will allow her to test the dysfunctional
expectation in her interaction with the therapist that asserting herself
in a *direct*, rather than indirect, fashion will have negative consequences. The fact that the patient is *now* able to explore her feelings
in the current interaction suggests that the therapist's stance has been
sufficiently validating (that is, sufficiently challenging to her dysfunctional interpersonal schema) to allow her to take more of a risk. In
response to the therapist's probe, she is now able to acknowledge
conflicting desires for the therapist's intervention to work and not
work—a crucial step in the process of accepting responsibility for her
actions. In future sessions, the patient's perception of whether the
therapist's response is schema-consistent or schema-inconsistent will
be critical in determining whether she can continue the process of
acknowledging her disclaimed action dispositions.

The patient has now taken responsibility for her current stance. This
process involves a full acknowledgment of her conflicting feelings
about the therapeutic task rather than a grim determination to engage
in the task no matter what she feels.

CHAPTER 9

General Clinical Issues

Maintaining a Therapeutic Focus

In more structured forms of therapy, the therapist plays an active role in maintaining a therapeutic focus by working out an agenda in collaboration with the patient and by structuring sessions to cover the agenda (Beck, Rush et al. 1979). In a more process-oriented approach to cognitive therapy, such as we describe, it is not always possible to structure sessions in advance. It is, nevertheless, essential to maintain a therapeutic focus, particularly in short-term therapy where there is little time for wasted sessions, but also in longer term therapy, because failure to maintain an appropriate therapy focus can produce directionless sessions that ultimately demoralize the patient.

Here we will summarize a number of guidelines for maintaining a therapeutic focus that have been articulated in this book. First, as suggested by a variety of psychodynamic theorists (for example, Mann 1973; Luborsky 1984; Strupp and Binder 1984), the determination of what Strupp and Binder have referred to as the "dynamic focus," or what Luborsky terms the "core conflictual relationship" theme, is vital in guiding the focus of the sessions. However, it is also important that the therapist not be blinded by his or her preconceptions of the patient's internal working model and that the formulation be refined continually. Formulations of the patient's internal working model should not be a procrustean bed; they should function as one of the pieces of background information that the therapist implicitly brings to bear on his or her appraisal of the continuing interaction.

Second, the therapist should engage in a continuing assessment of what takes place in the therapeutic interaction, and constantly ask: What are my feelings toward my patient? What is the patient's internal experience? What kind of impact is the patient intending to have on me?

Third, the therapist should constantly assess what is emotionally immediate and experientially real for the patient. Change is most likely to take place when the patient is processing experiences in an emotionally immediate way. Moreover, emotion is an indicator of those events and experiences that are subjectively meaningful to the patient. The therapist should thus always be tracking the patient's nonverbal behavior for clues of emotionality, such as changes in voice tone or body expression.

The therapist should continually track whether the patient is processing information at a more abstract, intellectual level or at more of an experiential level. The construct of *experiencing* (Klein, Mathieu-Coughlan, and Kiesler 1986) from the client-centered tradition is particularly relevant here. Processing information at a high level of experiencing has now been demonstrated to be related to good therapy outcome in a variety of different forms of psychotherapy (Klein et al. 1986). The experiencing construct involves two components. The first requires the patient to process information by coming into contact with inner experiences and feelings, rather than by analyzing it with intellectual detachment. The second requires processing information by appraising a problem in an open, exploratory way in terms of the propositions about the self. These components must be combined. That is, if patients are posing intellectualized questions about the self that do not call upon immediate experience and feelings, they will not be processing information in an experiential way.

If patients process experience by combining these components, however, they have the possibility of revising core beliefs about self in interaction with others. Processing the information in an emotional way implies that one is in contact with the true meaning of events for oneself because, as Frijda (1988) suggests, emotions reflect the values, goals, and concerns of the system as a whole.

Finally, the therapist should strive to increase the depth of the patient's experiencing by heightening and reflecting those aspects of an experience that are most subjectively important and meaningful to the patient. The therapist's empathic responses should thus be geared not only toward letting patients know that they are understood, but also, toward sharpening and heightening patients' experiences, which means that the therapist must take care to select and reflect feelings in a way that accurately empathizes with the subjectively important aspects of the patients' communications (Rogers 1961; Rice 1974; Gendlin 1981).

By attending to the foregoing guidelines, the therapist will increase the possibility of maintaining a therapeutic focus on core issues without imposing a structure that is insensitive to the unfolding therapeutic process.

Therapist Activity Level

In contrast to approaches such as client-centered therapy or psychodynamic therapy, the cognitive therapist has traditionally played an active and directive role in terms of structuring sessions for the patient, and assigning homework. There is no reason, in theory, for the therapist not to be active when it is appropriate. An unqualified prescription to be active, however, is as clinically problematic as an unqualified injunction for the therapist to assume a passive role. It is thus essential that therapists titrate their activity level to the needs of the specific patient.

Two general considerations can be useful in guiding this calibration. The first is the patient's core dysfunctional interpersonal schema. Depending upon its nature, the therapist's activity level has different meanings for the patient. If, for example, a patient believes he or she is helpless and that the therapist must always provide advice and support, a highly active therapist will be confirming the patient's dysfunctional interpersonal schema. Or, if a patient has a dysfunctional belief that any act of independence will be threatening to others, it is vital for the therapist to demonstrate, by encouraging the patient to act independently and by withholding unnecessary support, that he or she is not threatened.

If, on the other hand, a patient believes that any act of dependency will result in rejection or abandonment, the therapist who plays a relatively passive role and refuses to participate actively in the treatment will be confirming the patient's dysfunctional beliefs. Here, it is advisable for the therapist to play a much more active role, perhaps taking a stance similar to that traditionally taken by cognitive therapists.

A second general principle is the principle of optimal frustration (Kohut 1984). Ultimately it is in the patient's interest to learn to act autonomously and to learn to find support internally rather than indirectly through others (Perls 1973). The therapist should thus carefully calibrate the amount of activity or support given here in order to offer sufficient support in building a secure base for exploration that will allow the patient to learn to stand alone. On the other hand, the therapist should not provide so much support that it deprives patients of the opportunity to do for themselves what they are capable of doing. Patients often underestimate their own ability and exert a strong pull for support from their environment, so the therapist must constantly be gauging how much support is necessary to modulate the patient's anxiety and maintain an adequate working alliance to allow the patient to develop self-support. The optimal balance between support and frustration fluctuates continually, and the therapist must rely upon clinical judgment to calibrate this balance.

A related principle is what Luborsky (1984) describes as balancing the supportive and expressive aspects of therapy. Patients can only engage in a process of self-exploration if their anxiety level is sufficiently well modulated to permit this process. As Sullivan (1953) emphasized, anxiety obstructs the processing of both external and internal experience. The therapist must thus engage in an ongoing assessment of patients' anxiety levels to evaluate whether they are currently experiencing sufficient support and safety in the therapeutic relationship to continue the process of self-exploration.

If, in the therapist's assessment, the patient's self-exploration is blocked because of excessive anxiety caused by a lack of security in the therapeutic relationship, the therapist must then provide more support. As Luborsky (1984) suggests, a primary mode of supporting patients is through facilitating their experience of the therapeutic alliance.

The Role of the Rationale in Therapy

In cognitive and behavioral therapies a strong emphasis is placed on conveying the therapeutic rationale to the patient (Beck, Rush et al. 1979; Burns 1980; McMullin 1986). We believe this is an extremely useful component in any therapy approach and one that other approaches toward psychotherapy tend to underestimate. It may be useful, then, to examine the role that conveying the therapy rationale plays in the therapy process, because in doing so, we may discover considerations that would allow us to use this strategy in more refined and differentiated ways.

Essentially, the role that conveying the therapy rationale plays is one of facilitating the development of the therapeutic alliance (Luborsky 1984). If we conceptualize the therapeutic alliance in terms of Bordin's (1979) dimensions of task, goal, and bond, it becomes apparent that the process of conveying the therapy rationale can strengthen any or all three of these dimensions.

Thus, for example, speaking with the patient about the relationship between feelings and thoughts (Beck, Rush et al. 1979) and clarifying the value of becoming aware of feelings or thoughts, can facilitate agreement about the task dimension of the therapeutic alliance, whereas specifying treatment targets and setting an agenda for change relate to the goal dimension. In certain contexts the very act of responding to questions about the purpose of certain therapeutic procedures and reassuring patients that the therapist is sensitive to their concerns can facilitate the bond dimension of the therapeutic alliance.

For these reasons, as a way of fostering the growth of the therapeutic alliance at the outset of therapy, it is useful for the therapist to give a brief description of the therapeutic rationale and then to evaluate whether it makes sense to the patient. As therapy continues, whenever the therapist detects strain, one way of strengthening the alliance can be to clarify whether the patient understands what is going on in the therapeutic process and, if the patient is confused or uncertain, to explain it. In this way the therapist may alleviate concerns patients may have about being manipulated or help to reduce the anxiety they are experiencing as a result of confusion.

If, however, the therapist's initial attempt to facilitate the alliance by giving a rationale is not successful, it may well be that a more in-depth exploration of the patient's current experience of the therapeutic relationship is in order because, in this context, it is important for the therapist, rather than trying to persuade a skeptical patient, to explore feelings and perceptions underlying that skepticism.

When they are feeling skeptical or critical, it is not unusual for patients to say that they do not understand the rationale. Consequently, the interpersonal meaning of the exchange between the therapist and patient is much more important than the content of the exchange because the patients' ability to understand or make sense of a particular rationale in a specific context will be colored by their perception of the therapist and the meaning of the exchange.

Therapeutic Engagement

If patients are to benefit from therapy they must engage in the tasks of therapy. These range from concrete behavioral assignments to abstract, subtle cognitive/affective tasks. Examples of more subtle cognitive/affective tasks would include such activities as attempting to track one's inner experience, to experience one's true feelings, or to engage in a self-exploratory process with the objective of clarifying the true meaning of an event for oneself.

If a therapy task is tangible and concrete, it is fairly easy to determine whether or not the patient is engaging in that task. For example, if patients are assigned the homework task of monitoring and writing down self-critical thoughts between sessions, the act of bringing in the completed automatic thoughts record provides tangible evidence that the task has been completed. Or, if patients have been asked to place themselves in a situation they are phobic about, or to refrain from engaging in an obsessive ritual, it is fairly evident whether they have actually engaged in the task. In the more behaviorally oriented approaches, it is taken as a given that therapy cannot progress unless the patient engages in the prescribed task.

In the subtle cognitive/affective tasks, it is more difficult to determine whether the patient is truly and wholeheartedly engaging in the tasks. It is entirely possible for the patient to go through the motions of engaging in some overt behavioral task while not fully engaging in the task psychologically. For example, a patient may monitor and challenge automatic thoughts overtly, but not engage in this task fully at a psychological level. In an extreme case the patient may go through the motions of completing such a task with the covert agenda of demonstrating to the therapist that the therapy is not effective.

For these reasons, the therapist must be attuned not only to whether the patient is engaging in the tasks of therapy at a gross, tangible level, but also to whether the patient is engaging in the more subtle psychological tasks of therapy. If there is no engagement at this second level, the therapist may have to make it a major focus of therapeutic exploration. It is not unusual for a patient who approaches the tasks of therapy cynically to approach many of life's activities in the same way, for the kind of disengaged stance that is an obstacle to therapeutic progress can also block fulfillment in the patient's life and interpersonal relationships. In such a case, the therapist may have to rely upon his or her own feelings and observations of subtle nonverbal behaviors to generate hypotheses about what is occurring. Identifying and isolating patterns of this kind can thus be guided by the same principles that guide the identification of other cognitive-interpersonal cycles.

For example, in one case, the therapist found that although a patient was going through the motions of completing the various tasks of therapy, he was experiencing a subtle, nagging feeling of irritation with the patient. Exploring these feelings and the interpersonal markers evoking them helped him identify a faded, plaintive quality in the patient's style. To the therapist it felt as if the patient was subtly saying that she was doing what was being asked of her, but did not really see the point of it.

When the therapist spoke to the patient about his perception in a nonjudgmental way, the patient was then able to begin exploring her experience and to acknowledge that the therapist's perception did indeed reflect her experience. Further exploration helped to illuminate a general attitude of futility and hopelessness that also pervaded other parts of her life. Once the patient was clearly able to see how this attitude was affecting her experience both in therapy and in life in general, she was able to begin to experiment with participating in a more psychologically engaged way. Experimenting with this subtle shift in psychological perspective began to have an impact on the therapy, which led to an improvement in the therapeutic alliance, and change began to take place.

In some situations, the therapist may find it difficult to determine whether the patient is truly engaging in the tasks of therapy. It may be particularly difficult to assess this issue if the therapist has not been assigning tangible, concrete behavioral tasks. Here, a useful strategy can be to make a point of assigning such tasks because even if the patient does not acknowledge a lack of engagement in the tasks of therapy, failure to complete clear-cut behavioral tasks will become apparent. The therapist can bring this evidence to the patient's attention, which may then lead either to an exploration of the underlying expectations and attitudes related to this lack of engagement or to a clear confrontation in which the patient is called upon to make an existential choice, in full awareness, about whether he or she is willing to engage in the tasks of therapy at this time.

Challenging Security Operation Cognitions

It is vital for the cognitive therapist to be able to distinguish between dysfunctional cognitive appraisals that are direct reactions to a situation and those that play a role in maintaining the patient's core sense of self and subjective sense of interpersonal relatedness. If we assume an organizational/hierarchical perspective on cognitive processes, we recognize that different cognitive processes play different roles in the overall cognitive structure. At the core level are fundamental beliefs about the self and others and beliefs about how one has to be to maintain relatedness to others. At a peripheral level are cognitive structures and processes that function to maintain one's self-esteem and sense of potential interpersonal relatedness (Safran, Vallis et al. 1986). Thus, for example, one may engage in an exaggerated positive evaluation of oneself. Some cognitive therapists see the overly positive evaluation of the self as stemming from an unrealistically positive self-schema (for example, Winfrey and Goldfried 1986). It is vital, however, to distinguish between one's fantasy of how one would ideally like to be and one's fundamental sense of self. Horney (1950), for example, distinguished between the individual's real self and the idealized self. According to her, people develop an idealized fantasy of themselves to help compensate for a deep underlying sense of inadequacy. She theorized that the neurotic person puts his or her energy into trying to actualize this idealized self, and that the task of therapy involves shifting the energy back toward actualizing the real self.

In addition to an inflated sense of self which may function to help one compensate for an underlying feeling of vulnerability, people also engage in ongoing distortions of information to reduce their anxiety and increase self-esteem. As we have previously argued, cognitive operations of this kind can be thought of as security operations which help to reduce one's anxiety and maintain a subjective sense of potential interpersonal relatedness.

For example, a patient who was inept socially spoke repeatedly about the women who were extremely attracted to him. When the therapist asked how he knew this, he responded that he could "feel it." In the therapist's assessment, the patient's unrealistic appraisal of these situations stood in the way of developing the social skills that would allow him to have more meaningful relationships with women. She thus attempted to challenge his perception of the situation by asking him to specify the evidence on which his perception was based. The more she attempted to challenge his perception, however, the more entrenched the patient became in his beliefs.

In this situation, the therapist's attempt to challenge the patient's perception failed because his distortion of the situation played a functional role for him, by maintaining his self-esteem and subjective sense of interpersonal relatedness. It is thus not surprising that the attempt to challenge distortions failed, since this intervention did not address the underlying sense of personal inadequacy. Moreover, it is possible that the therapist's challenge was construed by the patient as another instance of precisely the kind of nonacceptance by females connected with his fundamental sense of underlying inadequacy. For the patient to relax his security operations in this situation, it would first be necessary for him to feel sufficiently comfortable about himself to do so. It would thus be essential for the therapist not to use a frontal attack on his security operations in helping the patient appraise reality more correctly, but rather to provide a sufficiently supportive and empathic environment to allow the patient to contact his underlying feelings of inadequacy and vulnerability.

Issues Related to Termination

As previously indicated, the approach described in this book can be employed in either long-term or short-term and time-limited therapy. In our experience, if one chooses to use a short-term therapy protocol, it is preferable to make a termination date in advance or to contract in advance for the number of sessions that will be provided, rather than negotiate the termination as the therapy proceeds (Beck, Rush et al. 1979; Mann 1973; Sifneos 1972). One reason for this is that failure to do so often results in the negotiation of the termination date becoming a dominant issue in therapy.

Of course, negotiation of a termination date also becomes an important therapeutic issue in long-term therapy. With a shorter time frame, however, there is an increased possibility that the patient may not wish to terminate when a short-term time span has elapsed (for example, six months). Here, negotiations on extending the time limit often take on an important symbolic meaning for patients who question whether the therapist cares enough about them to extend the therapy.

Setting the time limit or termination date in advance can actually facilitate the therapeutic process by creating a sense of urgency and goal directedness that may encourage patients to work in a more wholehearted way.

For many patients, the imminent arrival of termination activates important issues and concerns about the interpersonal meaning of separation (Mann 1973). For patients who have not progressed in therapy as much as they had initially hoped, the approach of the termination date can activate a number of complex, ambivalent feelings,

211

not just about whether they have got what they wanted from the therapy, but also whether they have got what they wanted from the therapist.

A fundamental assumption of our approach is that human beings have a wired-in propensity for interpersonal relatedness and that much of the maladaptive learning that takes place is shaped by attempts to avoid the disintegration of important interpersonal relationships. Because therapy is an interpersonal relationship of potential significance for patients, it is likely that complex feelings and characteristic (often maladaptive) ways of handling separations will emerge prior to termination or around termination. It is thus particularly important for the therapist to be mindful of the potential symbolic significance of termination for the patient and to use the approach of termination as an opportunity to explore the patient's characteristic way of responding to and managing separations.

If, in the early phases of therapy, the therapist is able to establish a reasonable working hypothesis regarding the patient's core interpersonal schemas, he or she will be better able to generate hypotheses about some of the potential themes that may be relevant for a particular patient around termination. This is especially important in cases where patients' previous histories suggest that they respond to interpersonal separations in an intense or maladaptive way. For example, one patient had a history of having difficulty in ending relationships and attempted to maintain contact years after the end of the relationship with ex-lovers who did not want to see her. Moreover, in her previous therapy she had developed an elaborate fantasy about having a romantic relationship with her therapist, and continued to try to re-establish contact with him six years after terminating treatment, even though the therapist had made it clear that he wished to have no contact with her.

The patient's personal history suggested that termination was particularly likely to be a problem for her and that it would be appropriate either to begin working on termination very close to the beginning of therapy or to assign her to longer term psychotherapy, where there would be adequate time to deal with her intense reaction to separations.

Although this is an extreme example, the prospect of termination often provides an opportunity to explore feelings, attitudes, beliefs, and interpersonal strategies associated with the patient's core interpersonal schema. For example, one patient characteristically maintained an independent stance to avoid the experience of being abandoned by others. Although this stance was adaptive for her in a certain sense, it was also dysfunctional in that it stood in the way of her forming a lasting romantic relationship with a man. On the basis of early interactions with her and knowledge about her relationship with her parents and other significant figures, the therapist hypothesized that she might have difficulty forming any kind of emotional attachment to him because of her fear of abandonment. About halfway through therapy, the therapist began talking about the prospect of termination and the patient, at first, indicated that she was not concerned at all about the prospect. Over time, however, it emerged that she, indeed, questioned the value of beginning to speak with the therapist about intimate matters because he would be leaving her in another ten sessions anyway.

This provided an opportunity to explore the ways in which she had difficulty being intimate with other people because of her overriding fear and anticipation of separation. In therapy, they explored the possibility that it might be worthwhile sharing herself more intimately with the therapist, even though separation was inevitable. Rather than attempting to avoid intimacy because of the fear of pain associated with the possibility of separation, therapy with this patient explored the alternative of accepting the pain of separation as an inevitable part of life and that one can only avoid this pain at the cost of avoiding intimacy. By being attuned to the potential meaning of termination for this patient, the therapist was able to help her explore and make changes in some of her fundamental beliefs and interpersonal strategies related to separation issues.

In some cases, the patient may not acknowledge concerns about termination even though the therapist hypothesizes that termination will be an issue for the patient at some level. Here, the therapist must not impose his or her perspective on the patient. The best policy is to invite patients to explore any feelings they may have about termination, but if they decline or say that there is no issue to discuss, to respect that position.

When a patient maintains that there are no concerns, it may well be that the therapist has simply been wrong in his or her hypothesis about the significance of termination for this patient and that, indeed, there are no concerns. In those cases where the therapist believes that the patient experiences anxiety around the possibility of termination, it may also be that the patient actually feels pleased about the possibility of terminating and proceeding independently of the therapist. As Weiss and colleagues (1987) have pointed out, some patients have a pathogenic belief that a display of independence may harm the significant other. Here, accepting the patient's words at face value can play an important role in disconfirming the patient's dysfunctional beliefs about interpersonal relationships.

One of the difficulties in doing short-term psychotherapy is the sense of pressure the therapist often feels to "accomplish" things. This is particularly true in cognitive therapy, which has a tradition of establishing clear-cut therapeutic targets at the beginning and then working toward these goals. In our experience, however, it is important for therapists to realize that every contact with a patient can potentially have a significant impact, yet at the same time to keep in mind that the role that they play in a patient's life is, on the grand scale of things, minuscule. Therapists must learn to leave the responsibility for change to their patients and to accept them wherever they are at the end of therapy.

The termination of the therapeutic contact is not necessarily the end of the change process for the patient, and in some cases more dramatic changes will take place after termination. This can be particularly true in short-term therapy. Sometimes, events that take place during therapy sow the seed for changes patients will make later on. Sometimes the therapeutic contact patients have had may help them become sufficiently trusting and optimistic about the possibility of change to return to therapy with a new therapist.

If one is able to keep this lifespan perspective in mind, it will help reduce the pressure to produce changes in the present and free one up to be more open and receptive to any subtle, but nevertheless important, changes that may take place during therapy. Conversely, the therapist who feels pressured to make large changes will be less aware of subtle and important changes that do occur and less able to accept patients wherever they are.

This is particularly difficult for therapists who, at the end of therapy, take the patient's view of progress as a reflection of their overall competence. Therapists must be accepting of both themselves and the patient. One must accept and believe that one has worked to the best of one's ability to facilitate the patient's growth given one's competence and knowledge at the time.

Unless therapists can develop this kind of accepting and compassionate stance toward themselves, it will be difficult for them to develop the accepting and compassionate, nonattached stance that is most helpful to patients. If, however, one can maintain a degree of nonattachment, one will be able to accept patients wherever they are at the end of therapy, which is particularly important when patients have not made the type of dramatic change initially hoped for.

Whatever emerges at termination should be systematically understood and explored as fully as possible in terms of its significance for the patient's internal working model and for his or her relationship with the therapist, rather than used as a measure of the therapist's competence.

Premature Termination

The same principle applies if the patient, in the therapist's view, wishes to terminate prematurely. The cardinal rule here is that the patient should not leave treatment feeling pathologized or blamed. There is no formula for handling this situation, but in general, the therapist should invite patients to explore their reasons for terminating and provide the appropriate climate to support and facilitate this exploration. Patients who have been feeling skeptical or critical of the therapist, and who have difficulty discussing these feelings, often give excuses for terminating rather than deal with these concerns directly. If the therapist is able to provide a facilitative climate that allows the patient to explore negative or ambivalent feelings, the reasons for termination may dissipate, and the patient may decide not to terminate.

Sometimes the exploration of the patient's ambivalence about therapy becomes the major focus of therapy. This ambivalence may, in turn, involve central concerns that the patient has about relating to other people. For example, a patient who tends to see others as dominating and manipulative and for this reason finds it hard to establish meaningful relationships may also have difficulty forming an adequate working alliance with the therapist. If the patient has a problem in talking with the therapist about these concerns because of the fear of abandonment or retaliation, there is no possibility of resolving the issue.

If, however, the therapist is sufficiently skillful in helping the patient explore these negative feelings, the very act of articulating negative feelings and observing that the therapist's behavior does not confirm their dysfunctional beliefs about interpersonal relationships can be an important part of the change process.

Although it is important for the therapist to provide the kind of facilitative climate that maximizes the possibility for exploring negative or ambivalent feelings and articulating them directly, it is equally

215

important for the therapist to respect the position of a patient who is unable or unwilling to explore these feelings. Also it is essential for therapists to remember that when one feels the patient's termination is a reflection on one's own competence, one can make interpretations which, although ostensibly offered in the patient's best interests, are ultimately harmful or destructive.

If one has done one's best to facilitate the patient's exploration of reasons for termination and finds that the patient still wishes to terminate, it is important to maintain a respectful nonintrusive stance until the end. A possibility is that one's hypothesis about the patient's reasons for termination is simply wrong. Alternatively, if they are unable or unwilling to explore their reasons for termination in greater detail, patients may well be doing what is necessary to protect themselves at that time. The therapist who is able to maintain a respectful stance under these circumstances will ultimately be more therapeutic than one who pushes that patient to stay in therapy, or makes an interpretation that is pathologizing.

A key factor in how therapists handle a termination that they consider premature, should be an evaluation of the patient's interpersonal schema. If, for example, the patient has an interpersonal schema centered around a belief that others will be hurt if the patient acts independently, the announcement of plans to terminate may be an important test of that dysfunctional expectation. Here, it would be important for the therapist to respect the patient's decision to act independently and to demonstrate to the patient that the therapist is not overly concerned.

If, however, patients have interpersonal schemas revolving around a belief that others do not care enough about them to exert any effort on their behalf, it may be important for the therapist to be more active in exploring their reasons for leaving, as a way of demonstrating care or concern. To the extent that therapists have a working hypothesis regarding a patient's interpersonal schema, they will have more information regarding the best way to handle an announcement of the intention to terminate. It is thus important for therapists to keep in mind that announcing a premature termination can have multiple meanings for patients and that keeping patients in therapy is not necessarily in their best interest.

The following transcript illustrates the use of impending termination as an opportunity to explore the patient's dysfunctional interpersonal schema and characteristic way of dealing with intimate interpersonal relationships. It is extracted from the fifteenth session of a twenty-session protocol. To this point, the course of therapy has been turbulent, with a fairly tenuous therapeutic alliance. The patient has by now, however, begun to develop some degree of trust in the therapist.

THERAPIST: Anything else stand out for you that you want to talk about, particularly relating to where we are right now and where we've come from? Where we are and where you want to go?

PATIENT: I don't know where else to go from here. I mean, I'm in your hands. I'm letting you lead the way.

THERAPIST: What's that like, letting me lead the way?

PATIENT: Well, I guess I'm putting some faith in you. Some trust. You know, I—guess that's not something I do very often.

THERAPIST: So that I get a sense of you taking somewhat of a risk?

PATIENT: Uh-huh.

THERAPIST: That you're by nature cautious.

PATIENT: Yeah.

THERAPIST: And you're saying—taking somewhat of a risk.

PATIENT: Uh-huh. That's right. You haven't hurt me this far, and it's been like fifteen sessions or whatever and I think, basically, I've gotten over the really tough points and all that—mistrust and everything else in the beginning. So I just figure you're not here to harm me. You're here to do me some good. The only person that can harm me is me. So that's where it stands.

THERAPIST: That whole process of coming to trust another person, I think, is an important process.

PATIENT: Yeah, it is. And it's a long one.

THERAPIST: Yeah.

PATIENT: Uh-huh. I don't know if other people are the same way, or if they trust easier, or they say they do and they really don't but it takes me a long time. I don't know why. Nobody, I could ever depend on really. Everything was left to me—or people have screwed up, you know. That's how I feel, anyways—along the way. You know, parents or family and stuff like that.

THERAPIST: So, you're used to being very self-reliant?

PATIENT: I think so, yeah.

THERAPIST: To not depending on anybody?

PATIENT: Uh-huh. Not emotionally. I comfort myself, you know. I talk to myself. I'm financially okay. My aunt's been around. Financially she—you know, she's that way. That's her way of caring. I don't think she can really say what she feels.

You know, she doesn't show, she doesn't touch me or anything like that. Or give me that—no hug, or whatever. My father hasn't been around. So—my mother hasn't been around—my sister hasn't been around, no grandparents.

I mean, I think I started out with it all, but somewhere along the way, it just all disappeared. I guess I was angry and hurt, and you know, depressed for a long time. And it always seemed like it just came, came down to *me*. You know—I had just *me* to make myself feel better. Nobody else could do it for me and I don't know if I did such a good job of it, but I did the best I could.

THERAPIST: Did the best you could.

PATIENT: Yeah.

THERAPIST: So for you to begin to trust somebody—to start depending on other people—to some extent is a big thing.

PATIENT: Uh-huh.

THERAPIST: Not an easy thing.

PATIENT: Yeah. I kind of felt that if you start to lean on somebody and trust somebody—like men, that they're gonna wind up, they're gonna leave me anyways. They're not gonna be around, or something's gonna happen. Just that fear that they're not gonna be there for you. And you know, you open up and you feel that way for somebody and all of a sudden they're gone again. And it's that hurt, that pain that comes afterwards and it takes a long time to get over.

THERAPIST: Yeah—so I'm wondering, along that line, any thoughts about what it'll be like when we stop—you know. Because we will be stopping in another five sessions.

PATIENT: Yeah.

THERAPIST: And I have a sense of your beginning to kind of open up and starting to share yourself.

PATIENT: Uh-huh.

THERAPIST: Any sense of what that's going to be like, to stop at that point?

PATIENT: I don't know. Maybe there'll be times when I'll need somebody to talk to again—I don't know. Probably. I guess I'll have to deal with that when I get to it. I mean, I guess I'm hoping to find ways that I won't feel that way, or that I can take care of myself, or know where else to go or—you know—what to do.

THERAPIST: Has that been on your mind at all? Sort of, the thought that we'll be stopping?

PATIENT: Actually, it crossed my mind, I think a couple of weeks ago. But it was just—yeah, I guess it was because I didn't see you for a couple of weeks and I thought, "geez," you know, "it seems strange." All these things that you want to say and there's really nobody else to say it to. I guess I have to learn how to say it to somebody else, I don't know. But I don't think I'll get the same response or be able to talk without being told "You're stupid. Don't have those crazy ideas—" or something.

In response to the therapist's question about her objectives for the rest of the therapy, the patient says she is placing herself in the therapist's hands. Already sensitized to the importance of the issue of trust versus mistrust or dependence/independence for this patient, the therapist attempts to explore what this experience is like for her, which leads to an exploration of her difficulty in trusting anybody because of her fear of abandonment. She focuses briefly on the way in which experiences of abandonment by family members have led to these fears, but this is not explored in detail here.

She also alludes to how difficult it is for her to trust men. This is particularly important because one of the key issues for her is the lack of a stable romantic relationship. The therapist empathizes with her experience, and then returns the focus to the exploration of this theme in the context of the therapeutic relationship and the impending termination.

Thereafter (in a segment omitted here for brevity), the patient returns to a more general focus on her feelings of sadness because of her experiences of loss and abandonment in the past and her fear that she will never have a stable interpersonal connection. When she interrupts her feelings of sadness in the session, the therapist begins to explore the fears and expectations that block her from fully experiencing them in the moment. At this point the session continues.

THERAPIST: What's your objection to experiencing those feelings of sadness?

PATIENT: If I showed you those feelings inside of me—then that would mean that I was opening myself up to you. But you're really not, you know, a friend. You're from the outside, or something like that. It's not to say that you don't care, but you—I don't know—but maybe it would stir up a feeling in me and I would be close to you. And then, again, you wouldn't be here. You know what I'm saying?

THERAPIST: I think so, yeah.

PATIENT: Yeah.

THERAPIST: That sounds important, right?

PATIENT: Yeah.

THERAPIST: That if you were to show some of the really intimate feelings inside of you, that would be like opening yourself up to me.

PATIENT: Uh-huh.

THERAPIST: And then, it's like I wouldn't be there for you anymore?

PATIENT: Yeah, it's like, you know me now, but then, later on, I'd just be another person. And I'd walk through your office—in and out. You know? I know that's why I'm here, but I just can't help the way I feel. That's the way it is.

THERAPIST: Yeah. Well, it sounds important.

PATIENT: Uh-huh. You know—I'll allow you to see so much, right? But then, not all of me. So, what am I doing here? Am I defeating the purpose? I don't know.

THERAPIST: I don't think you're defeating the purpose. And what you're saying—that sounds important.

PATIENT: Uh-huh.

THERAPIST: There's a real concern you have that needs to be respected.

PATIENT: Uh-huh.

In response to the therapist's probe, the patient discloses her fears of being abandoned by the therapist. This is not an abstract, intellectualized explanation but an emotionally immediate one taking place in the context of her *currently* interrupting her feelings of sadness. Rather than push her to share her feelings, the therapist conveys an understanding of and respect for her need for self-protection.

THERAPIST: That's why you're saying "I'll only allow so much. I'll only allow you to see so much."

PATIENT: Uh-huh.

THERAPIST: "If I were to show more, then it'd be like opening myself up. And you wouldn't be there for me. That's my concern."

PATIENT: Uh-huh. Yeah! I guess you'd have to mean more to me, basically, you know. I mean, I trust you this far, but then I'd have to even more. I don't know. It's like—I don't know. I guess when I get that far, it feels like I'm giving myself to somebody.

And what I'm saying is—just like in a relationship with me. They'll—you know—if I go to bed with somebody it's—because that's—you know, I want to be with them.

I'm giving myself to them, you know. And I guess I'm old-fashioned that way. You know, you go to bed with somebody you love and that's it. And that's supposed to be it. But it doesn't work that way. And that's why you get hurt afterwards.

THERAPIST: That's why you get hurt afterwards?

PATIENT: Yeah. Yeah, you just feel, you know. "I went to bed with that person. We shared this and that." And intimacy and all this jazz, and then they can just—you know—get up and walk away or something. And that really devastates me. I—you know—can't cope with that. I don't know. Just—letting—revealing—myself—and then it just seems so easy for other people just to walk away.

As the therapist empathizes with her need to protect herself, the patient spontaneously compares the current experience to the experience of becoming intimate with men in general. She speaks about the importance and difficulty of trusting and the pain of being disappointed in her trust. There is no need for the therapist to draw connections with other relationships. She is spontaneously using the therapeutic relationship as a vehicle for exploring her problematic interpersonal style.

THERAPIST: Okay, so that if you—you're speaking in general terms and also specifically about now, I think?

PATIENT: Uh-huh.

THERAPIST: Okay. So that if you were to really reveal yourself, you'd get hurt?

PATIENT: Uh-huh.

THERAPIST: All right. That in a sense, there's a reality to it, right? We've got five more sessions.

PATIENT: Uh-huh.

THERAPIST: All right. If you were really to reveal what's inside of you—at the end of five sessions, we're still going to be saying goodbye.

PATIENT: Uh-huh.

THERAPIST: So, you'd end up being hurt. You say—was the word you used devastated, or——?

PATIENT: Yeah.

THERAPIST: Devastated.

PATIENT: I don't know. I guess it's always been my experience that if I let myself go, or really open myself up to somebody, I'm opening myself up to hurt. I'd become vulnerable.

THERAPIST: So that's the risk?

PATIENT: Yeah. Now either I take on the attitude that—you know— "Toughen up" and that it doesn't mean much, or "Don't feel it." Or else, wind up feeling devastated and you know, "Eat your heart out." Two big choices.

THERAPIST: It seems like those are the only options for you?

PATIENT: Yeah.

THERAPIST: That you toughen yourself up. Which is what you seem to do a lot of the time, right?

PATIENT: Uh-huh.

THERAPIST: You kind of close off your feelings. And you're tough. Or you really open up and you end up getting devastated.

PATIENT: Yeah, extremes, you know. No halfway with me. It's either all the way or not at all.

THERAPIST: So, the question, it seems to me, is whether somehow we can find another possibility.

PATIENT: Uh-huh. That would be nice. Yeah. Something I know that I could feel comfortable with and some way of thinking that's not—you know—devastating and—you know—not feeling vulnerable, but not totally shut down either. It's like I'm always walking around with a suit of armor or something.

THERAPIST: Okay, so maybe, you know, if we're trying to get some kind of a focus for the time we've got together, my suggestion is that we could see if there's some way we could use this time to discover some alternative to either being totally shut down and protective versus being totally open and devastated.

PATIENT: Uh-huh.

THERAPIST: In other words, maybe you can even use our relationship as a way of testing out, trying out different possibilities to see if there's an alternative.

PATIENT: Yeah, sounds good.

THERAPIST: Okay?

PATIENT: Yeah.

THERAPIST: Okay, so let's stop here.

PATIENT: And we'll continue next week.

The therapist again makes sure to ground the exploration in the current interpersonal situation. ("You're speaking in general terms and also specifically about *now*, I think?'') In this final segment the patient reveals a style of dichotomous thinking about intimate relationships. (''I take on the attitude that—you know—'Toughen up' and it doesn't mean much, or 'Don't feel it.' Or else, wind up feeling devastated and you know, 'Eat your heart out.' Two big choices.'')

The therapist explicitly suggests using the current relationship to explore other alternatives. It is important to recognize that this exploration is experiential rather than rational. In other words, the very act of having spoken with the therapist about the dilemma to the extent that she has, and having him respond in an accepting fashion, is a new learning experience. This process begins to challenge her ''all-or-nothing thinking'' about intimate relationships in that even though therapy will still terminate at twenty sessions, the therapist's consistent empathic stance demonstrates that this is not quite the same as abandonment. Separation will inevitably involve some pain, but this is part of life. It is the desire to completely avoid this pain that is contributing to the problem. As an old Japanese poem says:

> Flowers opening
> Meet wind and rain;
> Human life
> Is full of parting.

The Therapist as Role Model (Revisited)

Throughout the course of this book we have emphasized the importance of the inner discipline of the therapist, and argued that one's relationship with oneself will ultimately influence one's relationship with the patient and the change process. Thus, for example, one who is able to accept one's own feelings of sadness and vulnerability will be able to empathize with similar feelings in others and thus help them to integrate these feelings into their sense of self. Being able to accept one's own feelings of anger helps one to acknowledge them when they emerge and to avoid being hooked into a struggle to demonstrate that one is not angry.

There is another, subtler way in which one's relationship with one's self influences the therapeutic process. As we have already discussed, cognitive-behavioral therapists have long recognized that therapists can provide important role models for patients. The characteristics

223

being modeled, however, are more than specific behavioral skills or specific cognitive strategies.

The basic values and philosophical perspective one has as a therapist are ultimately transmitted to the patient regardless of how much or how little one talks about them in therapy. This is particularly true in long-term therapy, where the patient has an extended period to infer the therapist's values and general beliefs about life from his or her reactions and behavior. Therapists who are, generally, accepting of themselves and their own imperfections as human beings, will, as therapists, model the kind of self-acceptance they are trying to promote in their patients, whereas therapists with little tolerance for their own shortcomings will have difficulty modeling the kind of self-acceptance they are promoting.

Because modeling is a natural part of the developmental process it is natural that the patient's values and beliefs will, to some extent, be influenced by the therapist's values and beliefs. In fact, as research on attitude change in psychotherapy demonstrates, the tendency for patients to change their values in the direction of their therapist's, is a consistent phenomenon in psychotherapy (Beutler, Crago, and Arrizmendi 1986). Given that this kind of modeling is an inevitable part of the therapy process, it is important to clarify the factors mediating whether this process is growth-enhancing or not.

If therapists can, genuinely, accept their patients in all their facets, their patients are likely to explore the values of their therapists with which they resonate. This process, which will ultimately have an impact on the value system a patient evolves over the course of therapy, is not a wholesale adoption of the therapist's values, but rather a gradual integration of some of their aspects with the patient's own value system, resulting in the ultimate synthesis of a world view that is distinctly the patient's. In contrast, if the therapist transmits a message to patients that to be truly accepted by the therapist, they must be a certain way, the values held by the therapist then become the patient's new contingencies for maintaining relatedness. Although the patient may adopt some of the therapist's values, this value adoption process parallels the one that was problematic for the patient in his or her childhood, obscuring different aspects of the patient's internal experience, rather than articulating them.

In the psychoanalytic literature the topic of modeling, dealt with under the general theme of internalization, is, as Eagle (1984) has pointed out, somewhat confusing because of the host of different theories of internalization and the lack of an adequate metapsychology.

Two processes of internalization, however, correspond to the two modeling processes we have described: identification and introjection (Meissner 1981; Schafer 1968).

In the process of identification, one explores the value system of the person one identifies with and ultimately integrates some aspects of it into one's own value system, while rejecting others. In this process one uses the value system of the person one identifies with to help clarify and sort out one's own value system. As Eagle (1984) expresses it, ultimately the distinguishing feature of identification is that one fully integrates the relevant values into an overall sense of self.

In introjection, however, one adopts the values of the person who is being modeled without fully integrating them into one's own self-organization. As a result, these introjected values are experienced in some sense as being outside of the self.

By viewing the internalization process in terms of the cognitive representation of self-other interactions, it is theoretically consistent with a cognitive framework: The process of introjection involves the cognitive representation of restrictive contingencies for interpersonal relatedness based on interaction with others. The process of identification involves articulating new values and standards that derive from an internally experienced locus rather than from the need to maintain interpersonal relatedness.

CHAPTER 10

Patient Selection for Short-Term Cognitive Therapy

Jeremy D. Safran, Zindel V. Segal, Brian F. Shaw, and T. Michael Vallis

Conducting short-term therapy heightens many of the themes and issues that emerge for both patients and therapists in long-term therapy. For patients, the knowledge of an imminent termination date heightens concerns related to the theme of separation and individuation. Closely related, of course, are concerns about trusting and depending on the therapist when the relationship is clearly time-limited. For therapists, operating within a short-term framework heightens the importance of developing an adequate case conceptualization and a clear therapeutic focus within a reasonable time limit while maintaining an openness to what is truly occurring for patients, without imposing preconceptions upon them.

Operating within a short-term framework can also create a sense of urgency in therapists to accomplish something within the available time. It is vital that therapists not allow this feeling to pressure them into pushing or manipulating patients to satisfy their own needs. For this reason it is important to maintain the kind of lifespan perspective discussed earlier, in which therapy is viewed as one event in a change process that can extend over a long period, rather than as the ultimate cure.

Because of the specific demands of a short-term therapy framework, it becomes important to have some way of evaluating whether a particular patient is suitable for this approach. From a historical perspective, it is important to acknowledge that other orientations have struggled with the question of determining in advance a patient's suitability for their form of treatment. The work of D. H. Malan (1976) was influential in establishing a trend toward brief psychotherapy in

Britain. Malan's process of selection involves taking a psychiatric and a psychodynamic history and determining how the patient reacts to initial interpretations of what appear to be the patient's core neurotic conflicts. The patient's acceptance of early interpretations is seen as an indication of how well the therapy process might proceed. The two selection criteria that emerge from this assessment are an estimate of the patient's initial motivation for change as well as of the focality of the patient's complaint. The latter is especially important and is considered a good predictor of suitability if the patient's complaints are of an oedipal nature (usually described as a triangulation involving elements of a goal the patient has, a moral injunction or threat against the goal, and a defense used to reduce anxiety).

At about the same time, on the other side of the Atlantic, the work of Peter Sifneos (1972) and David Mann (1973) was addressing the same issues. Sifneos developed a short-term, anxiety-provoking psychotherapy that aimed to produce enduring characterological changes through the resolution of neurotic conflicts. Sifneos's procedure was also more confrontational and directive in its application. To be accepted into the therapy the patient would be given an initial screening interview to determine his or her ability to: 1) engage rapidly, 2) tolerate anxiety provoked by probing their defenses, and 3) adopt an active working stance during the brief time frame of this approach. In addition, the following characteristics were thought to predict a good outcome with this therapy:

1. Above average intelligence
2. A history of at least one meaningful relationship during the patient's life
3. The ability to interact well with the evaluator
4. A circumscribed chief complaint
5. A motivation for change

The work of David Mann (1973) also shares commonalities with the other two approaches described, that is, an emphasis on identifying a central issue to focus on in therapy. For Mann, patients ideally suited to this approach often tend to be in the midst of a developmental crisis, for example, college students dealing with issues of separation from parents or the definition of social, sexual, and career identities. Mann is not as stringent as Sifneos in specifying the need for superior intelligence in his patients. Perhaps the most important suitability indicator for Mann is the ability to identify a core conflict that can be worked on in therapy. Mann describes a number of conflicts involving independence versus dependence, activity versus passivity, adequate self-esteem versus diminished self-esteem, and resolved versus unresolved grief as themes especially well suited for this type of therapy.

Recently H. Davanloo (1980) has articulated an approach that is more ambitious in its scope than those previously discussed. He has widened his selection criteria to include individuals who suffer from a number of chronic debilitating disorders, such as obsessive/compulsive disorder, phobic neuroses, and even characterological problems where a number of active conflicts often prevent therapy from focusing on a single issue. Davanloo also claims that change in these more intractable problems can be achieved in a fairly short period of time (up to a maximum of thirty one-hour sessions). The criteria Davanloo articulates for selecting patients into his therapy include:

1. The presence of meaningful relationships in the past
2. Ability to tolerate anxiety, guilt, and the like
3. A sense of psychological mindedness
4. Motivation to tolerate the uncovering and working through of character problems
5. Positive responses to trial interpretations during a pre-therapy evaluation interview
6. Problems that have a predominantly oedipal focus

As this brief survey has demonstrated, current variants of brief psychodynamic therapy share many features when they attempt to specify which patients would benefit most from treatment. The exclusion criteria adopted by these therapies are also similar and generally seek to screen out individuals with severe depression and schizophreniform psychotic disorders, protracted substance abuse, and borderline or other disruptive personality disorder diagnoses. This combination of inclusion and exclusion criteria has caused some to question what percentage of patients would be suitable for therapies of this sort. Sifneos (1979), himself suggests that about 20 percent of outpatients would be appropriate for his approach, while R. J. Silver (1982), through an examination of Malan's published work, has also estimated that 20 percent of outpatients would be suitable for his approach. Davanloo, in contrast, considers his approach to be valuable for well more than 20 percent of the troubled individuals who visit psychotherapists.

Selection Criteria for Cognitive Therapy

We expect, as cognitive approaches to treatment become increasingly established in the therapy mainstream, that there will be a greater need for specifying which patients are most suitable for this kind of intervention.

Beck and coworkers (1979) have tried to address this issue by specifying a number of criteria that would justify the administration of cognitive therapy alone for the treatment of depression, meaning that medication would not be indicated if the patient met the following criteria:

1. Failure to respond to adequate trials of two antidepressants
2. Partial response to adequate doses of antidepressants
3. Failure to respond or only a partial response to other psychotherapies
4. Diagnosis of major affective disorder
5. Variable mood reactive to environmental events
6. Variable mood that correlates with variable cognitions
7. Mild symptomatic disturbances (sleep, appetite, weight)
8. Adequate reality testing (for example, no hallucinations or delusions)
9. An adequate span of concentration and adequate memory functioning
10. Inability to tolerate medication side effects, or evidence that excessive risk is associated with pharmacotherapy

One striking aspect of these criteria is the relative absence of the kind of psychological variables represented to a greater degree in the suitability schemes discussed earlier. In addition, cognitive therapy is indicated only after medication or other forms of therapy have not proven helpful. The emphasis is thus on targeting suitable candidates by their lack of suitability for other modalities, rather than on identifying features that are positive prognostic indicators for cognitive therapy.

Two recent studies have empirically investigated predictors of outcome in short-term cognitive therapy. M. J. V. Fennell and J. D. Teasdale (1987) found that patients who responded positively to a written treatment rationale and who reported a positive response to homework assignments benefited more from short-term cognitive therapy than those who did not. Persons, Burns, and J. M. Perloff (1988) found the following factors to be predictive of outcome: 1) low initial scores on the Beck Depression Inventory, 2) compliance with homework assignments, and 3) absence of endogenous symptoms. They also found that premature termination was more likely in patients with personality disorders.

Our Approach

Over the last five years we have been developing selection criteria and an accompanying interview format for evaluating the suitability of patients for short-term cognitive therapy. At a practical level, our efforts were initially motivated by a desire to streamline referrals to the Cognitive Therapy Unit at the Clarke Institute of Psychiatry in Toronto. We had observed that one consequence of the policy of accepting all patients referred to us, without restriction, was that there were always a percentage for whom short-term cognitive therapy proved to be an unproductive modality. Furthermore, this realization often became apparent fairly early on in the treatment process, and yet once the patients had been seen for a number of treatment sessions, it was difficult to terminate and refer elsewhere without concluding the therapy protocol. We felt that it would be useful to devise a method that would minimize frustration for both the patient and the therapist, an interview or screening format that would allow us to select patients most suitable for treatment by our unit.

The criteria that we have formalized into the selection process naturally reflect the theoretical emphasis we have evolved in our clinic and articulated in this book. At the same time, however, this theoretical emphasis is consistent with more widespread developments taking place in the field of cognitive therapy, such as the emphasis on the role of emotion in the change process (Foa and Kozak 1986; Guidano 1987; Mahoney 1985; Rachman 1980), the growing emphasis on the therapeutic relationship (for example, Jacobson 1989; Young in press), and the recognition of the role of security operations in maintaining a coherent sense of self (Guidano and Liotti 1983), or a sense of interpersonal relatedness (Safran 1984a; 1984b; 1990a; 1990b). For this reason, we believe that the usefulness of the current selection procedure extends beyond the specific approach described in this book, although different therapists or researchers may wish to make specific alterations in the procedure to meet the demands of their specific setting.

In choosing the items to be included in our screening interview, we drew upon insights gleaned from previous work (see Budman and Gurman 1988; Horowitz et al. 1984), and the recognition that, at present, the most reliable predictor of outcome for psychotherapy is the quality of the therapeutic alliance.

Bordin's (1979) conceptualization of the therapeutic alliance as consisting of bond, task, and goal components provided an important starting point for our thinking. By attempting to clarify the important tasks and goals in our therapeutic approach we were able to identify specific characteristics that suitable candidates would be likely to require.

Over an extended period of time we oscillated among theory, observation of intake interviews, and evaluation of clinical outcome, modifying both our selection criteria and our intake interviews as we became clearer about what variables seemed to be most predictive of outcome. Eventually, we formalized ten criteria into a rating scale, and developed an accompanying interviewer's manual (see appendix I for the interviewer's manual and item descriptions; see appendix II for the interview rating scales; and see appendix III for the suitability rating form). The rating scale for each item consists of five detailed descriptive anchors that are designed to increase reliability of ratings. Half-point ratings are allowed. The interviewer's manual is designed to guide the interviewer in probing for information required to make reliable ratings. This interview is designed to be used in a clinically sensitive manner, and the order of items probed can be modified to meet the demands of the specific situation.

An important feature of the interview involves the use of "successive test probes" designed to increase the possibility that patients will display important strengths and capacities that may not be immediately apparent. For example, the patient who has difficulty gaining access to automatic thoughts about something that happened over the week may be able to tap into automatic thoughts about something currently taking place in the session. The interview is designed to be conducted within one hour, although a second interview is usually scheduled to give the patient feedback and to fill in any missing information. Another advantage to scheduling a second interview is that it permits the interviewer to assess whether the patient follows through on an assignment between sessions. The ten items are:

1. Accessibility of automatic thoughts
2. Awareness and differentiation of emotions
3. Acceptance of personal responsibility for change

4. Compatibility with cognitive rationale
5. Alliance potential: in-session evidence
6. Alliance potential: out-of-session evidence, including previous therapy
7. Chronicity of problems
8. Security operations
9. Focality
10. General optimism regarding therapy

Accessibility of automatic thoughts. Determining how easy or difficult it is for patients to report on their ongoing construals or appraisals in problematic situations is important because a central task in cognitive therapy involves helping patients learn to decenter themselves from these relatively automatic appraisals and experience their own role in construing reality.

Awareness and differentiation of emotions. This item gauges the patient's ability to label different emotional states in retrospect as well as the ability to experience emotion in the present. The detection of fluctuations in mood is an essential prerequisite for monitoring automatic thoughts. Moreover, the ability to experience the relevant emotion in session is important for gaining access to relevant cognitive processes and articulating tacit construals. This ability to re-experience situations in an emotionally alive way means that the kind of information processing characteristic of a past situation will likely re-occur in session and, therefore, be more available for exploration.

Acceptance of personal responsibility for change. This item taps the extent to which patients see themselves as playing a role in their own recovery. Possibilities here range from models of change that view professionals as doing something to patients (for example, prescribing medication, telling patients what the problem is) to models in which patients take a more active role in their own therapy. This item overlaps somewhat with the one that follows.

Compatibility with cognitive rationale. This item gauges the extent to which the patient sees the value of important tasks, such as exploring the relationship between feelings and thoughts, using the therapeutic relationship as a vehicle for self-exploration, testing out expectations, and doing homework assignments.

Alliance potential: in-session evidence and out-of-session evidence. The next two items assess the patient's potential to form a therapeutic alliance. In-session evidence is collected by judging the quality of the relationship between the therapist and patient, while out-of-session evidence is based on a history of previous meaningful relationships, including previous therapy. These items are compatible with Bordin's bond component.

Chronicity of problems. This item rates the duration of the patient's problems. The hypothesis here is that problems showing a chronic course will be more difficult to work with and will probably require more open-ended therapy. Therefore, patients who rate very low on this item are considered to be less suitable than those whose symptom picture indicates a more recent onset.

Security Operations. This item assesses security operations on the basis of in-session interaction between the therapist and patient. An attempt is made to gauge the extent to which the intensity of the patient's security operations will block a reasonable amount of self-exploration within the short-term context. If patients engage in security operations that seem likely to block self-exploration, the interviewer attempts to evaluate whether they seem receptive to metacommunication about these operations and their underlying experience. The interviewer manual (appendix I) suggests specific assessment probes for this purpose. Patients who do not seem receptive to self-exploration or metacommunication may well become so at a later date, but they may require a longer term therapeutic approach in which their anxiety becomes modulated as they develop a trusting relationship.

Focality. This item gauges the patient's ability to maintain a problem focus. This is particularly important in a short-term approach where time is limited. Patients who have difficulty identifying and working with a central underlying theme may require a longer term approach.

General optimism or pessimism regarding therapy. This item estimates how hopeful patients are that the process of therapy can lead to change in their lives.

For a more complete description of these items and an elaboration of the context in which they are probed during the interview, please refer to the interviewer's manual in appendix I and the rating scales in appendix II.

Reliability of the Coding Scheme

In a reliability study, three raters rated a total of eleven suitability interviews conducted by four different interviewers. All ratings were made by starting at the lowest anchor on the scale and, if the rater's judgment justified it, moving up the scale. This kind of value allocation is similar to that used with other psychiatric rating scales (for example, Global Assessment of Functioning Scale, DSM-IIIR). Intraclass correlation coefficients were calculated to determine the level of agreement among raters for each item. They are as follows:

Item	Reliability
1. Accessibility of automatic thoughts	.82
2. Awareness of emotion	.75
3. Acceptance of responsibility for change	.77
4. Compatibility with rationale	.86
5. In-session alliance	.82
6. Out-of-session alliance	.80
7. Chronicity	.98
8. Security operations	.76
9. Focality	.46
10. Optimism/pessimism	.76

These coefficients indicate reasonably good reliability among raters.

Factor Structure and Construct Validity

While the individual items for the suitability interview were generated on the basis of conceptual considerations thought to reflect the important tasks and goals in cognitive therapy, it still remains to be determined whether the individual elements cohere together in a meaningful fashion. In order to examine this, a factor analysis was conducted that utilized forty-two clinic patients as subjects and examined the degree of intercorrelation between items and the factor structure of the suitability interview. The optimism/pessimism item was not included in this analysis, since it was developed subsequent to the other items, and ratings were thus not available on all forty-two subjects. Subject characteristics of the sample indicated that 52 percent of the sample were males while 48 percent were females. Ages ranged from 23 to 62 years with approximately 73 percent of the sample falling within the boundaries of 23 to 42 years of age. In addition, 45 percent of the sample were married or had remarried, while 40 percent were single, and 8 percent each were separated or divorced. Anxiety-based disorders and unipolar depression were the predominant diagnostic categories.

Table 10.1   Factor Structure

Factors	Percentage of Variance
Compatibility with tasks and goals	34.8
Bond	15.4
Refractoriness to change	11.9
	62.1% Total

Rotated Factor Matrix	Factor 1	Factor 2	Factor 3
Accessibility of automatic thoughts	.89294	−.01400	.23871
Compatibility with cognitive rationale	.74485	.23034	−.21587
Awareness of emotions	.58566	.16279	.11463
In-session alliance	.23259	.76770	−.33295
Acceptance of personal responsibility	.07776	.74225	.25140
Out-of-session alliance	.20333	.60511	.52968
Chronicity	−.10897	−.07302	.73318
Focality	.28940	.16224	.57298
Security operations	.49586	.36616	.50521

A principle components factor analysis with a varimax rotation extracted three factors accounting for 62.1 percent of the variance (see table 10.1). Factor 1 was composed of the items measuring the accessibility of automatic thoughts, compatibility with cognitive rationale, and awareness and differentiation of emotions; it accounted for 34.8 percent of the variance. Factor 2 was composed of items measuring the in-session alliance, acceptance of personal responsibility for change, and out-of-session alliance; it accounted for 15.4 percent of the variance. Finally, the third factor was composed of items measuring chronicity of difficulties, focality, and security operations. It accounted for 11.9 percent of the variance.

The extracted factor structure appears to be conceptually meaningful. Factor 1 seems to reflect both the capacity for engaging in the tasks of cognitive therapy and a general conviction on the patient's part that the tasks and goals are relevant. While the accessibility of automatic thoughts and awareness and differentiation of emotions dimensions gauge capacity for specific types of self-exploration, the compatibility with cognitive rationale dimension gauges the extent to which the patient believes in the relevance of the various tasks and goals of the treatment in a more general sense.

Factor 2 appears to be more closely related to the bond component of the therapeutic alliance. The clustering of the acceptance of personal responsibility dimension with the two alliance dimensions may reflect the possibility that the existence of a certain level of personal responsibility for change may be prerequisite for establishing the type of role relationship that permits the formation of a good bond. Patients who adopt an externalizing stance toward their problems often experience themselves as victims and others (including the therapist) as malicious and/or unhelpful. This type of interpersonal schema can easily lead to suspicion and mistrust, which can make it difficult to establish a good therapeutic bond.

Factor 3 appears to tap the refractoriness of the problem to change. The clustering together of focality and security operations may reflect the fact that difficulties in focusing often stem from an avoidance of anxiety-provoking issues. The clustering of these two dimensions with chronicity is particularly interesting since the first two dimensions involve an assessment of in-session performance, while the second dimension involves a simple rating of problem duration. Whether more extreme security operations lead to more chronic problems or vice versa is a matter of speculation. One hypothesis, however, is that in extreme cases intense security operations in the past may have made the patient's problems refractory to change by preventing potentially therapeutic interpersonal experiences and may continue to be an obstacle to change in therapy.

A second analysis evaluated the correlation between the suitability interview and a self-report measure of the therapeutic alliance administered at the third session. This is an important comparison to determine whether the suitability interview provides nonredundant information with a simple self-report therapeutic alliance inventory. The Working Alliance Inventory (WAI) (Horvath and Greenberg 1986) was administered to patients at the end of the third interview, and separate correlations were calculated between the total score on the WAI and each of the dimensions of the suitability measure, as well as the mean suitability score. The only significant correlation was with the in-session alliance dimension in the suitability interview, $r = .47$ ($p < .05$). This suggests that: 1) the therapeutic alliance rating based on in-session evidence emerging in the suitability interview is related to the therapeutic alliance as assessed from the patient's perspective on the WAI, and 2) the other nine dimensions in the suitability interview add information that is nonredundant with the WAI. It thus provides preliminary evidence relevant to the convergent validity of the in-session alliance item and offers some support for the discriminant validity of the suitability interview as a whole.

Predictive Validity

Data bearing on the predictive validity of the suitability interview were analyzed by calculating Pearson correlations between the mean of the suitability ratings and global assessment measures (administered only at termination) and by calculating partial correlations (controlling for pre-therapy severity level) with outcome measures administered before and after therapy. (Negative partial correlations indicate a positive association between high suitability ratings and low levels of symptomatology at termination). All correlations to be reported were significant (see table 10.2). The mean suitability score correlated .34 with the therapist's global ratings of success and .33 with the patient's global ratings of success. The partial correlations between the mean suitability score and the therapist's ratings of target complaints and the patient's ratings of target complaints were −.55 and −.34 respectively.

The mean suitability score also correlated significantly with outcome as measured by a number of psychometric tests. The partial correlation between the mean suitability score and the Beck Depression Inventory at termination was −.46. The partial correlations with the two subscales of the Automatic Thoughts Questionnaire (Hollon and Kendall 1980) were −.54 (frequency of automatic thoughts) and −.54 (degree of belief). In addition, the total suitability score correlated significantly with change in certain personality characteristics as measured by the avoidant ($r = -.43$), dependent ($r = -.43$), and passive-aggressive ($r = -.45$) scales of the Millon Clinical Multiaxial Inventory (Millon 1981).

Summary

These data provide preliminary evidence for the construct validity and predictive utility of the suitability interview. The interview appears to have a theoretically meaningful factor structure and preliminary evidence relevant to convergent and discriminant validity has been obtained. In addition, significant correlations were found between the total suitability score and a number of outcome measures. The results compare quite favorably with other attempts to predict therapy outcome.

Table 10.2   Correlations between Mean Suitability Rating
and Measures of Therapy Outcome

	Mean Suitability Score
Global Success Ratings	
Therapist Global Success Rating	.34*
Patient Global Success Rating	.33*
Therapy Termination Scores	
Therapist Ratings of Target Complaints	−.55‡
Patient Ratings of Target Complaints	−.34*
Beck Depression Inventory	−.46*
Automatic Thoughts Questionnaire (Frequency)	−.54†
Automatic Thoughts Questionnaire (Degree of Belief)	−.54†
Millon Clinical Multiaxial Inventory:	
—Avoidant	−.43*
—Dependent	−.43*
—Passive Aggressive	−.45*

NOTE:
1. Pearson correlations were calculated between mean suitability scores and global success ratings.
2. Partial correlations were calculated with post-therapy scores on all other measures, controlling for pre-therapy scores.
3. Negative correlations indicate a relationship between high suitability scores and low levels of symptomatology at therapy termination.

*p < .05
†p < .01
‡p < .001

For example, Marmar and his colleagues (1986) report correlations in the range of .27 to .35 for the external judges' version of the California Therapeutic Alliance Rating System, and found that while there was some consistency in predicting global ratings of outcome, specific measures of symptom change were difficult to predict. Horvath and Greenberg (1986) found that the Working Alliance Inventory, while predictive of patient post-therapy reports of change, was not predictive of changes in specific symptoms or personality variables. The ability of the current suitability interview to predict outcome as measured from both patient and therapist perspectives on both global outcome measures, as well as measures of specific symptoms and personality variables, is thus encouraging. Future research will be required to replicate these findings with other samples.

CHAPTER 11

Conclusion

Summary of Central Principles

The therapeutic approach we have described draws upon a number of traditions, including cognitive therapy, interpersonal therapy, gestalt therapy, and client-centered therapy. It thus shares specific features in common with each of these approaches. Because of its integrative nature, however, it does not overlap completely with any one. In this chapter we summarize the main principles of our approach. A therapy adherence scale, which can be used for training purposes and for evaluating a therapist's adherence to treatment protocol in research investigations, can be found in appendix IV.

The central principles are:

1. This approach emphasizes phenomenological exploration rather than interpretation. We assume that only patients can be experts on their experience and that interpreting their experience for them deprives them of the important opportunity of articulating it for themselves. An interpretation, even if sufficiently accurate to be accepted by the patient, may still not capture the subtle nuances of the affective experience. Moreover, an interpretation may be sufficiently attuned to the patient's inner experience to be "allowed in," but subtly misattuned in a way that alters the nature of the experience. This parallels a phenomenon, referred to by Stern (1985) as "emotional theft," in which a mother attunes to the infant's state, establishes a

shared experience, and then changes the experience so that it is lost to the child.

2. It emphasizes accessing and modifying cognitive processes in an emotionally immediate way. It assumes that cognitive processes that are split off from patients' affective experiences do not fully represent their organismic experiences. For this reason, working in an emotionally immediate fashion is fundamental to change.

3. It emphasizes using the therapeutic relationship as a laboratory for exploring cognitive/affective processes and challenging interpersonal schemas. It does not, however, assume that patterns emerging in the therapeutic relationship will necessarily parallel other important patterns in the patient's life. It, therefore, advocates that therapists take responsibility for their role in the interaction.

4. It emphasizes the in-depth exploration of the patient's construal processes in context of the therapeutic interaction before explicitly identifying interpersonal patterns. As a rule, any linking of the therapeutic interaction to other interpersonal relationships occurs *after* a specific therapist/patient interaction has been explored in depth, the therapist has acknowledged his or her contribution to the interaction, and the patient has acquired a tangible sense of his or her own internal experience during this interaction. The patient can then monitor for similar experiences between sessions.

5. It advocates formulating an understanding of the patient's interpersonal schema and continually revising this understanding.

6. It advocates using the therapists' own feelings to generate hypotheses about interpersonal patterns that are characteristic for patients and to help identify interpersonal markers, or characteristic interpersonal acts and communications that play an important role in patients' cognitive-interpersonal cycles.

7. It emphasizes using interpersonal markers as junctures for cognitive/affective exploration.

8. It emphasizes promoting generalization, both through the in-depth exploration of out-of-session events, and through the assignment of experiments between sessions. Beliefs and expectations that are discovered by using the vehicle of the therapeutic relationship become topics for self-monitoring and further experimentation between sessions.

240

9. It advocates enlisting the patient as an active collaborator by exploring and testing out beliefs and expectations, both in the therapeutic relationship and outside of therapy. The therapist facilitates the processing of schema disconfirming information by using active cognitive interventions to articulate explicitly the patient's expectations and to draw the patient's attention to whether these expectations are being confirmed.

10. It emphasizes the importance of detecting and working through ruptures in the therapeutic alliance. Therapists continually monitor fluctuations in their experience of interpersonal distance from the patient and use this experience as a clue to the quality of the alliance. The healing of alliance ruptures is hypothesized to be a particularly potent change event.

11. It emphasizes the therapist's active role in exploring the patient's cognitive/affective processes and in designing experiments, while maintaining an ongoing receptivity to events emerging in the moment that signal a need to shift focus.

12. It emphasizes maintaining a therapeutic focus by paying careful attention to what is emotionally alive for patients and by using accurate empathic reflection to facilitate a deepening of experience, thereby helping patients to make contact with core issues. The therapist's assessment of what is salient at any given moment is determined by integrating several sources of information at a tacit level, including the patient's verbal content, nonverbal behavior, and level of emotional involvement, the therapist's own feelings about previous interactions with the patient, and the patient's interactions with other people.

Research Directions

Our approach suggests a number of important research directions, which can be divided into two general categories: psychotherapy outcome studies and psychotherapy process studies.

Outcome Studies

The first general strategy consists of using a conventional aggregate analysis, clinical trial approach to compare the efficacy of a more traditional cognitive therapy (for example, Beck, Rush et al. 1979) with the approach outlined here. In a study of this kind it is important to employ a wide variety of dependent measures to tap changes that, in theory, would be more likely to be activated by an integrative cognitive approach than by traditional cognitive therapy. For example, it may be that although traditional cognitive therapy results in the remission of depressive symptomatology, a more integrative approach would have impact on subtler areas of interpersonal functioning.

In this type of study it is critical to have an adequate follow-up period. While pure-form cognitive therapy and a more integrative approach may appear equally effective at termination, differences may emerge at follow-up. It may be that a pure-form cognitive therapist, although achieving symptom remission at termination, unwittingly confirms dysfunctional beliefs about self-other interactions by failing to attend adequately to the therapeutic relationship, thus increasing the risk of relapse. In contrast, integrative cognitive therapists may be able to effect more enduring changes in modifying core dysfunctional cognitive structures by disconfirming dysfunctional interpersonal expectations through their own behavior in the sessions. Differences between the two approaches that do not show up at termination may thus emerge at follow-up.

While this type of clinical trial study may have some utility for purposes of demonstrating the utility of a more integrative approach, the general failure of clinical trial studies to demonstrate consistent differences among different forms of psychotherapy suggests that an alternative research strategy may be required. A second research strategy involves identifying treatment failures in traditional cognitive therapy and evaluating them to see whether implementing the current approach can bring about change in those who have not benefited from treatment. This general research strategy has the advantage of capitalizing on an important intuition about why an integrative approach might be preferable to pure-form cognitive therapy. In any psychotherapy study there are always those patients who benefit from treatment and those who do not. Those patients who already benefit from a specific pure-form psychotherapy are not likely to receive incremental benefit from exposure to an integrative approach, but those who do not benefit from the pure-form psychotherapy (that is, those who have difficulty establishing an adequate therapeutic alliance or those who have difficulty gaining access to important cognitive processes) stand to gain from the implementation of an integrative approach.

Because any clinical trial comparing the efficacy of an integrative to a pure-form psychotherapy will find a large proportion of patients deriving substantial benefit from the pure-form psychotherapy, differences between the integrative and pure-form approaches may be washed out. Thus the conventional clinical trial strategy may not be powerful enough to detect differences between these two approaches because of its use of aggregate data and its failure to attend to relevant individual differences.

For this reason, a more powerful design may consist of beginning with a large number of patients in a more traditional cognitive therapy treatment condition and then identifying those who do not appear to be benefiting after a certain point in therapy. Once potential treatment failures have been identified, they can be randomly assigned either to continue in the original treatment or add integrative therapy components to their treatment.

A second alternative outcome research strategy is to identify patients in advance who are predicted to be potential treatment failures with traditional cognitive therapy (for example, patients with diagnosed personality disorders) and randomly assign them to traditional cognitive therapy or to the integrative approach in a clinical trial study.

Process Studies

Another important research direction involves evaluating hypotheses about the mechanisms through which change takes place, beginning with the basic hypothesis about the centrality of the therapeutic alliance to the therapeutic process. Preliminary findings in our clinic suggest that the quality of the therapeutic alliance does predict outcome when patients are treated with the approach described in this book (Safran 1989). Twenty-two patients diagnosed with depression and anxiety-related disorders were treated in a twenty-session protocol of this therapeutic approach. Both the Working Alliance Inventory (WAI) (Horvath and Greenberg 1986) and the California Psychotherapy Alliance Scale (CALPAS) (Marmar et al. 1987) were administered following the third session, and were found to predict outcome significantly on a number of dependent measures, including therapist and patient global success ratings, therapist target complaint ratings, and the Beck Depression Inventory. It will be important for future investigations to replicate these findings with larger samples.

Another important line of research involves investigating the process through which ruptures in the therapeutic alliance become resolved. Safran, Crocker, and coworkers (in press) have developed a preliminary model of this process, which consists of seven stages:

1. The therapist empathizes with negative feelings and establishes a focus on the here and now.
2. The patient engages in assertive behavior alternating with deference or dependency.
3. The therapist explores the patient's fears of directly expressing negative sentiments.
4. The patient accesses fears of expressing negative sentiments and self-assertion.
5. The therapist empathizes with these fears.
6. The patient expresses negative sentiments in a direct, self-assertive fashion.
7. The therapist validates the patient's experience and acknowledges his or her own role in the interaction.

We are currently refining the model through a combination of qualitative and quantitative research methodologies that involve operationalizing the stages with reliable process coding systems and looking for recurring patterns across cases. An important step will be to test a refined version of the model by evaluating whether the hypothesized stages are regularly associated with alliance ruptures that become resolved.

Another important research direction will involve evaluating the central hypothesis that therapist-patient interactions that disconfirm the patient's dysfunctional interpersonal schemas are positively related to both immediate and ultimate outcome. To do this, it will first be necessary to develop a procedure for reliably formulating the nature of the patient's core dysfunctional interpersonal schema and evaluating whether the therapist's actions are schema confirming or schema disconfirming.

This could be accomplished by adapting Weiss and colleagues' (1987) methodology for assessing pathogenic beliefs and relevant tests in psychodynamic therapy. Their series of studies has now demonstrated that patients' pathogenic beliefs can be formulated reliably, and that the disconfirmation of these pathogenic beliefs is related to both immediate and ultimate outcome. G. Silberschatz (1987), for example, demonstrated that the disconfirmation of pathogenic beliefs is significantly correlated with an immediate reduction in patient anxiety, an increase in patient relaxation, and an increase in the extent to which the patient confronts elaborate, bold, or nontrivial material. J. Caston, R. Goldman, and M. M. McClure (1987) found a relationship between the in-session disconfirmation of pathogenic beliefs and immediate increases in insight and the elaboration of nontrivial material. Silberschatz, P. B. Fretter, and J. T. Curtis (1986) found a relationship between immediate increases in patients' experiencing level and disconfirmation of pathogenic beliefs. They also found that good ultimate outcome was associated with a higher proportion of pathogenic belief disconfirming interventions to confirming interventions.

While there are certain theoretical differences between the conceptual framework of Weiss and colleagues and our approach, Collins and Messer (1988) have recently demonstrated that the basic Mount Zion Group methodology can be adapted for use with a different theoretical orientation. An important step would thus be to adapt Weiss and colleagues' methodology so that it can reliably assess the interpersonal schema construct as described in this book and evaluate the hypothesis that therapist interventions that are schema inconsistent are related to both immediate and ultimate outcome. A related investigation would involve evaluating the hypothesis that the quality of the therapeutic alliance is mediated by whether or not the therapist acts in a way that disconfirms the patient's interpersonal schema.

Still another line of investigation involves evaluating the hypothesis that one factor mediating the immediate outcome of traditional cognitive therapy challenging interventions (for example, examining the evidence or considering alternatives) is whether the intervention confirms or disconfirms the patient's dysfunctional interpersonal schema at a process level. A central thesis in our approach is that the impact of any intervention is the result of the interaction between the particular features of that intervention and the patient's interpersonal schema. Using an adaptation of Weiss and colleagues' (1987) methodology, this hypothesis could be evaluated by having independent raters appraise the amount of cognitive change that takes place following every challenging intervention, and then rate the extent to which these interventions are schema confirming or disconfirming. The current theory hypothesizes that any intervention (whether it is a challenging intervention in cognitive therapy or an interpretation in psychodynamic therapy) that confirms the patient's core interpersonal schema at a process level will lead to a poor immediate outcome, even if it is accurate or on target at a content level.

A final research direction involves developing measures of patients' interpersonal schemas and evaluating whether change on these measures is related to treatment outcome and maintenance of treatment gains. Safran, K. Hill, and C. Ford, in a pilot study (reported in Safran, Segal, et al. in press), developed a questionnaire to evaluate subjects' expectations of how three significant others (mother, father, and friend) would respond to a range of interpersonal behaviors that the subjects might present. Sixteen different interpersonal behaviors were derived from Kiesler's (1983) interpersonal circle. Each of these behaviors represented one of the sixteen segments of the interpersonal circumplex. Subjects were then asked to indicate the kind of response expected from each of the three significant others to each of the behaviors and to rate the desirability of each response. Ninety-nine college undergraduate subjects were administered the questionnaire and then divided into low-symptomatic versus high-symptomatic groups based on their responses to the Symptom Check List - 90 (SCL-90) (Derogatis 1977). It was found that low-symptomatic subjects expected significantly more desirable responses from each of the "others." Hill and Safran (1990) administered the same questionnaire to a sample of 216 undergraduate subjects, who were once again divided into low-symptomatic and high-symptomatic groups on the basis of the SCL-90. This study also found that low-symptomatic subjects expected significantly more desirable responses from the "others," and that, moreover, they expected responses that were significantly more sociable, affiliative, and trusting. In addition, the study found that low-symptomatic subjects tended to expect complementary responses to agreeable interpersonal acts, whereas high-symptomatic subjects tended to expect complementary responses to hostile or quarrelsome interpersonal acts. We are currently evaluating whether patients who show changes in their response to this instrument over the course of therapy show greater maintenance of treatment gains at follow-up than patients not reporting changes.

Summary

The field of cognitive therapy is currently undergoing a rapid expansion. This volume represents one attempt to systematize some of the changes taking place in clinical practice by broadening both theory and technique through the incorporation of principles from a number of different therapy traditions. In this chapter we have summarized the central principles of the current approach and outlined a number of relevant research directions. Our hope is to stimulate the kind of research investigation that will keep these and future developments empirically grounded, thereby facilitating the continuing vitality of the field.

Epilogue

All real living is meeting. The relation to the Thou is direct. No system of ideas, no foreknowledge, and no fancy intervene between I and Thou. The memory itself is transformed, as it plunges out of its isolation into the unity of the whole. No aim, no lust, and no anticipation intervene between I and Thou. Desire itself is transformed as it plunges out of its dream into the appearance. Every means is an obstacle. Only when every means has collapsed does the meeting come about.

—MARTIN BUBER

The Authentic Human Encounter

Because of the dysfunctional cognitive-interpersonal cycles that are characteristic of people seeking therapy, patients have difficulty meeting others in an authentic fashion. Because of the desperateness of their need for interpersonal relatedness, they disown parts of themselves. They also have difficulty accepting others as they are and attempt to shape them to meet their needs for human contact. Because of the dysfunctional strategies that they have learned for maintaining interpersonal relatedness, they have difficulty revealing their authentic selves to others. Others, in turn, are alienated by patients' lack of self-contact and by their dysfunctional interpersonal maneuvers, and behave in a way that confirms patients' worst fears about human relationships. Others have difficulty seeing the patient as a whole person and instead relate to the fragmented parts that are presented. They become ensnared in the patient's cognitive-interpersonal cycle and suppress or have difficulty fully accepting the confused and contra-

248

dictory feelings that are often aroused in them. They respond in various ways out of their own needs to maintain self-esteem.

People seeking help thus live in a state of alienation, both from themselves and from others. The purpose of therapy is to help them reduce this state of alienation. To do this, the therapist must overcome the obstacles to relatedness created by their alienation from themselves and their dysfunctional strategies for maintaining relatedness, and provide a relationship in which they can learn that they do not have to disown parts of themselves.

By not participating in their cognitive-interpersonal cycles, the therapist can provide patients with an experience that is lacking in their lives—an authentic human encounter, or what Buber referred to as an I-Thou relationship. In this kind of relationship, one accepts patients fully as they are. Rather than acting out of anger or desire to protect one's own self-esteem or to meet one's own needs, one attempts to use one's feelings as tools in the service of the patient. Rather than suppressing parts of oneself that one finds threatening, one attempts to harness them to the therapeutic process. Rather then attempting to use patients in therapy to maintain one's own self-esteem, one endeavors to accept them wherever they are—to meet them in their wholeness.

Throughout this book we have emphasized the centrality of the therapeutic relationship in promoting change. We have attempted to provide a theoretical framework for clarifying the connection between the relationship and the technical aspects of therapy. Indeed, we have argued that these two aspects of the process are ultimately inseparable. We have also provided technical suggestions to aid the therapist in making use of the therapeutic relationship to facilitate the change process.

Ultimately, however, it must be remembered that all theoretical concepts and techniques described in this book are merely tools; they are tools designed to help the therapist overcome the obstacles to having an I-Thou relationship with the patient. These tools themselves, however, can become obstacles if they are used to avoid authentic human encounters, rather than to facilitate them. As an old Zen saying puts it: "The right tools in the hands of the wrong man become the wrong tools." The wise therapist will thus not confuse the particular vehicle for change described in this book with the underlying essence of change.

Therapists who let concepts blind them to the reality of what is truly happening for their patients in the moment are relating to the patient as an object, or in Buber's phraseology, an "It" rather than a "Thou." Therapists who hide behind the security of the conceptual framework provided here rather than risking authentic human encounters, which could lead to therapists' transcending all roles and preconceptions about how they themselves should be, rule out the possibility of the very experiences in human relatedness that will be healing for their patients.

This does not mean that concepts and techniques are not important or that the therapist must never objectify the patient. The process of participant-observation, at times, requires treating both the patient and the self as objects. Ultimately, however, the therapist must be able to transcend this objectifying process to have a true meeting with the patient in which both parties become more fully human.

APPENDIX I

Suitability for Short-Term Cognitive Therapy Interview

Selection Criteria Manual

The purpose of this manual is to provide a general guideline for interviewing patients to evaluate their suitability for short-term cognitive therapy. The manual is to be used in conjunction with the selection criteria for short-term cognitive therapy, and its objective is to facilitate the process of eliciting information that will provide an adequate data base for rating the selection criteria on a nine-point scale. The dimensions to be rated by judges are:

1. accessibility of automatic thoughts
2. awareness and differentiation of emotions
3. acceptance of personal responsibility for change
4. compatibility with cognitive rationale
5. alliance potential (in-session evidence)
6. alliance potential (out-of-session evidence)
7. chronicity versus acuteness
8. security operations
9. focality
10. general optimism/pessimism about therapy

All dimensions are rated on a 9 (1–5 with half-point ratings) point scale. These rating scales are anchored so that 5 indicates the best prognosis and 1 indicates the worst prognosis.

The interview should take approximately one hour. It is important for the interviewer to have some basic biographical, historical, and diagnostic information *before* the interview. Obtaining advance information will permit the interviewer to focus on the specific areas that will yield information relevant to the selection criteria ratings.

There is no specific structure to the interview, and the interviewer should feel free to move back and forth among areas as he or she sees fit. This will allow the interviewer to take advantage of the natural flow of the interview to tap into different areas at clinically opportune times. For example, should the patient indicate that he or she is feeling anxious, the interviewer should feel free to probe for automatic thoughts, because this will provide important data on the patient's ability to gain access to these thoughts in the alive and controlled environment of the therapeutic situation.

An important feature of this interview is the use of "successive test probes." If, for example, the patient spontaneously discloses automatic thoughts, no further probing may be required in this area. If, however, automatic thoughts are not forthcoming, the interviewer may wish to encourage the patient to describe a problematic situation in concrete detail. If automatic thoughts are still not accessible, the interviewer may wish to explore the patient's thoughts about the interview situation. The basic idea is to provide patients with an optimal opportunity to reveal whatever therapy-relevant capacities they have.

Although there is no rigid structure, it is usually helpful to open the interview with a general question about the patient's present problems. Once the patient has provided a general description of current problems, it is useful to ask for an example as soon as possible. Once the patient provides a concrete example, the stage is set to probe for accessibility of automatic thoughts and awareness and differentiation of emotions.

Accessibility of Automatic Thoughts

Once the patient has described a specific problem situation, the therapist can use this opportunity to probe for automatic thoughts. Such questions as: "What were you thinking in that situation?" or "Do you recall what was going on in your mind?" are examples of simple and useful basic probes.

If the patient has difficulty recalling or reporting automatic thoughts, it can be useful to help him or her relive the situation in the present by having the patient describe the situation as concretely and vividly as possible. It may be useful to ask the patient to use imagery and to attempt to get a picture in mind of the exact situation and the events that took place.

Once the patient describes the situation vividly, the interviewer can ask questions such as "Can you see yourself in that situation right now?" If the patient indicates that he or she can, the therapist can ask: "What's going through your mind?" "Can you get a sense of the thoughts that are racing through your mind?"

A third alternative consists of probing for them in the session. Patients who have difficulty recalling automatic thoughts in past problem situations may be able to capture them in the immediacy of the therapeutic situation. Here, it can be useful for the therapist to probe for automatic thoughts if the patient reports a fluctuation in mood during the session (for example, "I'm feeling really anxious now" or "I'm feeling really sad"), or if the therapist notes nonverbal cues consistent with emotional fluctuations (for example, the patient begins to look extremely sad or clasps the chair tensely).

Although probing for automatic thoughts in the immediacy of the therapeutic situation may provide access to cognitive processes not accessible in the other two ways, one must remember that some patients may have more difficulty gaining access to automatic thoughts about the therapeutic interaction, because the process may be too threatening to them.

In general, the patient's ability to speak of his or her feelings and thoughts about the therapeutic interaction is a good prognostic indicator, because this kind of interaction is often essential in working out misunderstandings and communication problems that impede the development of a good therapeutic alliance.

Awareness and Differentiation of Emotions

Once the patient has described a specific situation, the interviewer can probe for the patient's ability to become aware of and label different emotional states and to notice fluctuations in emotions. Examples of relevant probes would be:

"Do you remember what you were feeling in that situation?"

"What was that feeling like?"

"Is that different from the way you normally feel?"

"How strong or intense was that feeling?"

"As you think about that situation or imagine it, can you get in touch with that feeling at all now?"

"If so, what does it feel like?"

These last two questions gauge not only the patient's ability to differentiate between different emotional states in retrospect, but also his or her ability to re-experience different emotional states in the present. This latter ability can be extremely useful for purposes of gaining access to mood dependent cognitions or "hot cognitions" in the therapy session.

In addition to asking the patient to recall emotional experiences from the past, it is useful for the therapist to be attentive to nonverbal markers of emotional fluctuations in the session. For example, if the interviewer notices the patient suddenly tensing in the interview, it can be useful for him or her to ask: "What are you experiencing now?" This kind of probe will help tap into the patient's ability to be aware of and report emotional fluctuations occurring in the present.

Acceptance of Personal Responsibility for Change and Compatibility with the Cognitive Rationale

We will deal with these together, because the same probes may yield information relevant to both criteria. The interviewer can begin to probe with general questions about the patient's understanding and expectations of psychotherapy in general and cognitive therapy specifically. For example: "What is your understanding of how cognitive therapy works?" If the patient appears to have a reasonable preliminary understanding of the way cognitive therapy works, the therapist may ask questions such as: "Does what you understand so far make sense to you?", "Is there anything unclear or confusing for you?"

This latter question can be a subtle way of assessing reservations and skepticism. For example, if the patient says, "I just don't understand how becoming aware of your negative thoughts is going to change the way you feel," the therapist may attempt to clarify this issue. If, after repeated attempts at clarification, the patient continues to be confused, this is a negative prognostic indicator.

If the patient appears to know nothing about cognitive therapy, the interviewer should provide a simple and basic description. *In an interpersonally oriented form of cognitive therapy, the therapist must supplement the standard cognitive therapy rationale (that is, the emphasis on examining the relationship between thinking and feeling, and active participation in experiments during the week), with the idea that the therapeutic relationship is often used as a laboratory for exploring cognitive and interpersonal processes.* Following a brief outline of the rationale, the therapist can ask the patient if there are any questions. If, after repeated attempts at clarification, the patient continues to be unclear or confused, this—again—is a negative prognostic indicator. In addition to the foregoing general questions, the interviewer can ask questions like, "What is your understanding of the role that the therapist plays in therapy?" or "What role do you see the patient playing in therapy?" This can elicit important information about the patient's understanding of who ultimately assumes responsibility for change in therapy.

Other relevant probes include questions like, "What is your understanding of what causes your problems?" This can yield important information about whether the patient attributes the problem to internal sources ("the way I look at myself") or to external sources ("It's a hormonal imbalance" or "I had a bad upbringing").

Alliance Potential (In-Session Evidence)

Although this dimension can often be rated without extensive probing, it may be useful for the interviewer to ask some basic questions about the patient's perception of the therapeutic interaction such as, "How are you feeling about what's going on right now?" or after the interview, "How are you feeling about our interview today?" It is particularly important to ask such questions if there appears to be a misunderstanding or if the communication appears blocked in any way. If the patient is able to deal directly with his concerns or reservations about the therapeutic interview, this can be a good prognostic indicator.

Alliance Potential (Out-of-Session Evidence)

For this rating, it is important for the interviewer to ask questions about both earlier and current intimate relationships. A variety of probes can be useful, ranging from questions about how the patient got along with and perceives his or her parents, the relationship with siblings, to the relationship with friends in school. In the past, has the patient had close intimate relationships and people in whom he or she could confide? Currently, is there anyone the patient can confide in? Such information can be useful to raters in assessing the dimension of trust versus mistrust, and whether the patient has been or currently is trusting enough to form the kind of alliance necessary for progress in short-term therapy.

One of the most important sources of information here is the history of previous therapeutic relationships. The interviewer should thus ask for a detailed description of previous therapeutic relationships, the outcome of those experiences, and the patient's perception of other therapists seen in treatment. Should the patient report that he or she has not benefited from a previous therapy experience or experiences, the therapist must then assess the patient's perception of what went wrong in those interactions. By probing for this information, one can detect whether the patient engages in externalizing or excessive blaming or in a pattern of idealizing and then devaluating the therapist. An overly positive evaluation of a previous therapy experience may reveal a tendency for the patient to idealize the therapist rather than to form a productive working alliance in which the patient assumes responsibility for change.

Chronicity versus Acuteness

Information about this dimension can be obtained with simple, basic probes about the onset, history, and course of the present problem.

Security Operations

The interviewer's task here is to note and observe the patient's security operations during the session. Security operations can be defined as psychological processes and behaviors that function to maintain the individual's self-esteem and to restore their sense of psychological security when it is threatened. A major theoretical assumption in a cognitive-interpersonal framework is that experiences that threaten the individual's self-esteem evoke anxiety, and that a variety of different styles of interaction may be employed to decrease that anxiety and maintain a positive view of self. These styles vary in kind, intensity, and degree to which they interfere with the integration of interpersonal situations and are potential obstacles to therapy. Although we do not attempt to categorize security operations, some examples may be useful: attempts to control the interview; tangential or circumlocutory talking that makes it difficult to deal with any one subject in depth; changing the topic; excessive confusion in the interview; preoccupation with topics that distract from themes associated with anxiety; dealing with issues in an overly rational way; blaming others for one's own weaknesses and vulnerabilities.

If the patient's security operations do not appear to constitute an obstacle to short-term cognitive therapy, no probes are required here. If, however, the interviewer determines that the communication process is sufficiently blocked by security operations to constitute a substantial obstacle to short-term therapy, it is then necessary to probe here to assess whether the patient can tolerate anxiety well enough to modulate these operations when they are drawn to his or her attention. For example, the therapist who notices that the patient skims superficially from topic to topic without ever dealing with an issue may draw this pattern to the patient's attention in a nonthreatening way and ask whether he or she is aware of it. Or, the interviewer who observes that the patient deals with an emotionally laden topic in an extremely rational and intellectually distant way, may draw this to the patient's attention and ask what his or her current experience is. Of course, the ability to probe appropriately in this context, requires a therapist who is adept at continuous monitoring of the therapeutic process and its communication fluctuations.

Focality

Focality refers to the patient's ability to work within a problem-oriented focus. A good deal of this work in cognitive therapy relies on the examination of patient behavior in specific problematic situations. The ability to be problem-focused involves starting with the situation at hand—not straying to other things that may have also happened in the patient's life—and being able to explore the situation with the therapist in depth. This item gauges how comfortable patients are at working in a framework where their problems are broken into subunits, or targets which are then explored in greater depth. Poor focality would be indicated by the inability to work within such a model. Evidence of such behavior is: wanting to work on everything at once, raising multiple problems while attempting to work on a single difficulty, or being unable to elaborate upon a situation of interest without bringing in tangential information from other situations.

Patient Optimism/Pessimism about Therapy

This item is intended to provide a global estimate of the degree to which the patient feels hopeful or hopeless about the possibility of therapy leading to change in his or her life. Raters will often have to rely on their global impressions or evaluations, because the information relevant to rating may not be probed directly, but permeate the interview as a whole. The item bears some resemblance to Frank's (1973) notion of the level of demoralization in a patient and its effect on the healing process. The question being asked is "In a general sense, how much does the patient feel he or she is likely to benefit from therapy?"

APPENDIX II

Suitability for Short-Term Cognitive Therapy Rating Scales

These anchored scales are to be used in conjunction with the suitability interview. High ratings indicate good prognosis and low ratings indicate poor prognosis. Although only 5 scale points are anchored, half point ratings (for example, 2.5) are permissible.

Ratings should not be made in the absence of adequate information. Thus, if the interviewer has not adequately probed an area and the patient does not spontaneously provide relevant information, a code of "0" should be assigned.

Accessibility of Automatic Thoughts

Instructions to Raters

In rating this item, *two* dimensions are considered:

a. The *ease* with which the patient accesses and articulates automatic thoughts and dysfunctional beliefs. This necessitates some consideration of the *quantity* and *quality* of probing by the therapist.
b. The *level* of self-reference reflected in the automatic thoughts the patient reports.

Score '1' when the patient is unable to gain access to *any* automatic thoughts (that is, is unaware of "self talk," does not report "mental pictures," and does not see the relationship between his or her own thinking and emotions).

Score '5' when the patient *spontaneously* reports automatic thoughts that appear to be core or central to the patient's conception of self.

Score '2' to '4' depending on the level of automatic thoughts reported. For example, a rating of '2' reflects automatic thoughts reported that are judged to be less core, less central than a rating of '4.'

0	0.5	1	1.5	2	2.5	3	3.5	4	4.5	5

0   Do *not* rate. Insufficient information.
1   Patient appears to be completely unable to gain access to automatic thoughts.
2   Patient is able to gain access to one or two automatic thoughts.
3   Patient is able to gain access to some automatic thoughts.
4   Patient is able to gain access to a number of important automatic thoughts.
5   Patient *readily* gains access to central automatic thoughts.

Awareness and Differentiation of Emotions

Instructions to Raters

This scale combines two dimensions. At the lower end of the scale it is concerned with the patient's ability simply to label and differentiate among emotional states. It is assumed that this ability helps the patient gain access to automatic thoughts. At the higher end of the scale it incorporates the additional dimension of "experiencing emotions in an emotionally immediate way." This dimension is more closely allied to the Experiencing Scale in experiential therapy. It is assumed that this kind of experiential processing is instrumental in helping patients gain access to tacit idiosyncratic meaning related to core cognitive processes and in helping them gain a tangible understanding of the impact that their cognitive processes have upon their experience (in other words, helping them to decenter). It is important to note that patients can receive a high score without necessarily displaying a wide range of emotions.

0	0.5	1	1.5	2	2.5	3	3.5	4	4.5	5

0   Do *not* rate. Insufficient information.
1   Patient appears completely unable to recognize fluctuations in emotional quality or intensity between sessions and is not able to verbalize changes in emotion during session. Appears completely cut off from emotional experience.
2   Patient reports some fluctuation in quality and intensity of mood outside of session, but with considerable difficulty.
3   Patient is able to report some fluctuation in emotional quality and intensity between sessions, and displays some ability to experience those feelings in session.
4   Patient can identify and experience fluctuation in emotional quality and intensity both in and out of session. Patient shows some ability to use emotions as a vehicle for further self-exploration.
5   Patient is extremely good at labeling and differentiating emotional experience, both in and out of session, and processes experience in session in an emotionally authentic fashion. Patient shows clear ability to use emotions in session as a vehicle for further self-exploration.

Acceptance of Personal Responsibility for Change

Instructions to Raters

This item gauges the patient's beliefs about his or her role in the change process. It is important to distinguish between self-blame and self-criticism and a willingness to accept responsibility for the change process, as patients may present with hopeless ideation but still recognize that they must play a role in the change process.

An important distinction between ratings of 2 and 3 relates to how genuine patients are in their remarks about personal responsibility. One example of a 2 rating would be a patient who first espouses the idea of taking personal responsibility and then contradicts that view at another point in the interview. A rating of 3 would be assigned to someone who is genuinely struggling with the issue of personal responsibility.

0	0.5	1	1.5	2	2.5	3	3.5	4	4.5	5

0   Do *not* rate. Insufficient information.
1   Patient does not accept responsibility for change, feeling instead that change will come from some external source, for example:
   a. "A magical solution."
   b. "The right combination of medication will be found and this alone will improve my mood."
   c. "The therapist will give me the answer."
2   Patient claims to be able to facilitate change through his or her actions, but there is a hackneyed quality or lip-service in these remarks.
3   Patient has some awareness that his or her efforts are important in the change process, but is honestly fluctuating between this recognition and an externalizing stance.
4   Patient generally accepts responsibility for the change process but may lapse into an externalizing stance slightly or occasionally.
5   Patient recognizes and endorses the role his or her efforts will play in the change process, for example:
   a. "You can point me in the right direction, but I know I have to do the work myself."
   b. "I know I'm the only one who can help myself."

Compatibility with Cognitive Rationale

Instructions to Raters

This item is intended to assess basic compatibility between the patient's conceptualization of the problem and the change process and the cognitive rationale provided by the therapist. It incorporates the task and goal dimensions of the therapeutic alliance. Relevant tasks in an interpersonally oriented form of cognitive therapy would include such activities as: monitoring thoughts and feelings, doing experiments between sessions, and using the therapeutic relationship as a laboratory for exploring thoughts, feelings, and interpersonal issues.

0	0.5	1	1.5	2	2.5	3	3.5	4	4.5	5

0   Do *not* rate. Insufficient information.
1   Patient does not see a relationship between thinking and feeling and/or clearly subscribes to an alternative model (for example, biological or psychoanalytic, which he or she views as incompatible) or clearly rejects central tasks (for example, homework, self-monitoring) or goals (for example, believes that twenty sessions will not be adequate). Patient rejects the value of the central tasks.
2   Patient has difficulty in understanding the cognitive rationale and/or in seeing the value in the tasks of cognitive therapy.
3   Patient *appears* to understand cognitive rationale, but still has some reservations or questions about the model or its applicability.
4   Patient responses indicate an openness to the role of cognitive factors in distress and some willingness to experiment with the tasks of cognitive therapy.
5   Patient indicates genuine acceptance of the role of cognitive factors in distress and very clearly sees the value of important tasks such as homework, monitoring cognitions, exploring the therapeutic relationship, and so forth.

Alliance Potential (In-Session Evidence)

Instructions to Raters

This dimension focuses on the bond component of the therapeutic alliance. Although bond, task, and goal are somewhat interdependent, the task and goal components are assessed more explicitly on dimensions like *compatibility with cognitive rationale*. On *this* scale the rater should focus on dimensions such as *degree of engagement between patient and therapist, evidence of empathic resonance between therapist and patient,* and *mutual warmth.* Remember that the alliance is an interactional concept and that if the interviewer appears to be contributing an excessive proportion of the variance to a poor alliance, this should be taken into account.

0	0.5	1	1.5	2	2.5	3	3.5	4	4.5	5

0   Do *not* rate. Insufficient information.
1   Patient clearly exhibits a lack of trust or confidence in the interviewer or explicitly expresses negative sentiments about the interview, or appears very guarded. No evidence of any rapport is evidenced during interview.
2   Patient appears withdrawn or somewhat guarded or somewhat irritable or defensive. There is little evidence of engagement during the interview.
3   Patient appears to be engaged with the interviewer, but remains somewhat untrusting.

4   There is little evidence of negative sentiments toward therapist or therapy, and the patient is reasonably involved in the interview process. There is evidence that the patient feels understood.
5   Patient appears to be *actively* engaged with the therapist and seems to feel valued and understood. There appears to be an empathic resonance or signs of mutual warmth between patient and therapist.

Alliance Potential (Out-of-Session Evidence)

Instructions to Raters

This item gauges patients' ability to form trusting relationships with others, on the basis of their description of various relationships in their lives. This basic capacity mediates the ease with which the patient can engage in self-exploration in therapy. Particularly relevant information relates to the patient's ability to confide intimacies to friends and the way in which he or she handles conflict situations with friends (for example, complete withdrawal versus some attempt to work things out). Important relationships to probe for are:

—Previous therapy contacts (an important source of information)
—Parents, siblings
—Current/past confidants, lovers, boy/girlfriend, spouse
—Coworkers, doctor

Information might be solicited with general probes such as:

1. Everyone has conflicts in relationships; when you and _____ have conflicts, how is it handled? What happens?
2. When this relationship ended, how did it end? What happened?

0	0.5	1	1.5	2	2.5	3	3.5	4	4.5	5

0   Do *not* rate. Insufficient information.
1   Extremely poor history of interpersonal relationship. Few if any sustained relationships, all marked with mistrust or ambivalence.
2   Shows evidence of some capacity to establish stable relationships, but there is a marked tendency toward mistrust or ambivalence.
3   Patient displays moderate evidence of ability to establish stable, trusting relationships but clearly lapses into a state of mistrust when conflict arises.
4   Shows good evidence of sustained, trusting relations with some tendency to mistrust, withdraw, or avoid conflict situations.
5   Patient may have interpersonal difficulties, but there is good evidence of sustained, trusting, intimate relationships and ability to maintain good interpersonal contact in conflict situations.

Chronicity of Problems

Instructions to Raters

In rating this item, the rater should consult the patient's list of target complaints and consider the most important complaints or problems presented. The assumption here is that the more chronic problems will be less amenable to treatment in a short-term framework than the more acute problems.

0	0.5	1	1.5	2	2.5	3	3.5	4	4.5	5

0   Do *not* rate. Insufficient information.

1   A nearly lifelong difficulty with at least one of the main complaints.

2   Long-lasting difficulties with at least one of the main complaints for at least five years.

3   Patient reports main problems or complaints lasting most of the past two years *or* during at least two episodes of six months each.

4   Patient reports that main complaints or problems have existed for more than six months, but less than two years.

5   A relatively recent (that is, within past six months) onset of the main complaints.

Security Operations

Instructions to Raters

This item gauges the extent to which the patient's security operations will serve as a potential obstacle to the process of therapy. Security operations can be defined as psychological and/or behavioral operations that function to reduce anxiety and raise self-esteem. Examples of security operations are: avoidance of topic, circumstantiality, preoccupation with fine details, selective inattention, presenting oneself in an exaggeratedly favorable light, and discussion of emotional issues in an intellectually distanced way. An important dimension to gauge here is how amenable patients appear to be to metacommunication about their security operations.

0	0.5	1	1.5	2	2.5	3	3.5	4	4.5	5

0   Do *not* rate. Insufficient information.

1   The patient's security operations appear to be sufficiently disruptive to constitute a substantial barrier to the therapeutic process. For example, the patient displays marked avoidance of difficult or potential anxiety-producing areas. This style is displayed consistently with a high degree of intensity over the course of the interview.

2   The patient displays security operations that are moderately disruptive, but there do seem to be some points at which he or she is able to deal with potentially anxiety-provoking issues openly and directly.

3   The patient displays mildly disruptive security operations. There appears

to be some openness to dealing with potentially anxiety-provoking topics, but the rater is left with some concern that certain operations on the part of the patient might ultimately interfere with short-term cognitive therapy.

4 There is some evidence of disruptive security operations, but the interviewer is left with the impression that these are not a *major* obstacle to short-term cognitive therapy.

5 There is no reason to believe that the patient's security operations will constitute an obstacle to short-term cognitive therapy.

Focality

Instructions to Raters

This dimension concerns the extent to which the patient is able to remain task-oriented and focused during the session, particularly when working with the therapist on a circumscribed problem. Is the patient able to explore a particular theme in depth, or is there a tendency to shift from issue to issue without maintaining focus? If the patient appears without focus, is he or she responsive to prompting from the therapist to help maintain a focus or to attempt to clarify the factors making it difficult to focus (for example, anxiety about dealing with underlying theme).

0	0.5	1	1.5	2	2.5	3	3.5	4	4.5	5

0 Do *not* rate. Insufficient information.

1 The patient is unable to focus on a specific situation being worked on during the session, the style is loose and rambling, and the patient is unresponsive to the therapist's attempts to stay with the event being worked on.

2 The patient is poor at focusing on a specific problem. There is some degree of looseness and rambling in the patient's attempts to discuss the situation in particular. Therapist prompting is still needed to maintain the problem focus.

3 The patient is able to focus on a specific problem without prompting by the therapist to stay on task.

4 The patient shows very good ability to maintain a problem focus in the absence of therapist prompting, and feels comfortable working within such a structure.

5 The patient shows very good ability to work within a problem focus without therapist prompting and shows an ability to work with this structured aspect of cognitive therapy to delineate or explore fully a specific situation of importance.

Patient Optimism/Pessimism
Regarding Therapy

Instructions to Raters

Unlike the compatibility with cognitive rationale item, which gauges the patient's expectations about a *specific* approach, this item taps into a more general sense of optimism versus pessimism about the possibility of change. Examples of relevant information would be accounts of having changed in the past or spontaneously optimistic or pessimistic statements (for example, ''I know I can get over this with the right help,'' or ''I just can't imagine changing.'')

0	0.5	1	1.5	2	2.5	3	3.5	4	4.5	5

0   Do *not* rate. Insufficient information.
1   The patient does not believe in the possibility of therapy being able to help change things in his or her life.
2   The patient seems skeptical or pessimistic about therapy being of value.
3   The patient displays some degree of hope that therapy will be helpful.
4   The patient is optimistic that therapy will be of value.
5   The patient is very optimistic and hopeful that therapy can help achieve change in his or her life.

Suitability for Short-Term Cognitive Therapy Rating Form

1 = negative prognosis
5 = positive prognosis
0 = insufficient information
(Half ratings are allowed, for example, 1.5)

Date _____   Interviewer _____

Patient Name _____   Rater _____

Item	Rating (1–5)
1. Accessibility of automatic thoughts	
2. Awareness and differentiation of emotions	
3. Acceptance of personal responsibility for change	
4. Compatibility with cognitive rationale	
5. Alliance potential (in-session evidence)	
6. Alliance potential (out-of-session evidence, including previous therapy)	
7. Chronicity of problems	

8. Security operations

9. Focality

10. Patient optimism/pessimism
    regarding therapy

APPENDIX IV

Therapy-Adherence Rating Scale

This therapy-adherence scale is to be employed to train therapists and to evaluate how closely therapists are adhering to the central treatment principles of the approach described in this book. The first part of the scale, divided into two sections, consists of principles and behaviors that are regarded as "on task" or appropriate to this therapeutic approach.

The first section, in this part, lists six general principles that should be adhered to in all sessions. The second section consists of a variety of on-task therapist behaviors to be employed in the relevant context. Not every behavior described here will be appropriate for every session. For example, a session that focuses primarily on the exploration of out-of-session events may not require the explicit exploration of the therapeutic relationship if there are no problems in the therapeutic alliance. Over the course of several sessions, however, the therapist should receive high ratings on most items.

The second part of this scale consists of five off-task items or common therapist behaviors that are considered inappropriate to this particular approach. Consistently high ratings on these items highlight important problem areas to be worked on in supervision.

On Task Items

I. The following general principles are relevant to all sessions.
   1. Establishes concrete focus within reasonable timeframe.
      The problem focus can be on either an out-of-session event or an in-session event (that is, some aspect of the therapeutic interaction), or both.
      a) in-session

1	2	3	4	5
none	some	moderate	much	very much

267

b) out-of-session

1	2	3	4	5
none	some	moderate	much	very much

2. Maintains problem focus.
   The therapist maintains a problem focus by actions such as redirecting the patient's attention if necessary, clarifying the connection among apparently different themes, or exploring patient anxieties or concerns that may lead to a change of focus.

1	2	3	4	5
none	some	moderate	much	very much

3. Is appropriately active while maintaining continuous receptivity to the patient's experience.

1	2	3	4	5
none	some	moderate	much	very much

4. Makes use of openings for exploration.
   The therapist detects and makes use of openings for exploration, such as changes in voice quality and nonverbal behavior indicating momentary deepening of experience or accessibility of affective experience (for example, the sound of tears in the voice, a slowing of conversational pace that suggests an inward deployment of attention).

1	2	3	4	5
none	some	moderate	much	very much

5. Uses empathic reflection to heighten focus on core issues.
   This involves accurate empathy that tunes into salient features of the patient's experience and deepens the patient's experience and articulation of associated tacit meaning.

1	2	3	4	5
none	some	moderate	much	very much

6. Therapist acknowledges his or her contribution to the interaction when appropriate.

1	2	3	4	5
none	some	moderate	much	very much

II. The following principles and therapist actions need not all be implemented in every session. The therapist should, however, have high ratings on at least some items in every session, and over the course of three or four sessions should have high ratings on most of them.

7. Therapist conveys own feelings to help the patient become aware of his or her impact on others and role in the interaction.

1	2	3	4	5
none	some	moderate	much	very much

8. Therapist conveys own feelings to the patient to probe for his or her internal experience.

1	2	3	4	5
none	some	moderate	much	very much

9. Therapist identifies and points out the patient's interpersonal markers to help the patient become aware of his or her role in the interaction.

1	2	3	4	5
none	some	moderate	much	very much

10. Therapist uses identified interpersonal marker as a juncture for cognitive-affective exploration.

1	2	3	4	5
none	some	moderate	much	very much

11. Explores important interpersonal schema.

1	2	3	4	5
none	some	moderate	much	very much

Please identify: _____

_____

_____

12. Explores negative self-statements or "shoulds" in an emotionally immediate fashion.

1	2	3	4	5
none	some	moderate	much	very much

13. Facilitates decentering process in one of the following ways:
a) Cognitive challenging interventions with out-of-session focus.

1	2	3	4	5
none	some	moderate	much	very much

b) Facilitates tangible experience of dysfunctional construal style.

1	2	3	4	5
none	some	moderate	much	very much

c) Actively works with patient to test out dysfunctional interpersonal schema in therapeutic relationship.

1	2	3	4	5
none	some	moderate	much	very much

14. Invites collaborative exploration of shared experience.

1	2	3	4	5
none	some	moderate	much	very much

15. Explores alliance rupture.

1	2	3	4	5
none	some	moderate	much	very much

16. Links exploration of therapeutic interaction to out-of-session events by assigning relevant tasks and experiments.

1	2	3	4	5
none	some	moderate	much	very much

Off-Task

The following items rate the frequency of commonly observed therapist actions that are regarded as off-task in the therapeutic approach described in this book. High ratings on these items are considered problematic.

1. Uses interpretation.

1	2	3	4	5
none	some	moderate	much	very much

2. Makes links among interpersonal situations (for example, the therapeutic relationship and other relationships) before exploring patient's phenomenology in a specific situation.

1	2	3	4	5
none	some	moderate	much	very much

3. Does not intervene actively when appropriate.

1	2	3	4	5
none	some	moderate	much	very much

4. Does not establish and maintain focus.

1	2	3	4	5
none	some	moderate	much	very much

References

Ainsworth, M. D. S. 1982. Attachment: Retrospect and prospect. In *The place of attachment in human behavior,* ed. C. M. Parkers and J. Stevenson-Hinde. New York: Basic Books.

Alba, J. W., and Hasher, L. 1983. Is memory schematic? *Psychological Bulletin* 93:203–31.

Alberti, R. E., and Emmons, M. L. 1974. *Your perfect right: A guide to assertive behavior,* 2d ed. San Luis Obispo, California: Impact Publishers.

Alden, L., and Cappe, R. 1981. Nonassertiveness: Skill deficit or selective self-evaluation? *Behavior Therapy* 12:107–14.

Alexander, J. F. et al. 1976. Social reinforcement in the modification of agoraphobia. *Archives of General Psychiatry* 19:423–27.

Alexander, F., and French, T. M. 1946. *Psychoanalytic therapy: Principles and application.* New York: Ronald Press.

Allen, J. et al. 1984. Scales to assess the therapeutic alliance from a psychoanalytic perspective. *Bulletin of the Menninger Clinic* 48:383–400.

Alloy, L. B., and Abramson, L. Y. 1979. Judgment of contingency in depressed and nondepressed students: Sadder but wiser? *Journal of Experimental Psychology* 42:1114–26.

Arkowitz, H., Holliday, S., and Hutter, M. 1982. *Depressed women and their husbands: A study of marital interaction and adjustment.* Paper presented at the annual meeting of the Association for Advancement of Behavior Therapy, Los Angeles, California.

Arnkoff, D. G. 1980. Psychotherapy from the perspective of cognitive theory. In *Psychotherapy process: Current issues and future directions,* ed. M. J. Mahoney, 339–62. New York: Plenum Press.

———. 1983. Common and specific factors in cognitive therapy. In *Psychotherapy and patient relationships,* ed. M. J. Lambert, 85–125. Homewood, Ill.: Dorsey.

Arnold, M. B. 1960. *Emotion and personality.* 2 vols. New York: Columbia University Press.

———. 1970. *Feelings and emotions.* New York: Academic Press.

271

References

Ausubel, D. P. 1963. *The psychology of meaningful verbal learning*. New York: Grune & Stratton.

Ayllon, T., and Michael, J. 1959. The psychiatric nurse as a behavioral engineer. *Journal of the Experimental Analysis of Behavior* 2:323–34.

Bandura, A. 1969. *Principles of behavior modification*. New York: Holt, Rinehart, & Winston.

———. 1971. Psychotherapy based upon modeling principles. In *Handbook of psychotherapy and behavior change: An empirical analysis*, ed. A. E. Bergin and S. L. Garfield. New York: Wiley & Sons.

———. 1977. Self-efficacy: Towards a unifying theory of behavior change. *Psychological review* 84:191–215.

Bartlett, F. C. 1932. *Remembering*. Cambridge, England: Cambridge University Press.

Beck, A. T. 1967. *Depression: Clinical, experimental, and theoretical aspects*. New York: Harper & Row.

Beck, A. T., and Emery, G. 1985. *Anxiety disorders and phobias: A cognitive perspective*. New York: Basic Books.

Beck, A. T., Rush, A. J. et al. 1979. *Cognitive therapy of depression*. New York: Guilford Press.

Beck, A. T., Hollon, S. D. et al. 1985. Treatment of depression with cognitive therapy and amitryptyline. *Archives of General Psychiatry* 42:142–48.

Beck, A. T., and Young, J. E. 1985. Depression. In *Clinical handbook of psychological disorders*, ed. D. Barlow, 206–44. New York: Guilford Press.

Bedrosian, R. C. 1981. Ecological factors in cognitive therapy: The use of significant others. In *New directions in cognitive therapy*, ed. G. Emery, S. D. Hollon, and R. C. Bedrosian. New York: Guilford Press.

Beidel, D. C., and Turner, S. M. 1986. A critique of the theoretical basis of cognitive therapy theories and therapy. *Clinical Psychology Review* 6:177–97.

Benjamin, L. S. 1974. Structural analysis of social behavior. *Psychology Review* 81:392–425.

Bergin, A. E. 1970. The deterioration effect: A reply to Braucht. *Journal of Abnormal Psychology* 75:300–302.

Berman, J. S., Miller, R. C., and Massman, P. J. 1985. Cognitive therapy versus systematic desensitization: Is one treatment superior? *Psychological Bulletin* 97:451–61.

Beutler, L. E., Crago, M., and Arrizmendi, T. G. 1986. Research on therapist variables in psychotherapy. In *Handbook of psychotherapy and behavior change*, 3d ed., ed. S. L. Garfield and A. E. Bergin, 257–310. New York: Wiley & Sons.

Biglan, A. et al. 1985. Problem solving interactions of depressed women and their husbands. *Behavior Therapy* 16:431–51.

Blatt, S. J., and Erlich, H. S. 1982. Levels of resistance in the psychotherapeutic process. In *Resistance: Psychodynamic and behavioral approaches*, ed. P. L. Wachter. New York: Plenum Press.

Bordin, E. S. 1979. The generalizability of the concept of working alliance. *Psychotherapy: Theory, Research, and Practice* 16:252–60.

Bower, G. H. 1981. Mood and memory. *American Psychologist* 31:129–48.

Bower, G. H., and Mayer, J. D. 1985. Failure to replicate mood-dependent retrieval. *Bulletin of the Psychonomic Society* 23:30–42.

Bowers, R. S., and Meichenbaum, D. 1984. *The unconscious reconsidered*. New York: Wiley & Sons.

Bowlby, J. 1963. Pathological mourning and childhood mourning. *Journal of the American Psychoanalytic Association* 11:500–541.

——. 1969. *Attachment and Loss*. Vol. 1, *Attachment*. New York: Basic Books.

——. 1973. *Attachment and Loss*. Vol. 2, *Separation, anxiety, and anger*. New York: Basic Books.

——. 1980. *Attachment and Loss*. Vol. 3, *Loss: Sadness and depression*. London: Hogarth Press.

Brazelton, T. B., Koslowski, B., and Main, M. 1974. The origins of reciprocity: The early mother-infant interaction. In *The effect of the infant on its caregiver*, ed. M. Lewis and L. A. Rosenbaum. New York: Wiley & Sons.

Bretherton, I. 1985. Attachment theory: Retrospect and prospect. *Monographs of the Society for Research in Child Development* 209 (50, nos. 1–2). Chicago: University of Chicago Press.

Breuer, J., and Freud, S. [1895] 1955. Studies on hysteria. In *The standard edition of the complete psychological works of Sigmund Freud*. Vol. 2. Ed. and trans. J. Strachey, 1–170. London: Hogarth Press.

Brown, G. W., and Harris, T. 1978. *Social origins of depression*. London: Tavistock.

Bucci, W. 1985. Linguistic evidence for emotional structures: Manuals and methods. In *Psychoanalytic process research strategies*, ed. H. Kaechele. New York: Springer.

Buck, R. 1980. Nonverbal behavior and the theory of emotion: The facial feedback hypothesis. *Journal of Personality and Social Psychology* 38:811–24.

Budman, S. H., and Gurman, A. S. 1988. *Theory and Practice of Brief Therapy*. New York: Guilford Press.

Burns, D. D. 1980. *Feeling Good: The New Mood Therapy*. New York: William Morrow.

Butler, S. F., and Strupp, H. H. 1986. Specific and nonspecific factors in psychotherapy: A problematic paradigm for psychotherapy research. *Psychotherapy* 23:30–40.

Campos, J., and Sternberg, C. 1980. Perception of appraisal and emotion: The onset of social referencing. In *Infant social cognition*, ed. M. E. Lamb and L. Sherrod. Hillsdale, N. J.: Erlbaum.

Carson, R. C. 1969. *Interaction concepts of personality*. Chicago: Aldine.

——. 1982. Self-fulfilling prophecy, maladaptive behavior, and psychotherapy. In *Handbook of interpersonal psychotherapy*, ed. J. C. Anchin and D. J. Kiesler. New York: Pergamon Press.

Caston, J., Goldman, R., and McClure, M. M. 1987. The immediate effects of psychoanalytic interventions. In *The psychoanalytic process: Theory, clinical observation and empirical research*, ed. J. Weiss, H. Sampson, and The Mount Zion Psychotherapy Research Group. New York: Guilford Press.

Claxton, G. 1987. Meditation in Buddhist psychology. In *The Psychology of Meditation*, ed. M. A. West. Oxford: Clarendon Press.

Collins, W. D., and Messer, S. B. 1988. *Transporting the plan diagnosis method to a different setting: Reliability, stability, and adaptability*. Paper presented at the annual conference of the Society for Psychotherapy Research, Santa Fe, New Mexico.

273

References

Coyne, J. C. 1976. Depression and the response of others. *Journal of Abnormal Psychology* 85:186–93.

Coyne, J. C., and Gotlib, I. H. 1983. The role of cognition in depression: A critical appraisal. *Psychological Bulletin* 94:472–505.

———. 1986. Studying the role of cognition in depression: Well-trodden paths and cul-de-sacs. *Cognitive Therapy and Research* 10:695–705.

Coyne, J. C. et al. 1987. Living with a depressed person: Burden and psychological distress. *Journal of Consulting and Clinical Psychology* 55:347–52.

Dane, B., Walcott, C., and Drury, W. H. 1959. The form and duration of the display actions of the goldeneye (*Bucephala clangula*). *Behavior* 14:265–81.

Danzinger, K. 1976. *Interpersonal communication*. Elmsford, N. Y.: Pergamon Press.

Davanloo, H. 1980. A method of short-term dynamic psychotherapy. In *Short-term dynamic psychotherapy*, ed. H. Davanloo, 43–71. New York: Jason Aronson.

Deikman, A. J. 1982. *The Observing self: Mysticism and psychotherapy*. Boston: Beacon Press.

Derogatis, L. R. 1977. *SCL-90 administration, scoring and procedure manual*. Johns Hopkins University School of Medicine.

Dixon, N. F. 1981. *Preconscious processing*. New York: Wiley & Sons.

Donee, L. H. 1973. *Infants' development scanning patterns of face and non-face stimuli under various auditory conditions*. Paper presented at the meeting of the Society for Research in Child Development, Philadelphia, Pennsylvania.

Dreyfus, H. L., and Dreyfus, S. E. 1986. *Mind over machine*. New York: Free Press.

Dunn, J. 1982. Comment: Problems and promises in the study of affect and intention. In *Social interchange in infancy*, ed. E. T. Tronick. Baltimore, Md.: University Park Press.

Dunn, J., and Kendrick, C. 1979. Interaction between young siblings in the context of family relationships. In *The child and its family*. Vol. 2, *The genesis of behavior*, ed. M. Lewis and I. Rosenbaum. New York: Plenum Press.

———. 1982. *Siblings: Love, envy and understanding*. Cambridge, Mass.: Harvard University Press.

D'Zurilla, T. J., and Goldfried, M. R. 1971. Problem solving and behavior modification. *Journal of Abnormal Psychology* 78:107–26.

Eagle, M. M. 1984. *Recent developments in psychoanalysis*. New York: McGraw-Hill.

———. 1987. The psychoanalytic and the cognitive unconscious. In *Theories of the unconscious and theories of the self*, ed. R. Stern. Hillsdale, N. J.: Analytic Press.

Ekman, P., ed. 1972. *Darwin and facial expression: A century of research in review*. New York: Academic Press.

Elkin, I. et al. 1986, May. *NIMH treatment of depression collaborative research program: Major outcome findings*. Paper presented to the American Psychiatric Association Conference, Washington, D. C.

Ellis, A. 1983. Rational-Emotive Therapy (RET) approaches to overcoming resistance. I: Common forms of resistance. *British Journal of Cognitive Psychotherapy* 1(1):28–38.

——. 1984. Rational-emotive therapy. In *Current psychotherapies.* 3d ed., ed. R. J. Corsini. Itasca, Ill.: Peacock.

Emde, R. N. 1983. *The affective core.* Paper presented at the Second World Congress of Infant Psychiatry, Cannes, France.

Emde, R. N., and Sorce, J. E. 1983. The rewards of infancy: Emotional availability and maternal referencing. In *Frontiers of infant psychiatry.* Vol. 2. Ed. J. D. Call, E. Galenson, and R. Tyson. New York: Basic Books.

Emde, R. N. et al. 1978. Emotional expression in infancy: I. Initial studies of social signaling and an emergent model. In *The development of affect,* ed. M. Lewis and L. Rosenblum. New York: Plenum Press.

Erdelyi, M. H. 1974. A new look at the new look: Perceptual defense and vigilance. *Psychological Review* 81:1–25.

——. 1985. *Psychoanalysis: Freud's cognitive psychology.* New York: Freeman.

Erdelyi, M. H., and Goldberg, B. 1979. Let's not sweep repression under the rug: Toward a cognitive psychology of repression. In *Functional disorders of memory,* ed. J. F. Kihlstrom and F. J. Evans. Hillsdale, N. J.: Erlbaum.

Eysenck, H. 1969. *The effects of psychotherapy.* New York: Science House.

Fantz, R. 1963. Pattern vision in newborn infants. *Science* 140:296–97.

Fennell, M. J. V., and Teasdale, J. D. 1987. Cognitive therapy for depression: Individual differences and the process of change. *Cognitive Therapy and Research* 11:253–72.

Field, T. M. et al. 1982. Discrimination and imitation of facial expression by neonates. *Science* 218:179–81.

Foa, E. B., and Emmelkamp, P. M. G. 1983, eds. *Failures in behavior therapy.* New York: Wiley & Sons.

Foa, E. B., and Kozak, M. J. 1986. Emotional processing of fear: Exposure to corrective information. *Psychological Bulletin* 99:20–35.

——. In press. Emotional processing: Theory, research and clinical implications for anxiety disorders. In *Emotion and the process of therapeutic change,* ed. J. D. Safran and L. S. Greenberg. Orlando: Academic Press.

Foa, E. B. et al. 1983. Treatment of obsessive-compulsives: When do we fail? In *Failures in behavior therapy,* ed. E. B. Foa and P. M. G. Emmelkamp. New York: Wiley & Sons.

Foreman, S. A., and Marmar, C. R. 1985. Therapist actions that address initially poor therapeutic alliances in psychotherapy. *American Journal of Psychiatry* 142:922–26.

Frank, J. D. 1973. *Persuasion and Healing.* Baltimore, Md.: Johns Hopkins Univ. Press.

——. 1979. The present status of outcome studies. *Journal of Consulting and Clinical Psychology* 47:310–16.

——. 1982. Therapeutic components shared by all psychotherapies. In *Psychotherapy research and behavior change,* ed. J. H. Harvey and M. M. Parks, 5–37. Washington, D. C.: American Psychological Association.

Fransella, F. 1985. Resistance. *British Journal of Cognitive Psychotherapy* 2:1–11.

Freud, S. [1900] 1953. The interpretation of dreams. In *Standard edition,* vols. 4 and 5, ed. and trans. J. Strachey. London: Hogarth Press.

——. [1912] 1958. *The dynamics of transference.* In *Standard edition,* vol. 12. ed. and trans. J. Strachey. London: Hogarth Press.

———. [1909] 1959. *Five lectures on psycho-analysis.* In *Standard Edition,* vol. 11, ed. and trans. J. Strachey. London: Hogarth Press.

———. [1940] 1964. *An outline of psycho-analysis.* In *Standard Edition,* vol. 23, ed. and trans. J. Strachey. London: Hogarth Press.

Friedlander, B. Z. 1970. Receptive language development in infancy. *Merrill-Palmer Quarterly* 16:7–51.

Frijda, N. H. 1988. The laws of emotion. *American Psychologist* 43:349–58.

Gardner, H. 1985. *The mind's new science.* New York: Basic Books.

Gendlin, E. T. 1962. *Experiencing and the creation of meaning.* New York: Free Press of Glencoe.

———. 1981. *Focusing.* New York: Bantam.

———. In press. On emotion in therapy. In *Emotion and the process of therapeutic change,* ed. J. D. Safran and L. S. Greenberg. Orlando: Academic Press.

Gibson, E. J. 1969. *Principles of perceptual learning and development.* New York: Appleton-Century-Crofts.

Gill, M. M. 1976. Metapsychology is not psychology. In *Psychology versus metapsychology,* ed. M. M. Gill and P. S. Holzman. New York: International Universities Press.

———. 1982. *Analysis of transference,* vol. 1, Theory and technique. New York: International Universities Press.

Goldfried, M. R. 1980. Towards the delineation of therapeutic change principles. *American Psychologist* 35:991–99.

———. 1982. Resistance and clinical behavior therapy. In *Resistance: Psychodynamic and behavioral approaches,* ed. P. L. Wachtel, 95–114. New York: Plenum Press.

Goldfried, M. R. 1983. Behavioral assessment. In *Clinical methods in psychology.* Vol. 2. Ed. I. B. Weiner, 231–81. New York: Wiley & Sons.

Goldfried, M. R., and Davison, G. C. 1976. *Clinical behavior therapy.* New York: Holt, Rinehart, & Winston.

Goldfried, M. R., and Robins, C. 1983. Self schemas, cognitive bias, and the processing of therapeutic experiences. In *Advances in cognitive-behavioral research and therapy.* Vol. 2. Ed. P. Kendall. New York: Academic Press.

Goldfried, M. R., and Safran, J. D. 1986. Future directions in psychotherapy integration. In *Handbook of eclectic psychotherapy,* ed. J. C. Norcross. New York: Brunner/Mazel.

Goldstein, A. P., Heller, K., and Sechrest, L. 1966. *Psychotherapy and the psychology of behavior change.* New York: Wiley & Sons.

Gomes-Schwartz, B. 1978. Effective ingredients in psychotherapy: Prediction of outcome from process variables. *Journal of Consulting and Clinical Psychology* 46:1023–35.

Gotlib, I. H., and Asarnow, R. F. 1979. Interpersonal and impersonal problem-solving skills in mildly and clinically depressed university students. *Journal of Consulting and Clinical Psychology* 47:86–95.

Gotlib, I. H., and Colby, C. A. 1987. *Treatment of depression: An interpersonal systems approach.* New York: Pergamon Press.

Greenberg, J. R., and Mitchell, S. A. 1983. *Object relations in psychoanalytic theory.* Cambridge, Mass.: Harvard University Press.

Greenberg, L. S., and Safran, J. D. 1980. Encoding, information processing, and cognitive behaviour therapy. *Canadian Psychologist* 21:59–66.

——. 1981. Encoding and cognitive therapy: Changing what clients attend to. *Psychotherapy: Theory, Research, and Practice* 18:163–69.

——. 1984. Integrating affect and cognition: A perspective on the process of therapeutic change. *Cognitive Therapy and Research* 8:559–78.

——. 1987. *Emotion in psychotherapy.* New York: Guilford Press.

——. 1989. Emotion in psychotherapy. *American Psychologist* 44:19–29.

Greenson, R. R. 1967. *The technique and practice of psychoanalysis,* vol. 1. New York: International Universities Press.

Guidano, V. F. 1987. *Complexity of the self: A developmental approach to psychopathology and therapy.* New York: Guilford Press.

——. In press. Affective change events in a cognitive therapy system approach. In *Emotion and the process of therapeutic change,* ed. J. D. Safran and L. S. Greenberg. Orlando: Academic Press.

Guidano, V. F., and Liotti, G. 1983. *Cognitive processes and emotional disorders.* New York: Guilford Press.

Haley, J. 1963. *Strategies of psychotherapy.* New York: Grune & Stratton.

Harlow, H. F. 1958. The nature of love. *American Psychologist,* 13:673–85.

Hartman, L. M., and Blankstein, K. R. 1986. *Perception of self in emotional disorder and psychotherapy: Advances in the study of communication and affect.* Vol. 2. New York: Plenum Press.

Hasher, L., and Zacks, R. T. 1979. Automatic and effortful processes in memory. *Journal of Experimental Psychology: General* 108:356–88.

Hautzinger, M., Linden, M., and Hoffman, N. 1982. Distressed couples with and without a depressed partner: An analysis of their verbal interaction. *Journal of Behavior Therapy and Experimental Psychiatry* 13:307–14.

Higgins, E. T. 1987. Self-discrepancy: A theory relating self and affect. *Psychological Review* 3:319–40.

Hill, C., and Safran, J. D. 1990. *A self-report measure of the interpersonal schema.* Manuscript submitted for publication.

Hinchcliffe, M., Hooper, D., and Roberts, F. J. 1978. *The melancholy marriage.* New York: Wiley & Sons.

Hollon, S. D., and Beck, A. T. 1986. Cognitive and cognitive-behavioral interventions. In *Handbook of psychotherapy and behavior change,* 3d ed., ed. S. L. Garfield and A. E. Bergin. New York: Wiley & Sons.

Hollon, S. D., and Kendall, P. C. 1980. Cognitive self-statements in depression: Development of an automatic thoughts questionnaire. *Cognitive Therapy and Research* 4:383–95.

Hollon, S. D., and Kriss, M. R. 1984. Cognitive factors in clinical research and practice. *Clinical Psychology Review* 4:35–76.

Hollon, S. D., and Najavits, L. 1988. Review of empirical studies on cognitive therapy. In *Review of Psychiatry.* Ed. A. J. Frances and R. E. Hales, Vol. 7. 643–67. Washington, D. C.: American Psychiatric Press.

Hooley, J. M., Orley, J., and Teasdale, J. D. 1986. Levels of expressed emotion and relapse in depressed patients. *British Journal of Psychiatry* 148:642–47.

Horney, K. 1950. *Neurosis and human growth.* New York: W. W. Norton.

Horowitz, M. J. 1979. *States of mind.* New York: Plenum Press.

Horowitz, M. J., and Marmar, C. 1985. The therapeutic alliance with difficult patients. In *Review of Psychiatry*, vol. 4, ed. A. J. Frances and R. E. Hales, 573–85. Washington, D. C.: American Psychiatric Press.

Horowitz, M. J. et al. 1984. Brief psychotherapy of bereavement reaction: The relationship of process to outcome. *Archives of General Psychiatry* 41:438–48.

Horvath, A., and Greenberg, L. S. 1986. The development of the working alliance inventory. In *The psychotherapeutic process: A research handbook*, ed. L. S. Greenberg and W. Pinsof. New York: Guilford Press.

Ingram, R. E., and Hollon, S. D. 1986. Information processing and the treatment of depression. In *Information processing approaches to clinical psychology*, ed. R. E. Ingram. Orlando, Fla.: Academic Press.

Ingram, R. E., and Kendall, P. C. 1986. Cognitive clinical psychology: Implications of an information processing perspective. In *Information processing approaches to clinical psychology*, ed. R. E. Ingram. Orlando, Fla.: Academic Press.

Izard, C. E. 1971. *The face of emotion*. New York: Appleton-Century-Crofts.

———. 1977. *Human emotions*. New York: Plenum Press.

Jacobson, N. S. 1989. The therapist-client relationship in cognitive behavior therapy: Implications for treating depression. *Journal of Cognitive Psychotherapy*. 3:85–96.

Jung, C. G. 1963. *Memories, dreams, reflections*. New York: Pantheon Books.

Kahn, J., Coyne, J. C., and Margolin, G. 1985. Depression and marital disagreement: The social construction of despair. *Journal of Social and Personal Relationships* 2:447–61.

Kahneman, D., and Tversky, A. 1972. Subjective probability: A judgement of representativeness. *Cognitive Psychology* 3:430–54.

Kaiser, H. 1965. The problem of responsibility in psychotherapy. In *Effective psychotherapy: The contribution of Hellmuth Kaiser*, ed. L. B. Fierman. New York: Free Press.

Kasin, E. 1986. Roots and branches. *Contemporary Psychoanalysis*, 22:452–57.

Kiesler, D. J. 1966. Some myths of psychotherapy research and the search for a paradigm. *Psychological Bulletin* 65:110–36.

———. 1979. An interpersonal communication analysis of relationship in psychotherapy. *Psychiatry* 42:299–311.

———. 1982a. Interpersonal theory for personality and psychotherapy. In *Handbook of interpersonal psychotherapy*, ed. J. C. Anchin and D. J. Kiesler. Elmsford, N. Y.: Pergamon Press.

———. 1982b. Confronting the client-therapist relationship in psychotherapy. In *Handbook of interpersonal psychotherapy*, ed. J. C. Anchin and D. J. Kiesler. Elmsford, N. Y.: Pergamon Press.

———. 1982c. Supervision in interpersonal communication in psychotherapy. Virginia Commonwealth University, Richmond, Virginia.

———. 1983. The 1982 interpersonal circle: A taxonomy for complementarity in human transactions. *Psychological Review* 90:185–214.

———. 1986. Interpersonal methods of diagnosis and treatment. In *Psychiatry*, ed. J. D. Cavenar. Philadelphia: Lippincott.

———. 1988. *Therapeutic Metacommunication: Therapist impact disclosure as feedback in psychotherapy*. Palo Alto, Calif.: Consulting Psychologists Press.

Kihlstorm, J. 1984. Conscious, subconscious, unconscious: A cognitive perspective. In *The unconscious reconsidered*, ed. K. S. Bowers and D. Meichenbaum, 149–211. New York: Wiley & Sons.

Klein, G. S. 1976. *Psychoanalytic theory: An exploration of essentials*. New York: International Universities Press.

Klein, M. H., Mathieu-Coughlan, P., and Kiesler, D. J. 1986. The experiencing scales. In *The psychotherapeutic process: A research handbook*, ed. L. S. Greenberg and W. Pinsof. New York: Guilford Press.

Klerman, G. L., Rounsaville, B., Chevron, E., and Weissman, M. 1984. *Interpersonal psychotherapy of depression*. New York: Basic Books.

Klinnert, M. D. 1978. *Facial expression and social referencing*. Ph.D. diss., Psychology Department, University of Denver.

Klinnert, M. D. et al. 1983. Emotions as behavior regulators: Social referencing in infancy. In *Emotion: Theory, research and experience*. Vol. 2. Ed. R. Plutchik and H. Kellerman. New York: Academic Press.

Kohut, H. 1977. *The restoration of the self*. New York: International Universities Press.

———. 1984. *How does analysis cure?* Ed. A. Goldberg and P. Stephansky. Chicago: University of Chicago Press.

Krantz, S. E. 1985. When depressive cognitions reflect negative realities. *Cognitive Therapy and Research* 9:595–610.

Krasner, L. 1962. The therapist as a social reinforcement machine. In *Research in psychotherapy*, vol. 2, ed. H. H. Strupp and L. Luborsky. Washington, D. C.: American Psychological Association.

Kuiper, N. A., and Olinger, L. J. 1986. Dysfunctional attitudes and a self-worth contingency model of depression. In *Advances in cognitive-behavioral research and therapy*, ed. P. C. Kendall, 115–42. Orlando, Fla.: Academic Press.

Lachman, R., and Lachman, J. 1986. Information processing psychology: Origins and extensions. In *Information processing approaches of clinical psychology*, ed. R. E. Ingram. Orlando, Fla.: Academic Press.

Lambert, M. J., ed. 1983. *Psychotherapy and patient relationships*. Homewood, Ill.: Dorsey Press.

———. 1986. Implications of psychotherapy outcome research for eclectic psychotherapy. In *Handbook of eclectic psychotherapy*, ed. J. C. Norcross, 436–61. New York: Brunner/Mazel.

Lambert, M. J., Shapiro, D. A., and Bergin, A. E. 1986. The effectiveness of psychotherapy. In *Handbook of eclectic psychotherapy*, ed. J. C. Norcross, 436–61. New York: Brunner/Mazel.

Lang, P. J. 1983. Cognition in emotion: Concept and action. In *Emotion, cognition and behavior*, ed. C. Izard, J. Kagan, and R. Zajonc. New York: Cambridge University Press.

Lazarus, A. A. 1971. *Behavior therapy and beyond*. New York: McGraw-Hill.

Lazarus, A. A., and Fay, A. 1982. Resistance or rationalization? A cognitive behavioral perspective. In *Resistance: Psychodynamic and behavioral approaches*, ed. P. L. Wachtel, 115–32. New York: Plenum Press.

Leary, T. 1957. *Interpersonal diagnosis of personality*. New York: Ronald.

Leventhal, H. 1979. A perceptual motor processing model of emotion. In *Advances in the study of communication and affect*, ed. P. Pliner, K. Blankestein, and I. Spigel. New York: Plenum Press.

———. 1984. A perceptual-motor theory of emotion. In *Advances in experimental social psychology*, ed. L. Berkowitz. New York: Academic Press.

Lewicki, P. 1986. *Nonconscious social information processing*. Orlando, Fla.: Academic Press.

Liotti, G. 1987. The resistance to change of cognitive structures: A counterproposal to psychoanalytic metapsychology. *Journal of Cognitive Psychotherapy* 2:87–104.

———. In press. Attachment and cognition: A guideline for the reconstruction of early pathogenic experiences in cognitive psychotherapy. In *Handbook of cognitive psychotherapy*, ed. C. Perris, I. Blackburn, and H. Perris. New York: Springer.

Lloyd, G. C., and Lishman, W. 1975. Effect of depression on the speed of recall of pleasant and unpleasant memories. *Psychological Medicine* 5:173–80.

Luborsky, L. 1984. *Principles of psychoanalytic psychotherapy: A manual for supportive-expressive treatment*. New York: Basic Books.

Luborsky, L., Singer, B., and Luborsky, L. 1975. Comparative studies of psychotherapies: Is it true that "Everyone has won and all must have prizes"? *Archives of General Psychiatry* 32:995–1008.

Luborsky, L. et al. 1980. Predicting the outcome of psychotherapy: Findings of the Penn psychotherapy project. *Archives of General Psychiatry* 37:471–81.

———. et al. 1983. Two helping alliance methods for predicting outcomes of psychotherapy. *Journal of Nervous and Mental Disease* 17:480–91.

———. et al. 1985. Therapist success and its determinants. *Archives of General Psychiatry* 42:602–11.

———. et al. 1986. Do therapists vary much in their success? Findings from four outcome studies. *American Journal of Orthopsychiatry* 56:501–12.

McMullin, R. 1986. *Handbook of cognitive therapy techniques*. New York: W. W. Norton.

Mahoney, M. J. 1974. *Cognition and behavior modification*. Cambridge, Mass.: Ballinger.

———. 1977. Reflections on the cognitive-learning trend in psychotherapy. *American Psychologist* 35:5–13.

———. 1982. Psychotherapy and human change processes. In *Psychotherapy research and behavior change*, vol. 1, ed. J. H. Harvey and M. M. Pars. Washington, D. C.: American Psychological Association.

———. 1983. Cognition, consciousness and the process of personal change. In *Advances in clinical behavior therapy*, ed. K. D. Craig and R. J. McMahon. New York: Brunner/Mazel.

———. 1985. Psychotherapy and human change processes. In *Cognition and psychotherapy*, ed. M. J. Mahoney and A. Freeman. New York: Plenum Press.

———. 1990. *Human change processes*. New York: Basic Books.

Mahoney, M. J., and Gabriel, T. J. 1987. Psychotherapy and the cognitive sciences: An evolving alliance. *Journal of Cognitive Psychotherapy* 1:39–59.

Mahoney, M. J., and Thoresen, C. E. 1974. *Self-control: Power to the person*. Belmont, Calif.: Brooks/Cole.

Main, M. 1983. Exploration, play, and cognitive functioning related to infant-mother attachment. *Infant Behavior and Development* 6:167–74.

Malan, D. H. 1976. *The frontiers of brief psychotherapy.* New York: Plenum Press.

Mann, J. 1973. *Time-limited psychotherapy.* Cambridge, Mass.: Harvard University Press.

Markus, H. 1977. Self-schemata and processing of information about the self. *Journal of Personality and Social Psychology* 35:63–78.

Markus, H., and Nurius, P. 1986. Possible selves. *American Psychologist* 41:954–69.

Marlatt, G. A., and Gordon, J. R. 1980. Determinants of relapse: Implications for the maintenance of behavior change. In *Behavioral medicine: Changing health lifestyles,* ed. P. Davidson and S. Davidson, 410–52. New York: Brunner/Mazel.

Marmar, C. R., Gaston, L., Gallagher, D., and Thompson, L. W. 1987, June. *Therapeutic alliance and outcome of behavioral, cognitive, and brief dynamic therapy of later-life depression.* Paper presented at the Society for Psychotherapy Research, Ulm, West Germany.

Marmar, C. R. et al. 1986. The development of the therapeutic alliance rating system. In *The psychotherapeutic process: A research handbook,* ed. L. S. Greenberg and W. M. Pinsoff. New York: Guilford Press.

Mathews, A. M. et al. 1976. Imaginal flooding and exposure to real phobic situations: Treatment outcomes with agoraphobic patients. *British Journal of Psychiatry* 129:362–71.

Mathews, S. A., and Macleod, C. 1985. Selective processing of threat cues to anxiety states. *Behavioral Research and Therapy* 23:563–69.

Mead, G. H. 1934. *Mind, self, and society.* Chicago: University of Chicago Press.

Meddin, J. 1982. Cognitive therapy and symbolic interactionism: Expanding clinical potential. *Cognitive Therapy and Research* 6:151–65.

Meichenbaum, D., and Gilmore, J. B. 1982. A perspective on the dynamic contributions. In *Resistance: Psychodynamic and behavioral approaches,* ed. P. Wachtel. New York: Plenum Press.

———. 1984. The nature of unconscious processes: A cognitive-behavioral perspective. In *The unconscious reconsidered,* ed. K. S. Bowers and D. Meichenbaum. New York: John Wiley & Sons.

Meissner, W. 1981. *Internalization in psychoanalysis.* New York: International Universities Press.

Millon, T. 1981. *Millon Clinical Multiaxial Inventory Manual,* 3rd ed. Minneapolis, Minn.: National Computer Systems.

Murphy, C. M., and Messer, D. J. 1977. Mothers, infants, and pointing: A study of gesture. In *Studies in mother-infant interaction,* ed. H. R. Schaffer. London: Academic Press.

Murphy, G. E. et al. 1984. Cognitive therapy and pharmacotherapy, singly and together in the treatment of depression. *Archives of General Psychiatry* 41:33–41.

Nash, E. et al. 1965. Systematic preparation of patients for short term psychotherapy. II. Relation of characteristic of patient, therapist, and the psychotherapeutic process. *Journal of Nervous and Mental Disease* 140:374–83.

Neisser, U. 1967. *Cognitive psychology.* New York: Appleton-Century-Crofts.

———. 1976. *Cognition and reality: Principles and implications of cognitive psychology.* San Francisco: Freeman.

———. 1980. Three cognitive psychologies and their implications. In *Psychotherapy process*, ed. M. J. Mahoney. New York: Plenum Press.

———. 1982. *Memory observed: Remembering in natural contexts*. San Francisco: W. H. Freeman.

Nelson, K., and Greundel, J. M. 1981. Generalized event representations: Basic building blocks of cognitive development. In *Advances in developmental psychology*, vol. 1, ed. M. E. Lamb and A. L. Brown. Hillsdale, N. J.: Erlbaum.

Newell, A., and Simon, H. 1972. *Human problem solving*. Englewood Cliffs, N. J.: Prentice-Hall.

Nisbett, R., and Ross, L. 1980. *Human inference: Strategies and shortcomings of social judgment*. Englewood Cliffs, N. J.: Prentice-Hall.

Norcross, J. C. 1986. Eclectic psychotherapy: An integration and overview. In *Handbook of eclectic psychotherapy*, ed. J. C. Norcross, 3–24. New York: Brunner/Mazel.

Orlinsky, D. E., and Howard, R. I. 1986. The relation of process to outcome in psychotherapy. In *Handbook of psychotherapy and behavior change*, 3rd ed., ed. S. L. Garfield and A. E. Bergin. New York: Wiley & Sons.

Pastor, D. L. 1981. The quality of mother-infant attachment and its relationship to toddler's initial sociability with peers. *Developmental Psychology* 17:326–35.

Perls, F. S. 1973. *The gestalt approach: An eyewitness to therapy*. Palo Alto, Calif.: Science and Behavior Books.

Perris, C. 1989. *Cognitive therapy with schizophrenic patients*. New York: Guilford Press.

Persons, J. B., and Burns, D. D. 1985. Mechanisms of action in cognitive therapy: The relative contributions of technical and interpersonal interventions. *Cognitive Therapy and Research* 9:539–57.

Persons, J. B., Burns, D. D., and Perloff, J. M. 1988. Predictors of dropout and outcome in cognitive therapy for depression in a private practice setting. *Cognitive Therapy and Research* 12:557–76.

Peterfreund, E. 1978. Some critical comments on psychoanalytic conceptions of infancy. *International Journal of Psychoanalysis* 59:427–41.

Peters, R. S. 1960. *The concept of motivation*. New York: Humanities Press.

Pilkonis, P. A., Imber, S. D., Lewis, P., and Rubinsky, P. 1984. A comparative outcome study of individual group and conjoint psychotherapy. *Archives of General Psychiatry* 41:431–37.

Piper, W. E. et al. 1984. A comparative study of four forms of psychotherapy. *Journal of Consulting and Clinical Psychology* 52:268–79.

Plutchik, R. 1980. *Emotion: A psychoevolutionary synthesis*. New York: Harper & Row.

Rabavilas, A. D., Boulougouris, J. C., and Perissaki, C. 1979. Therapist qualities related to outcome with exposure in vivo in neurotic patients. *Journal of Behavior Therapy and Experimental Psychiatry* 10:293–99.

Rachlin, H. 1977. Reinforcing and punishing thoughts: A rejoinder to Ellis and Mahoney. *Behavior Therapy* 8:678–81.

Rachman, S. 1980. Emotional processing. *Behavior Research and Therapy* 18:51–60.

Reich, W. 1949. *Character analysis*. New York: Noonday.

Reik, T. 1948. *Listening with the third ear*. New York: Farrar, Straus, & Giroux.

Rice, L. N. 1974. The evocative function of the therapist. In *Innovations in client-centered therapy*, ed. D. Wexler and L. N. Rice. New York: Interscience.

———. 1984. Client tasks in client-centered therapy. In *Client-centered therapy and the person-centered approach: New directions in theory, research, and practice*, ed. R. F. Levant and J. M. Shlien. New York: Praeger.

Rice, L. N., and Greenberg, L. S. 1984. *Patterns of change: Intensive analysis of psychotherapeutic process*. New York: Guilford Press.

Ricks, D. F. 1974. Supershrink: Methods of a therapist judged successful on the basis of adult outcome of adolescent patients. In *Life history research in psychopathology*. Vol. 3. ed. D. Ricks, M. Roff, and A. Thomas. Minneapolis, Minn.: University of Minnesota Press.

Rogers, C. R. 1951. *Client-centered therapy*. Boston: Houghton Mifflin.

———. 1961. *On becoming a person*. Boston: Houghton Mifflin.

Rosenthal, D., and Frank, J. D. 1956. Psychotherapy and the placebo effect. *Psychological Bulletin* 53:294–302.

Roth, D., and Rehm, L. P. 1980. Relationships among self-monitoring processes, memory and depression. *Cognitive Therapy and Research* 4:149–58.

Rush, A. J. 1983. Cognitive therapy for depression. In *Affective and schizophrenic disorders: New approaches to diagnosis*, ed. M. Zales. New York: Brunner/Mazel.

Ryle, A. 1979. The focus on brief interpretive psychotherapy: Dilemmas, traps, and snags. *British Journal of Psychiatry* 134:46–54.

Sacco, W. P., and Beck, A. T. 1985. Cognitive therapy for depression. In *Handbook of depression: Treatment, assessment, and research*, ed. E. Beckham and W. R. Leber, 3–38. Homewood, Ill.: Dorsey Press.

Safran, J. D. 1982. The functional asymmetry of negative and positive self-statements. *The British Journal of Clinical Psychology* 21:223–24.

———. 1984a. Assessing the cognitive-interpersonal cycle. *Cognitive Therapy and Research* 87:333–48.

———. 1984b. Some implications of Sullivan's interpersonal theory for cognitive therapy. In *Cognitive psychotherapies: Recent developments in theory, research, and practice*, ed. M. A. Reda and M. J. Mahoney. Cambridge, Mass.: Ballinger.

———. 1985, June. *A task analysis of change events in cognitive therapy*. Paper presented at the Society for Psychotherapy Research, Evanston, Illinois.

———. 1986, June. *A critical evaluation of the schema construct in psychotherapy research*. Paper presented at the Society for Psychotherapy Research, Boston, Massachusetts.

———. 1989, June. The relationship between the therapeutic alliance and outcome in cognitive therapy. Paper presented at the Society for Psychotherapy Research, Toronto, Canada.

———. 1990a. Towards a Refinement of Cognitive Therapy in Light of Interpersonal Theory: I. Theory. *Clinical Psychology Review* 10:87–105.

———. 1990b. Towards a Refinement of Cognitive Therapy in Light of Interpersonal Theory: II. Practice. *Clinical Psychology Review* 10:107–21.

Safran, J. D., and Greenberg, L. S. 1982a. Cognitive appraisal and reappraisal: Implications for clinical practice. *Cognitive Therapy and Research* 6:251–58.

———. 1982b. Eliciting "hot cognitions" in cognitive behavior therapy: Rationale and procedural guidelines. *Canadian Psychology* 23:83–87.

———. 1986. Hot cognition and psychotherapy process: An information processing/ecological perspective. In *Advances in Cognitive-Behavioral Research and Therapy*, vol. 5, ed. P. C. Kendall, 143–77. Orlando: Academic Press.

———. 1987. Affect and the unconscious: A cognitive perspective. In *Theories of the unconscious*, ed. R. Stern, 191–212. Hillsdale, N. J.: Analytic Press.

———. 1988. Feeling, thinking, and acting: A cognitive framework for psychotherapy integration. *Journal of Cognitive Psychotherapy* 2:109–30.

———. 1989. The treatment of anxiety and depression from an affective perspective. In *Negative Affective Conditions*, ed. P. C. Kendall and D. Watson, 455–89. New York: Academic Press.

Safran, J. D., and Greenberg, L. S., eds. In press. *Emotion and the process of therapeutic change*. New York: Academic Press.

Safran, J. D., Greenberg, L. S., and Rice, L. N. 1988. Integrating psychotherapy research and practice: Modelling the change process. *Psychotherapy* 25:1–17.

Safran, J. D., Crocker, P. et al. In press. The alliance rupture as a therapy event for empirical investigation. *Psychotherapy*.

Safran, J. D., Segal, Z. V. et al. In press. Refining strategies for research on self-representations in emotional disorders. *Cognitive Therapy and Research*.

Safran, J. D., Vallis, T. M. et al. 1986. Assessing core cognitive processes in cognitive therapy. *Cognitive Therapy and Research* 10:509–26.

Scaife, M., and Bruner, J. S. 1975. The capacity for joint visual attention in the infant. *Nature* 253:265–66.

Schafer, R. 1968. *Aspects of internalization*. New York: International Universities Press.

———. 1983. *The analytic attitude*. New York: Basic Books.

Segal, Z. V. 1988. Appraisal of the self-schema construct in cognitive models of depression. *Psychological Bulletin* 103:147–62.

Segal, Z. V., and Shaw, B. F. 1986a. Cognition in depression: A reappraisal of Coyne and Gotlib's critique. *Cognitive Therapy and Research* 10:671–93.

———. 1986b. When cul-de-sacs are more mentality than reality: A rejoinder to Coyne and Gotlib. *Cognitive Therapy and Research* 10:707–14.

Segal, Z. V., and Vella, D. D. In press. Self-schema in major depression: Replication and extension of a priming methodology. *Cognitive Therapy and Research*.

Segal, Z. V. et al. 1988. A structural analysis of the self-schema construct in major depression. *Cognitive Therapy and Research* 12:471–85.

Shank, R. C., and Abelson, R. 1977. *Scripts, plans, goals and understanding*. Hillsdale, N.J.: Erlbaum.

Shapiro, D. A., and Shapiro, D. 1982. Meta-analysis of comparative therapy outcome studies: A replication and refinement. *Psychological Bulletin* 92:581–604.

Shapiro, E. R. 1978. The psychodynamic and developmental psychology of the borderline patient: A review of the literature. *American Journal of Psychiatry* 135:1305–15.

Shaw, R., and Bransford, J. 1977. *Perceiving, asking, and knowing: Toward an ecological psychology.* Hillsdale, N. J.: Erlbaum.

Shevrin, H., and Dickman, S. 1980. The psychological unconscious: A necessary assumption for all psychological theory? *American Psychologist* 35:421–34.

Shiffrin, R. M., and Schneider, W. 1977. Controlled and automatic human information processing. II: Perceptual learning, automatic attending, and a general theory. *Psychological Review* 84:127–90.

Sifneos, P. E. 1972. *Short-term psychotherapy and emotional crisis.* Cambridge, Mass.: Harvard University Press.

———. 1979. *Short-term dynamic psychotherapy: Evaluation and technique.* New York: Plenum Press.

Silberschatz, G. 1987. Testing pathogenic beliefs. In *The Psychoanalytic process: Theory, clinical observation, and empirical research,* ed. J. Weiss, H. Sampson, & The Mount Zion Psychotherapy Research Group. New York: Guilford Press.

Silberschatz, G., Fretter, P. B., and Curtis, J. T. 1986. How do interpretations influence the process of psychotherapy? *Journal of Consulting and Clinical Psychology* 54:646–52.

Silver, R. J. 1982. Brief dynamic psychotherapy: A critical look at the state of the art. *Psychiatric Quarterly* 53:275–82.

Sloane, R. B. et al. 1975. *Psychotherapy versus behavior therapy.* Cambridge, Mass.: Harvard University Press.

Smith, D. 1982. Trends in counselling and psychotherapy. *American Psychologist* 37:802–9.

Spence, D. P. 1982. *Narrative truth and historical truth: Meaning and interpretation in psychoanalysis.* New York: W. W. Norton.

Spitz, R. 1946. Anaclitic depression: An inquiry into the genesis of psychiatric conditions in early childhood, II. *Psychoanalytic Study of the Child* 2:313–42.

Sroufe, L. A. 1979. Socioemotional development. In *Handbook of infant development,* ed. J. D. Osofsky. New York: Wiley & Sons.

Staats, A. W. 1970. Social behaviorism, human motivation and the conditioning therapies. In *Progress in experimental personality research,* ed. B. Maher. New York: Academic Press.

Steinbrueck, S. M., Maxwell, S. E., and Howard, G. S. 1983. A meta-analysis of psychotherapy and drug therapy in the treatment of unipolar depression with adults. *Journal of Consulting and Clinical Psychology* 51:856–63.

Steketee, G., and Foa, E. B. 1985. Obsessive-compulsive disorder. In *Clinical handbook of psychological disorders,* ed. D. Barlow. New York: Guilford Press.

Sterba, R. 1934. The fate of the ego in analytic therapy. *International Journal of Psychoanalysis* 15:117–26.

Stern, D. N. 1985. *The interpersonal world of the infant.* New York: Basic Books.

Stolorow, R. D., Brandhoft, B., and Atwood, G. E. 1983. Intersubjectivity in psychoanalytic treatment. *Bulletin of the Menninger Clinic* 47:117–28.

Strachey, J. 1934. The nature of the therapeutic action of psychoanalysis. *International Journal of Psychoanalysis* 15:127–59.

References

Strupp, H. H. 1980. Success and failure in time-limited psychotherapy: A systematic comparison of two cases. *Archives of General Psychiatry* 37:595–603.

Strupp, H. H., and Binder, J. L. 1984. *Psychotherapy in a new key: A guide to time-limited dynamic therapy*. New York: Basic Books.

Sullivan, H. S. 1953. *The interpersonal theory of psychiatry*. New York: W. W. Norton.

———. 1954. *The psychiatric interview*. New York: W. W. Norton.

———. 1956. *Clinical studies in psychiatry*. New York: W. W. Norton.

Sulloway, F. 1979. *Freud: Biologist of the mind*. New York: Basic Books.

Swan, G. E., and MacDonald, M. L. 1978. Behavior therapy in practice: A national survey of behavior therapists. *Behavior Therapy* 9:799–807.

Sweet, A. A. 1984. The therapeutic relationship in behavior therapy. *Clinical Psychology Review* 4:253–72.

Taylor, S. E., and Brown, J. D. 1988. Illusion and well being: A social psychological perspective on mental health. *Psychological Bulletin* 103:193–210.

Teasdale, J. D., and Fennell, M. J. V. 1982. Immediate effects on depression of cognitive therapy interventions. *Cognitive Therapy and Research* 6:343–51.

Tinbergen, N. 1953. *Social behavior in animals*. London: Methuen.

Tomkins, S. S. 1962. *Affect, imagery, consciousness*. Vol. 1. New York: Springer.

———. 1963. *Affect, imagery, consciousness*. Vol. 2. New York: Springer.

Toukmanian, S. 1986. A measure of client perceptual processing. In *The psychotherapeutic process: A research handbook*, ed. L. S. Greenberg and W. Pinsoff. New York: Guilford Press.

Trevarthan, C., and Hubley, P. 1978. Secondary intersubjectivity: Confidence, confiders and acts of meaning in the first year. In *Action gesture and symbol*, ed. A. Lock. New York: Academic Press.

Tronick, E. Z. 1989. Emotions and emotional communication in infants. *American Psychologist* 44:112–19.

Tronick, E. Z., and Cohn, J. F. 1989. Infant-mother face to face interaction: Age and gender differences in coordination and the occurrence of miscoordination. *Child Development* 60:85–92.

Tulving, E. 1972. Episodic and semantic memory. In *Organization of memory*, ed. E. Tulving and W. Donaldson. New York: Academic Press.

Ullman, L. P., and Krasner, L. 1965. *Case studies in behavior modification*. New York: Holt, Rinehart, & Winston.

Wachtel, P. L. 1977. *Psychoanalysis and behavior therapy*. New York: Basic Books.

———. 1982. *Resistance: Psychodynamic and behavioral approaches*. New York: Plenum Press.

Watts, A. W. 1957. *The way of Zen*. New York: Vintage Books.

Watzlawick, P., Weakland, J., and Fisch, R. 1974. *Change*. New York: W. W. Norton.

Weiss, J., Sampson, H., and The Mount Zion Psychotherapy Research Group. 1987. *The psychoanalytic process: Theory, clinical observation and empirical research*. New York: Guilford Press.

Weissman, M. M., and Paykel, E. S. 1974. *The depressed woman: A study of social relationships*. Chicago: University of Chicago Press.

Werman, D. S. 1984. *The practice of supportive psychotherapy.* New York: Brunner/Mazel.

Williams, J. M. G., Watts, F. N., MacLeod, C., and Mathews, A. 1988. *Cognitive psychology and emotional disorders.* New York: John Wiley.

Wilson, G. T. 1984. Clinical issues and strategies in the practice of behavior therapy. In *Annual review of behavior therapy,* vol. 9, ed. G. T. Wilson, C. M. Franks, K. D. Brownell, and P. C. Kendall. New York: Guilford Press.

——. 1987. Clinical issues and strategies in the practice of behavior therapy. In *Annual review of behavior therapy,* vol. 11, ed. G. T. Wilson, C. M. Franks, P. C. Kendall, and J. P. Foreyt, 288–317. New York: Guilford Press.

Wilson, G. T., and Evans, I. M. 1976. Adult behavior therapy and the therapist-client relationship. In *Annual review of behavior therapy,* vol. 4, ed. C. M. Franks, and G. T. Wilson, 771–92. New York: Brunner/Mazel.

——. 1977. The Therapist-client relationship in behavior therapy. In *The therapist's contribution to effective psychotherapy: An empirical approach,* ed. A. S. Gurman and A. M. Razin. New York: Pergamon Press.

Winfrey, L. P. L., and Goldfried, M. R. 1986. Information processing and the human change process. In *Information processing approaches to clinical psychology,* ed. R. E. Ingram. Orlando, Fla.: Academic Press.

Wolberg, L. R. 1988. *The technique of psychotherapy.* Toronto: Grune & Stratton.

Woody, G. E. et al. 1983. Psychotherapy for opiate addicts: Does it help? *Archives of General Psychiatry* 40:639–45.

Young, J. E. In press. Schema-focused cognitive therapy for personality disorders. In *Cognitive therapy for personality disorders,* ed. A. Beck and A. Freeman. New York: Guilford Press.

Zajonc, R. B., and Markus, H. 1984. Affect and cognition: The hard interface. In *Emotions, cognition and behavior,* ed. C. E. Izard, J. Kagan, and R. B. Zajonc, 73–102. Cambridge, Eng.: Cambridge University Press.

Zetzel, E. 1956. Current concepts of transference. *International Journal of Psychoanalysis* 37:369–76.

Zigler, E., and Phillips, L. 1961. Psychiatric diagnosis and symptomatology. *Journal of Abnormal and Social Psychology* 63:69–75.

Index